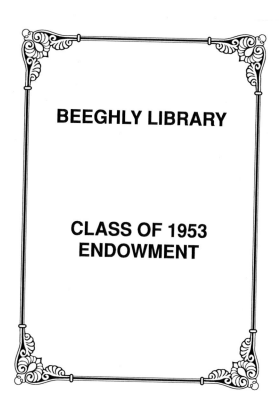

Gender, Indian, Nation

Gender, Indian, Nation

The Contradictions of Making Ecuador, 1830–1925

Erin O'Connor

The University of Arizona Press   Tucson

The University of Arizona Press

Library of Congress Cataloging-in-Publication Data
O'Connor, Erin, 1965–
Gender, Indian, nation : the contradictions of making Ecuador,
1830–1925 / Erin O'Connor.
p. cm.
Includes bibliographical references and index.
ISBN 978-0-8165-2559-1 (hardcover : alk. paper)
1. Indians of South America—Ecuador—Social conditions.
2. Indians of South America—Ecuador—Government relations.
3. Indians of South America—Ecuador—Politics and government.
4. Indian women—Ecuador—Social conditions. 5. Sex role—Ecuador.
6. Patriarchy—Ecuador. 7. Ecuador—Social conditions. 8. Ecuador—
Politics and government. 9. Ecuador—Ethnic relations. I. Title.
F3721.3.S65O36 2007
305.898'0866—dc22   2006039157

Publication of this book is made possible in part by a grant from
Bridgewater State College.

Manufactured in the United States of America on acid-free,
archival-quality paper containing a minimum of 50% post-consumer
waste and processed chlorine free.

12 11 10 09 08 07   6 5 4 3 2 1

I dedicate this book to
people who have profoundly influenced my view of the world:

The indigenous women and men of Ecuador,
whose struggles, past and present, have taught me so much.
May they together create a more equitable future.

And to my mother, Martha O'Connor,
the strongest woman I know.

Contents

Maps

Preface

The Present, the Past, and Patriarchy

> We women fight alongside our husbands, our sons, and
> our brothers.... We are often father and mother at the same time:
> we are responsible for everything. Because of the many tasks we have to
> complete, we are not able to participate fully in [political] meetings
> or cooperative work.
>
> —Mujeres Indígenas de la CONAIE[1]

Until recently, few scholars outside Ecuador studied the country's history. Since the 1980s, however, the rising tide of indigenous activism in Ecuador has brought unprecedented attention to this once overlooked nation. The Confederación de Nacionalidades Indígenas del Ecuador (CONAIE) has worked since 1986 to protect Indian rights, dignify indigenous cultural identities, and redefine democracy; the organization has become an important part of Ecuadorian national politics.[2] Since 1990 CONAIE activists successfully used the *paro* strategy—blocking roads to bring the nation to a halt—to make congresses and presidents negotiate with them; more recently, some members have been elected to congress through the newly created political party Pachakutik.[3] In January 2000, CONAIE's leadership (under Antonio Vargas) joined with members of the military to overthrow then-president Jamil Mahuad, whose neoliberal policies were highly unpopular with Ecuador's poor. Though the coup lasted less than twenty-four hours, it was a historic moment in which Indian activists were partners rather than followers in a coup.[4] Despite these accomplishments, wealthy white-mestizos continue to dominate national politics, and indigenous peoples continue to struggle daily to subsist, fight racism, gain respect for their cultures, and address gender inequalities. Historical studies of Ecuador have been proliferating to better understand why this small north Andean nation has produced one of Latin America's most prominent ethnic rights movements and to discover the roots of ongoing problems.

Gender issues in the movement are particularly complex, because indigenous women are central to and yet often marginalized within indigenous activism. Indian women, much more consistently than Indian men, symbolize authentic ethnic identity through dress, language, food preparation, and child rearing. Because of women's pivotal role in the maintenance of ethnic identity, and CONAIE's commitment to equitable social relations more generally, the organization has pledged to foster gender equality and has made an effort to incorporate women in all levels of organization and leadership.[5] Ironically, the very qualities that make women critical to preserving Indian identity are often the same ones that leave them politically vulnerable. Despite the rise of some women to prominent leadership positions, many indigenous women find themselves too busy with responsibilities in the home to attend meetings on a regular basis. Others have encountered resistance from male activists who express concern that if Indian women become too involved with politics, they will abandon the home—and thus their role in maintaining cultural identity.[6] Gender divisions create potential obstacles in realizing shared objectives or, at the very least, keep a potentially important interest group (women) unable to contribute fully to the movement.

The Present and the Past

Indigenous women's paradoxical position in the new politics of ethnicity raises key questions about Ecuadorian history. What past events and developments help to explain the simultaneous importance and marginalization of women within contemporary indigenous activism? Do recent problems result from a constant historical undercurrent, or can one find a particular point of departure, a period in which indigenous men gained a clear upper hand over women in negotiations with the state?

Certainly, to have women represent authentic identity in a way that highlights their importance to cultural identity while limiting their power to act on their symbolic authority is not new, nor is it unique to Latin America. Partha Chatterjee's path-breaking work on India highlighted a similar process in late nineteenth-century nationalism there, where the divide between the West and India, world and home, male and female, solved a critical dilemma of nationalism. When male nationalists struggled to differentiate their movements from Western nationalism, their answer was to distinguish between the worldly, political realm that was Western and male versus the *inner spirit* of Indian national culture that was associated with the home and with middle-class women.[7] Paula Hyman found similar patterns with Jewish assimilation in late nineteenth- and early twentieth-century Europe and the United States, when it became Jewish women's obligation to maintain cultural identity by keeping an authentically Jewish home.[8]

While the dilemma facing Ecuador's indigenous women is familiar, to understand the specific reasons for women's complex relationships to political activism requires an in-depth examination of exact conditions in the Ecuadorian past. CONAIE challenges the so-called uninational state in Ecuador based on Western political concepts, which benefits mainly white elite men. In its place, activists call for a multinational state that would give greater voice to a variety of ethnic groups and incorporate indigenous political culture as well as Western values.[9] Because activists seek to transform national politics, a focus on nation-state development is crucial for understanding the history behind contemporary Indian-state relations. For that reason, my foray into Ecuadorian Indian-state relations led me to investigate the century following Independence, roughly 1830–1925, in which the first meaningful nation-making projects took shape.[10]

This monograph examines multilayered links between gender and Indian-state relations in the nineteenth century, focusing on three key episodes in nation-state formation: the tribute dilemma from 1830 to 1857, conservative state building under Gabriel García Moreno from 1860 to 1875, and the liberal regime from 1895 to 1925. Gender influenced nineteenth-century sociopolitical behavior in various ways, providing a means through which interethnic struggles and negotiations played out in the process of making Ecuador. It presented Ecuadorian statesmen with a way to justify Indians' ongoing exclusion from the nation-state, while indigenous peoples manipulated gender concepts to advance their own interests vis-à-vis the state. Gender likewise shaped the *intra*ethnic encounters that went along with nation making. It gave local and central government officials ways to challenge each other's claims to political power and influence, and it provided competing political parties with fodder for their criticisms of each other. Among indigenous peoples, overlapping state and indigenous patriarchal concepts often disrupted balances of power between men and women, while differences between the two gender systems tended to foster solidarity between Indian men and women. Over time, the processes of nation making increased Indian men's ability to negotiate with the state, while Indian women's capacities were not similarly extended despite their importance within indigenous communities. The masculinization of Indian-state relations that surfaced by the early twentieth century laid foundations for the development of later indigenous movements and women's contradictory place within them.

Although indigenous women and their relationships to the state and to indigenous men concern me, it is not women's history per se but gender analysis that is the central feature of the present study. In the late 1980s, Joan Scott developed the now-standard definition of gender when she described it as both "a constitutive element of social relationships based on perceived differences between the sexes" and "a primary field within which or by means of which power is articulated."[11] Gender therefore encompasses practices (relations between men and women) and ideas (rules or assumptions about the sexes on which broader power relations are based)—both of which are socially constructed rather than bio-logically determined. Neither gender practices nor ideas are fixed: they have to reflect concerns and experiences of the society using them, or they would lose all meaning. Because of this, the social concept of gender has to be constantly reconstructed to adapt to continuously changing social, political, and economic atmospheres. Within the broader category of gender, the history of Ecuadorian Indian-state relations mandates a close consideration of *patriarchy*, which on its most basic level is "the manifestation and institutionalization of male dominance . . . in society in general," based on the assumption that men are the natural authority figures in the nuclear family.[12] In studying colonial Peru, Bianca Premo noted that patriarchy connected state and household governance through an intricate set of legal and social power relations.[13] This holds for nineteenth-century Ecuadorian Indian-state relations as well: law and custom alike bound multiple and conflicting patriarchal ideas to the question of Indians' status within the nation and determined Indian men and women's ability to engage with the developing nation-state.

As with any aspect of gender, patriarchy is both historically specific and adaptable, and these characteristics of patriarchy are the most complex—and most frequently misinterpreted. Studying struggles among Indian men, Indian women, and the state has led me to consider more closely the malleable, dynamic, and culturally informed meanings of patriarchy as it functioned "in historical motion."[14] In nineteenth-century Ecuador, interpretations of male authority were constantly being reconstructed and renegotiated in connection with other political, economic, and social transformations. Further, these fluctuating patriarchal concepts were culturally specific: though indigenous gender ideas in many ways paralleled the white-mestizo patriarchal precepts outlined in civil law, indigenous patriarchy tended to be more flexible than the concepts upheld by the formative state. Thus, rather than examine how a single and categorical patriarchy related to the history of Ecuadorian Indian-state relations, I examine overlapping, conflicting, and ever-evolving *patriarchies*—emphasizing class and cultural distinctions in patriarchal attitudes as well as changes in these structures and ideas over time.[15]

Sources, Voices, and Silences

I used various political and legal sources to investigate how gender and Indian-state relations were viewed from above and below in nineteenth-century Ecuador. Political sources, such as presidential speeches and decrees, congressional debates, and ministerial reports, offered critical information on central-state perspectives of the Indian and woman problems in Ecuadorian history. Laws themselves often revealed how elite-driven gender and racial ideologies shaped the formative nation-state. My other set of legal documentation, court cases, came from the Archivo Nacional de la Historia in Quito (for Supreme Court cases), and the Archivo Nacional de la Historia in Riobamba (for superior court records). I also examined tribute and hacienda records, and some government correspondence, in these archives. Taken together, these sources highlight the importance of addressing Indian-state relations from multiple vantage points: in addition to taking Indians' as well as state officials' views into account, one must also collect various state views from the historical records rather than relying on official central-state correspondence alone.

Political sources are vital to any study of the nation-state. Presidential speeches, ministerial reports, and congressional debates, for example, offer the official version of a politician's stance on Indians' place within the nation and how best to promote national unity and progress. I examined such sources for key years when debates over Indians and women were raging in Ecuador—mainly in the 1850s, 1870s, and 1895–1918. Laws produced out of these debates also had to be taken into account, and I followed roughly the same pattern of selection. I approach laws as multidimensional: besides setting the parameters within which Indian-state interactions took place, they are fused with sociocultural significance. Laws reflected lawmakers' own values, including deeply embedded gender assumptions. Both Tanja Christiansen and Rossana Barragán Romano have argued that these ideological underpinnings had further sociocultural implications, because laws were a means through which elites attempted to spread their own ideals throughout society.

Laws therefore cannot be considered "merely ideological or divorced from reality."[16] A final layer of top-down views of nation-state formation came via perusal of Ecuador's national newspapers, which provided valuable insights regarding the political culture of nation making.

Indigenous perspectives of nation-state formation came through interrogation of court records, mainly civil and criminal cases that offered information on the intersection of gender and indigenous history. Sometimes these cases included women's direct involvement, but contests between men that called on gender concepts were crucial as well. Also important were trials in which court officials manipulated gender ideologies to evaluate inter- or intraethnic disputes involving Indians. Though court cases show how laws were put into effect and expose discrepancies between central-state laws and regional practices, their greatest significance is in bringing to light how less-powerful groups engaged with formative nation-states. As Chambers observed, court cases help one analyze negotiations involved in the transformation of former colonies into nations, because not only did commoners regularly face members of the state in the courts, but, in doing so, their responses to and interpretations of national development are apparent.[17] More specifically, Charles Walker has asserted that trials were "an important weapon of the peasantry, and the records of trials provide valuable material for historians."[18] That commoners, including peasants, readily and repeatedly brought both inter- and intraethnic disputes to law courts confirms that they thought of the courts as an effective and meaningful way to address grievances. Such cases also show that indigenous peoples did not condone their treatment at the hands of powerful local authorities.[19] This was true even though they did not necessarily win their cases, and many contests were between indigenous peoples rather than against powerful outsiders.[20]

Court cases also provide some of the most readily available and reliable evidence about indigenous peoples' everyday lives and views. Criminal cases are especially informative regarding everyday life and gender relations among Indians, as well as about the unusual events that the cases describe.[21] These cases are not without their problems, and one must take particular care to avoid developing a skewed view of indigenous communities based on crimes that occurred. Christiansen has pointed out that we must further be on the lookout for signs that commoners were aware of elite views and tailored their statements to highlight elite values in the hopes of succeeding with their suits.[22] Civil cases—usually land disputes—though less overtly provocative than criminal cases discussing slander, injury, or homicide, were essential for understanding how indigenous men and women responded to threats to their communal or personal landholdings, and some cases exposed vital information concerning the extent to which indigenous peoples accepted, rejected, or reinterpreted state-sanctioned gender norms.

Summary of the Chapters

In the historical narrative forged out of these various sources, the first chapters focus on the stages of nation-state formation and the Indian problem. Chapter 1 presents the puzzle of Indians' relation to nation-state formation in Ecuador and identifies the relationship between this history and broader concerns in the history of Latin American nation-state formation. In closing, it highlights the importance of gender analysis to studies of Indian-state relations, noting the specific contribution the current work makes to the fields of Indian-state and gender studies for Latin America. Chapter 2 then examines how notions of manliness were pivotal to both state and indigenous manipulations of the tribute debate from 1830 to 1857. In particular, this chapter presents the image of Indians as "child-men" that emerged in the early to mid-nineteenth century and haunted nation-state making in Ecuador for decades to come. Though subsequent regimes evaluated Indian men differently according to their own agendas and in relation to important historical changes, the ongoing struggle to make "proper men" of Indians was central to the processes of nation-state making. Chapter 3 addresses how gender ideas helped to justify indigenous peoples' increasing marginalization and the rising tensions between the state and Indian communities during Gabriel García Moreno's rule, particularly in its second phase from 1869 to 1875. It also explores how Indian men and women often manipulated state-generated gender ideas to advance their own interests in contests with local authorities. Finally, chapter 4 explores how assertions about the need to save Indians during the liberal regime from 1895 to 1925 were ripe with gender implications. Although both Indians and women were subjects of liberal discourses, Indian women were often overlooked. Therefore, while Indian men gained significant new possibilities for negotiating with the state during liberal rule, Indian women did not, and this gender gap laid foundations for later developments in twentieth-century indigenous activism.

The next chapters examine how gender functioned in theory and practice within Indian communities themselves. Chapter 5 scrutinizes social relations within indigenous peasant communities, identifying how indigenous gender ideals sometimes paralleled and at other times diverged from the state-sponsored gender ideologies. Over time Indian men, sometimes to protect their communities and at others to advance their own personal interests, more often incorporated and condoned state-generated ideas about male prerogatives and individual rights. Chapter 6 moves on to examine gender relations among indigenous peoples living and working on large estates, exploring the importance of gender ideas not only to relations between Indian men and women on these estates, but also to estate workers' relationships with hacendados and the state. Overall, hacienda paternalism placed Indian men in a paradoxical position regarding their own patriarchal authority, while it more consistently disadvantaged Indian women.

The book closes by returning to the interplay between history and the present, and to the importance of approaching gender as a multifaceted force operating in Latin American societies. Chapter 7 summarizes findings from the main body of the monograph, and it addresses how the multiple and conflicting patriarchies in Ecuadorian history relate to broader studies of nation making in Latin America. The chapter then uses secondary sources to consider critical developments in

Indian-state relations from 1940 to 1964 and the rise of indigenous activism since 1980. The concluding analysis attends to the ways in which indigenous peoples' recent gender dilemmas are rooted in nineteenth-century transformations in Indian-state relations.

Examining gender during Ecuadorian nation-state making from above and from below does more than show how perceptions of the nation differed according to one's ethnicity or gender. It uncovers important processes of interaction and agency during a critical period in Ecuadorian national history, in which conflicts between Indian men and women, Indians and the state, and even members of the state itself all took part in giving birth to the Ecuadorian nation. The nation that emerged by 1925 was essentially Western in its fundamental concepts; Indian men and (more marginally) women at that time had the power only to help determine how these Western laws and structures would be put into practice, not to define or question the premises on which they were constructed. In the long run, however, this formative period opened doors for more meaningful indigenous political activism, culminating in an ambitious movement that questions the very nature of Western-based nationalism itself.

By Way of Thanks

My quest to understand the gendered past of Ecuadorian Indian-state relations began as a dissertation project. Little did I know then how many years it would take me to transform the dissertation into a book, or how many institutions, colleagues, friends, and family members would so generously buoy me during this lengthy process (my "longest gestation"). A Boston College dissertation fellowship made the original research (1993–1994) possible, in combination with a Janet James Memorial Award in women's studies that helped defray photocopying costs. I returned to Ecuador in 1999 and 2000 with help from faculty start-up funds from West Chester University. A 2000 Spring Local grant from WCU enabled me to make headway on early revisions. A faculty and librarian research grant from Bridgewater State College (BSC) in 2006 provided time and money to help me complete revisions for publication.

In Ecuador, the Facultad de Ciencias Sociales (FLACSO) offered me affiliation that facilitated my research. Doctora Grecia Vasco at the Archivo Nacional de la Historia in Quito and arquitecto Franklin Cárdenas at the Casa de la Cultura in Riobamba allowed me access to historical archives. Likewise Father Julián Bravo at the Biblioteca Ecuatoriana Aurelio Polit in Cotocollao allowed me access to invaluable published primary sources. The staff at all these institutions were very helpful. In Riobamba, I found good and true friends in the archives and beyond; among the most important of these were señora Luz América de Burgos, Susana Bustos, Karina Rojas, and—especially—Piedad Zurita.

Numerous mentors and colleagues have encouraged and influenced my intellectual development, and their contributions have made this a better book than it would otherwise have been. When I was an undergraduate, Nick Racheotes and Paul Gootenberg inspired and encouraged me. As a graduate student, I was privileged to work with Karen Spalding, John Tutino, and Mrinalini Sinha. Fellow Ecuadorianists Marc Becker, Christiana Borchart, Kim Clark, Karen Powers, Aleezé Sattar, Debbie Truhan, and Derek Williams have been wonderful colleagues and friends. Linda Alexander and Jaime Rodriquez also encouraged me when I met them in Quito one summer. I am particularly indebted to Marc Becker, Kim Clark, Nick Racheotes, and John Tutino for their careful reading of the manuscript at different points in the revision process. Members of the Washington Area Symposium on the History of Latin America offered useful suggestions on portions of the manuscript during revision; special thanks there to Vince Peloso and Brian Owensby. At West Chester University, Karin Gedge, Lisa Kirchenbaum, Maria VanLiew, Loretta Rieser-Danner, and Susan Gans offered ideas on early versions of this work. I am fortunate to have colleagues in the history department at BSC who inspire me in all my endeavors, and I thank our department secretary, Caroline Whitney, for her efficiency and friendship. Special thanks at BSC go to Duilio Ayalamacedo, Diana Fox, Andy Harris, Andy Holman, Ellen Ingmanson, Maggie Lowe, and Catherine Womack for their camaraderie. Leo Garofalo and Jama Lazerow have been loyal friends and generous colleagues for many years. Of course, any flaws in the book are my responsibility alone.

I was fortunate to have a wonderful experience with everyone at the University of Arizona Press. Patti Hartmann was especially efficient, encouraging, and helpful from the start. I thank the two anonymous reviewers, whose comments inspired me to think about my work in new ways. I am grateful to manuscript editor Nancy Arora and assistant managing editor Alan M. Schroder for their expert advice. My copyeditor, Melanie Mallon, was meticulous and friendly, and I was fortunate to work with her. Maps appear thanks to the excellent work of Don Larson at Mapping Specialists. I would also like to thank *The Americas* for permission to reprint portions of my article "Widows' Rights Questioned: Indians, the State, and Fluctuating Gender Ideas in Central Highland Ecuador, 1870–1900" (vol. 59, no. 1 [July 2002]: 87–106) in chapters 3 and 5.

Family and friends have given me so much over the years that it's hard to know where to begin thanking them. My parents, Martha and Gerald O'Connor, have been there for me even as I have forged ever deeper into academic terrain that is foreign to them. My many siblings—Kaethi (Cole), Steve, Chris, Mike, Tim, Pat, and Kevin—have cheered me on. Many friends have provided critical distraction from my work at one time or another, among them Ilana Katz, Barbara Kelley, Fernando Larrea, Nancy Mae, David Poulten, Jennie Ruth, Debra Sutton, Deborah Schocket, Laurie Stuhlbarg, Mark and Linda Tomilson, and Gabriela Torres. Debra Abrams and Kate Reist provided pivotal support during the final year of revisions.

My greatest personal debts, aside from those to my parents, lie with my husband and children. Howard Brenner was at my side as I wrote the dissertation then transformed it into a monograph; I'm not sure that I could have done it without him. Our children are woven into the saga of this book as well: I began important revisions while Samuel was a baby, and I came under contract with Arizona while on maternity leave with Anya. My children, more than anyone, give me hope for the future. They also remind me, whenever and however they get the chance, that they are more important than my work. On that note, I should take my leave to go play with them.

Gender, Indian, Nation

⇒ 1 ⇐

National Dilemmas

The Specter of Liberal Individualism in Ecuador

As long as all the classes ... do not have equal rights and duties;
as long as there is a class with duties and without rights,
the Constitution is a joke, the Republic is a lie.
—Minister of the Interior Francisco Icaza, 1856[1]

Indians presented a major challenge to nation-state builders in nineteenth-century Ecuador. Before 1857, Indian tribute stood out as the glaring example of Indians' failure to gain equal status with non-Indians in Ecuador. As the opening quotation shows, the 1856 minister of the Interior identified such racial inequality as an insurmountable obstacle in the quest to make Ecuador into a true nation. Though tribute was abolished a year later, by 1915 statesmen were still bemoaning Indians' marginal status within the nation, this time focusing on the plight of indigenous debt peons on large estates. In 1915, politician and scholar Agustín Cueva identified debt peonage as "the negation of common laws of human nature, the corrosive and thinning substance that retards the formation of national unity."[2] In both eras, liberal statesmen cited specific laws or practices that prohibited Indians from participating fully in the nation, arguing that liberating Indians from oppression was a prerequisite for nation building.[3] The seemingly ahistorical nature of Ecuador's Indian problem can be seen in other ways as well: in both the nineteenth and early twentieth centuries, for example, reforms were slow in coming and limited in impact. Members of the central state had desired the abolition of tribute since Independence, but the Indian head tax remained intact until 1857, and its elimination intensified rather than solved Indians' problems in Ecuador. Similarly, liberals took twenty-three years to abolish imprisonment for debts, and the law failed to change the basic socioeconomic structures to which indigenous workers were subjected on large estates. Yet statesmen of both periods claimed to have solved the Indian problem with their legislative acts and pressed forward with other agendas in their quest to build a strong state and (with it) a coherent nation.

Despite these parallel themes, historians—myself included—are skeptical that such dynamics are ever static. What, then, explains the continuities within Indian-state relations as the Ecuadorian nation was taking shape? What changes marked the passage from one regime to another, as well as the ways in which Indian-state relations were restructured over time? More broadly, what does the Ecuadorian case have to offer to the important and ever-evolving studies of Indians and the nation, and gender and nation, in Latin America? To address these questions requires not only an overview of Ecuadorian Indian-state relations, but also consideration of how Ecuador fits within the broader context of theoretical and historical literature on nation-states, Indians, and gender.

The Problem of Nation-States in Latin America

Studying—even defining—nation-states is challenging, because building a nation is a multilayered, contradictory, and constantly evolving project.[4] States themselves are complex entities, as Philip Abrams noted when he differentiated between the *state system*, which encompasses government infrastructure, hierarchy and policies, and the *state idea*, which comprises a set of ideologies aimed at legitimizing a given ruling regime. Abrams suggested that this emphasis on legitimacy was a "triumph of concealment ... it conceals the real history and relations of subjection behind an a-historical mask of legitimating illusion."[5] This

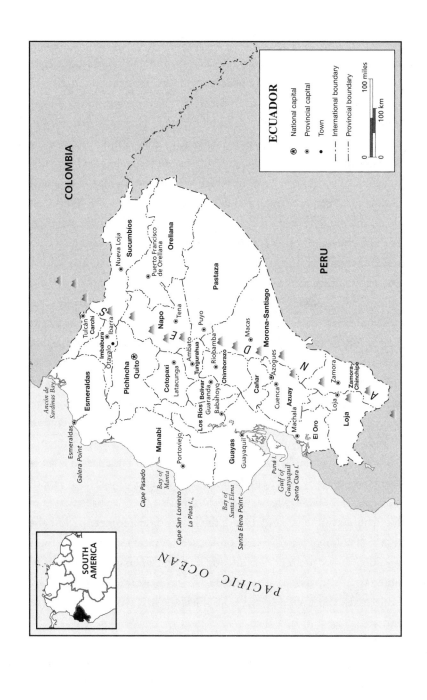

ECUADOR

⊛ National capital
◉ Provincial capital
• Town
–··– International boundary
–···– Provincial boundary

0   100 miles
0   100 km

COLOMBIA

PERU

SOUTH
AMERICA

PACIFIC OCEAN

Ancón de Sardinas Bay

Esmeraldas

Galera Point

Cape Pasado

Bay of Manta

Cape San Lorenzo

La Plata I.

Bay of Santa Elena

Santa Elena Point

Puná I.

Gulf of Guayaquil

Santa Clara I.

Tulcán
Carchi
Ibarra
Imbabura
Otavalo

Nueva Loja
Sucumbíos

Puerto Francisco de Orellana
Orellana

Pastaza

Napo
Tena
Puyo

Pichincha
Quito
Cotopaxi
Latacunga
Ambato
Tungurahua
Bolívar
Guaranda
Riobamba
Chimborazo
Babahoyo
Los Ríos

Macas
Morona-Santiago

Cañar
Azogues
Cuenca
Azuay

Zamora
Zamora-Chinchipe

Loja
Loja

Machala
El Oro

Esmeraldas

Manabí
Portoviejo

Guayas
Guayaquil

triumph of concealment typically justified limiting the political nation to certain social groups while asserting the state's right and power to represent and control all the people within its physical boundaries. In Ecuador, the state system was in the hands of elite white-mestizo men, and the state idea used elite cultural values to justify the exclusion of Indians, women, and the poor from participation within the nation.[6]

The course of Ecuadorian state formation was entangled with the dilemma of nation making, in which statesmen attempted to create an imagined community of people from different classes, regions, cultures, and genders. For a true nation to emerge, a majority of members of these diverse groups would have to develop a sense of belonging with each other and with the state, despite the large size, social inequalities, and exploitation that are all central to the nation.[7] Latin America has an especially complicated relationship to the history and theories of nationalism, as anthropologist Mark Thurner observed when he wrote, "Latin America's republics were 'old' like some European nations, but they were also postcolonial like the African and Asian 'new states' of the twentieth century."[8] Even the language of nation making has been more convoluted in Latin America than elsewhere, given that terms such as *república* simultaneously referred to the colonial-based republic of Indians as well as to the modern notion of republican government.[9] Adding to the complications was Latin American state leaders' acute awareness that they were emulating European and United States models of nation making. Especially problematic was their assertion that they could achieve equality before the law and render meaningless the legacy of colonial legal distinctions based on race. Colonial structures would give way to an era of individual rights, when citizens would be unfettered by corporate identities. Yet Latin American nation-making projects fell short of equality before the law, particularly with regard to Indians' place in the nation.

This elusive quest to replace colonial corporatism with individual equal rights haunted Latin American nations, leading me to refer to it as the specter of liberal individualism.[10] This Latin American dilemma was based as much on tensions within European liberal theory as it was on colonial racial policies. Uday Mehta noted that "In its theoretical vision, liberalism ... has prided itself on its universality and politically inclusionary character. And yet, when it is viewed as a historical phenomenon ... the period of liberal history is unmistakably marked by its systematic and sustained political exclusion of various 'groups' or 'types' of people."[11] Mehta found the answer not in the contradiction between liberal theory and practice, but within liberal theory itself, because liberals suggested that universal rights and freedoms rested on preconditions—notably the ability to reason. The assumptions that women, lower classes, children, or colonized peoples lacked the ability to reason meant that they could be "excluded from the political constituency, or what amounts to the same thing, they can be governed without their consent."[12] In this sense, the universal liberal individual, unburdened by the weight of group identity, never existed. Small wonder, then, that Ecuadorian statesmen found it difficult to adapt European individualism to their own nation, since their archetype was constructed and fictional rather than natural and original.

Not only were indigenous peoples (and peasants more generally) marginalized within elite nation-making discourses, but until the past few decades, scholars too identified them as detached from central-state politics and nationalism. Since the 1980s, however, numerous studies have shown that these groups were engaged with the process of nation-state formation. This interaction was most pronounced when wars threatened the nation—foreign invasion especially, but sometimes also periods of internal struggle.[13] Indigenous and peasant political leaders, whose roles bridged the colonial and national periods, mediated between rural commoners and state officials in the transformation from colony to republic.[14] Even indigenous peasant uprisings are coming under new scrutiny, particularly how insurgents related to concepts such as nation and republic. While it is true that rebel leaders called on elite-generated national discourses, they also adapted these ideas, merging them with national views that were shaped by their local economic, political, and cultural experiences, needs, and values.[15]

Together, these examinations of Indians, peasants, and nations have done far more than add the marginalized to the history of nation-state formation in Latin America. They have placed indigenous peoples and peasants at the center of national histories, and many of them have called into question basic assumptions in earlier studies of nation-states. Historians and anthropologists have taken us into the realm of what Thurner aptly describes as the "unimagined community"—the nation as indigenous peoples perceived it, which was quite different from elite perspectives.[16] Even the term "nationalism" has become more complicated: Florencia Mallon and Peter Guardino have argued persuasively that "alternative" or "popular" nationalisms coexisted with state-generated nationalisms in Latin America, and peasant nationalisms sometimes affected government policies.[17] In sum, though rural peoples may not have made the laws or run post-Independence governments, they were actively involved in shaping the state idea behind nationalism; in fact, they influenced nationalism even when they ignored rather than employed state ideas or policies. Their silence speaks to the failure of ruling regimes to build programs that took regional realities into account, and indigenous peoples' refusal to act on state-driven ideas or policies set limits on the reach of the national project as it was envisioned by political elites.[18]

As with all scholarly advances, these path-breaking studies of Indian and peasant engagement with nationalism have their limits. Gender remains one of the least developed facets of these studies, though Mallon's study of postcolonial Mexico and Peru, and Greg Grandin's examination of Guatemala, both evaluate how patriarchy related to peasant or indigenous involvement with nation-state formation.[19] Second, much more is known about subaltern leaders and intellectuals than about the aspirations, views, or strategies of indigenous and peasant commoners.[20] Finally, geographic treatment of these issues is quite uneven: to date, we know much more about how Indians and peasants engaged with formative nation-states in Peru or Mexico than we do in most other areas of Latin America, including Ecuador.

Though scholars have begun to identify the significance of the Indian problem to Ecuadorian political development, or examined ways in which Indians interacted with the formative state, analysis of Indians' roles in the course of Ecuadorian nation making is still in its early stages.[21] As the history of Ecuadorian Indians and the nation unfolds, interesting discoveries are being made regarding popular perceptions of and participation in politics.[22] For example, A. Kim Clark's study of the liberal period demonstrated that the failure of any one elite group to dominate the process of nation making "created the openings that allowed subordinate groups to pursue their own interests within the bounds of the liberal project."[23] Studying past relations between Indians and the state is important not only because of Indians' political activism in the current day, but also because Ecuador's national development was markedly different from that of nations like Mexico or Peru. Ecuador did share certain similarities with its Andean neighbors Peru and Bolivia in the early nineteenth century, when Indians in all three nations remained legally separate from non-Indians through the continuing collection of tribute. Yet in most ways Ecuador was uncommon: unlike either Mexico or Peru, in Ecuador there was no foreign invasion for peasants to resist as a means of expressing their own vision of nationalism; nor was Ecuadorian state formation in the nineteenth century led by a liberal government, as was the case in most other parts of Latin America. Instead, Ecuadorian political turbulence was generated solely from within, and state centralization began under the conservative rule of Gabriel García Moreno, since liberalism came later to Ecuador than to most other Latin American countries. Studying a less-well-researched nation like Ecuador promises to highlight broad patterns versus regional discrepancies in the history of Latin American Indian-state relations.

To see how Ecuadorian Indian-state relations functioned in the era of nation-state formation, as well as to understand how and why gender analysis figures centrally in these developments, it is necessary to explore the complicated processes of nation making in nineteenth-century Ecuador. This again raises the dilemma posed at the beginning of the chapter—why and how did Indian problems plague Ecuadorian statesmen for more than a century? Attending to this question takes one from the colonial foundations of the Indian problem, through the 1857 abolition of Indian tribute, and into the contradictions of state building from 1861 to 1925.

From Colony to Tribute-Laden Republic

Though the Indian problem was a specifically republican dilemma, its roots were in the colonial period. The Spanish created the category of "Indian" to facilitate their rule, but actual Indian identity and culture was a product of encounters, negotiations, and conflicts between Spanish colonizers and indigenous peoples.[24] "Indian," however, was also a meaningful legal category that shaped colonial encounters, allowing the Spanish crown to justify European rule and manage its American colonies. One of the most important aspects of Spain's Indian policies was the division of the American colonies into separate Spanish and Indian republics, in which each group had different obligations and rights before the law. Spanish settlers were privileged and had rights to indigenous labor, but they were also supposed to protect and convert indigenous peoples. Indians were periodically conscripted to work for the Spanish, and all Indian men between the ages of eighteen and fifty had to pay tribute to the Spanish crown and *diezmos* (first fruits) to the Catholic Church (through state collectors). Local indigenous leaders (*caciques*, or *kurakas*) helped to link the two republics; they assisted the Spanish with tribute collection, meted out justice in their communities, and represented community interests to Spanish officials. To keep caciques from gaining too much power, the Spanish created indigenous *cabildos* (town councils), which were elected annually to oversee local customs and mediate civil disputes. Indian leaders' strategies varied: some were primarily concerned with protecting and serving their communities, whereas others emphasized Spanish colonial interests over those of community members.[25]

In addition to creating a juridical category of Indian that transcended pre-Columbian cultural and political divisions, the system of two republics also provided fertile ground for the development of racial stereotypes. Indians were secondary and inferior to members of the Republic of Spaniards, who were exempt from tribute and labor obligations, were given preferential treatment in commerce, and controlled all upper levels of politics. This essential inequality was based at first primarily on religious principles, emphasizing that it was necessary to rule over Indians and limit their rights and powers in order to bring them the true faith. Over time, justifications more clearly identified Indians as *niños con barbas* (bearded children) who, although they reached physical maturity, in other ways remained forever childlike and therefore required European guidance, protection, and rule. Indians were generally categorized by their culture, payment of tribute, and—for the vast majority—poverty and rural life. By the late colonial period, stereotypes emerged throughout Spanish America that identified indigenous peoples with numerous bad qualities, such as a propensity to drunkenness and idleness, which only strict supervision and rule could keep in check.[26]

Indigenous peoples also provided the backbone of the colonial and republican economies, which developed to exploit Indian laborers and natural resources. In the Ecuadorian highlands, the temperate and relatively dry climate led to an economy dominated by large estates geared toward textile production, with labor performed primarily by indigenous indebted workers (*conciertos*). By the late seventeenth century, there were approximately two hundred textile *obrajes* (workshops), with most found in the north-central highlands.[27] The tropical coastal climate favored the development of cacao plantations, which spread in the late eighteenth century. Around this time, however, highland obrajes were in decline, making it possible for highland Indians to provide much of the labor force for the cacao boom, since highland hacendados and obraje owners did not need as many Indian workers as they had in more prosperous periods.[28] Economic crises in the north-central highlands often presented opportunities for coastal landowners since Indians would migrate from the highlands in search of work.[29] The opposite was also true: a prosperous highland economy led to labor scarcity on coastal estates. This pattern of alternating economic advantages between the coast and the highlands continued throughout much of the nineteenth century.[30]

Indians too could benefit from economic crises that hit the highland elite. For example, the decline of obrajes created business opportunities for some Indian peasants to provide home-produced textiles for local markets. Since the relative decline of large estates typically meant more secure and autonomous peasant production, the late colonial and early republican periods look better if viewed from indigenous rather than elite perspectives. The extent to which indigenous peoples could take advantage of changing economic and political conditions, however, differed based on demographics, especially the ratio of poor peasants to large estates. In the northern highlands, fewer peasants experienced economic crises that pushed them into debt peonage, whereas in the central highland province of Chimborazo, there were more poor Indians in need of loans than there were positions on large estates. Therefore, estate owners in the northern highlands competed for workers, while indigenous peoples in the central highlands competed for work. Even though the system of two republics gave the generic category of "Indian" real legal meaning, a diverse range of indigenous lives, customs, and opportunities flourished under colonial administration.

Indian commoners did find ways to make colonial life manageable and sometimes beneficial despite the exploitative nature of the system of two republics. In return for ethnically specific obligations, Indians were exempt from military service, most other taxes, and the majority of court fees—all of which made subsistence easier to maintain. The tribute system also helped indigenous communities preserve communal land rights and local indigenous political officials, as the state deemed both necessary to allow Indians to meet tribute requirements. Indians who found tribute too burdensome sometimes fled their home communities, becoming *forasteros* who escaped the heaviest obligations to the state. Still more Indians used the colonial court system to protest excessive exploitation or abuse: given the crown's proclaimed goal of protecting indigenous peoples, court cases could bring sufficient relief from the most onerous burdens and abuses. When peaceful means failed, Indian communities resorted to violence, though rebellions sought to address specific problems rather than reject the colonial system as a whole. Despite the inherent contradictions of the system of two republics, and the complications of the dual system with the rise of mestizo and forastero populations, the structure proved enduring because it could be manipulated from both above and below.[31] For the state, the separate republics, along with the conversion of native peoples to Catholicism, justified ethnic divisions and inequalities inherent in the colonial project. The system's emphasis on protection, however, also gave indigenous peoples outlets to defend their communities, subsistence, and local autonomy.

Independence brought an end to the precarious balance between Indians and the state. Independence leaders had identified Spanish rule as tyrannical and identified (often justifiably) Spanish policies as the source of racial inequalities. Yet they were not inclined to change the socioeconomic and racial hierarchies from which they benefited, nor did they think that Indians should enjoy a direct political voice in the nation. In short, early Ecuadorian statesmen were caught between their proclaimed desire to fashion a nation out of liberal individuals and their deeply embedded conviction that Indians were unfit for inclusion in the nation. Indian tribute stood out as the most glaring example of Ecuador's failure to overcome its colonial legacy in the early nineteenth century because it rested on colonial-style corporatism. National politicians therefore viewed it as the primary obstacle to creating a nation based on the tenets of liberal individualism.

Although the tax troubled statesmen, indigenous peoples' views of tribute were mixed. On the one hand, many indigenous communities found the tribute system preferable because it provided exemptions from other taxes and secured communal and cultural rights. On the other hand, there were individuals during the period who struggled to escape tribute payments, either because they were unable to shoulder the tax burden or perhaps because of looser cultural ties within their communities. In the long run, it was economic necessity, not elite politics or indigenous concerns, that kept the tribute system alive. Protracted and expensive Independence wars, followed by economic stagnation in the 1830s and 1840s, left the new national government with few sources of revenue to keep it afloat. During this time, tribute accounted for 35 percent of state income, making it impossible for legislators to abolish the head tax.[32] Only in the 1850s, when rising cacao exports meant that tribute accounted for a mere 8.5 percent of the government's total financial resources, did Ecuadorian statesmen more seriously consider doing away with it.[33] With financial confidence and emphatic declarations that the Indian was being liberated from centuries of colonial oppression, Congress abolished tribute in October 1857.[34] The abolition of tribute complicated rather than solved the Indian dilemma in Ecuadorian nation making, but Indians' formal equality before the law paved the way for García Moreno's state-building projects in the 1860s and 1870s.

Indians, the Nation, and Garcianismo

Historians have long classified Gabriel García Moreno as a conservative, and certain aspects of his rule uphold this categorization, most notably the prominent role of the Church in Garcian state building. Although García Moreno's commitment to the Catholic Church was strongly influenced by his religious upbringing and education, religion also provided him with a powerful political tool to unify a fragmented country.[35] Rather than point to the supremacy of law, García Moreno held that only God was infallible, hence only God's laws could provide a truly stable foundation for Ecuadorian society; republicanism therefore had to be infused with Catholicism.[36] The relationship between Church and state during this period was mutually beneficial: an 1862 concordat with Rome gave the Church property as well as control of education and censorship, while García Moreno had the right to expel many Ecuadorian religious officials from their posts, replacing them with foreign priests and nuns.[37] The introduction of foreign Church officials rested on García Moreno's admiration of the French Catholic Brothers' educational strategies; perhaps it was also related to his careful distinction between "uncorrupted Catholic faith and corruptible Catholic authorities."[38] Religion further provided García Moreno with a tool for social control, a means to augment state (and his own personal) power, and justification for political repression.[39] By the second phase of Garcian rule, from 1869 to 1875, Catholicism was even a requirement for Ecuadorian citizenship.[40]

Yet to label García Moreno simply as a conservative, particularly to associate him with backward-looking or colonial-style government, based on the centrality of religion to his rule would be a mistake. Historian Derek Williams has argued that Garcian religious policies were neither simply strategic nor seeking to bring back an earlier style of rule. Instead, he asserts that García Moreno aspired to an age of "Catholic Modernity" and used Catholicism to unite Ecuador into a single national community.[41] If García Moreno fused state formation with Catholicism, he did so in such a way as to ensure that the state was the dominant partner; he manipulated religion to bring coherence to the fractured nation and to increase the power of the central government. Similarly, his administrative goals were centered on national growth and modernization, as his commitment to improving roads and building railroads showed. Garcian educational projects also embraced the modern nation, given that García Moreno's proclaimed goal was to improve the opportunities for all Ecuadorians and to expand the political nation by raising literacy rates. Even García Moreno's relationship to different elite sectors defied simple conservative categorization. If highland hacendados had the greatest direct influence in national politics during Garcianismo, the government also supported cacao exports and lightened trade restrictions—both policies that benefited coastal landowners.

At the same time that Garcianismo supported religious corporatism and social hierarchies, it was a political project emphasizing individual responsibility and equality before the law, even though it identified this equality as an evangelical rather than secular national community.[42]

Morality-based equality before the law meant that the specter of liberal individualism haunted this conservative state, and as usual the core difficulty lay with the plight of Indians in the nation. Though the Indian problem was supposedly solved by the abolition of tribute, Garcian policies (especially from 1869 to 1875) led to increased tensions between Indians and the state. After the abolition of tribute, Indians were obliged to pay taxes from which they formerly had been exempt, and the new requirements were frequently more burdensome than tribute had been. Moreover, by the late 1860s the central state stopped recognizing, let alone supporting, indigenous protective laws, communal lands, or indigenous leaders. At the same time, indigenous workers were the primary labor force for infrastructural projects, marking the continuation of ethnically distinct obligations in the nation. The central government response to Indians' contradictory status was silence: within the space of a few years, Indians' plight went from being a prominent national concern to an issue that was rarely mentioned in Quito.

Indians did not passively accept their fate during this time of mounting crisis. Those who could afford to do so sought titles that would protect their land rights. Others went to court to complain that large estate owners had either taken their land or had blocked their access to vital resources—these cases, however, typically failed because of hacendados' dominance of local political and judicial processes. Without recourse against hacienda owners, most Indians were left to either squabble with each other over remaining lands or turn to haciendas for employment (temporary or permanent) to meet subsistence needs. Occasionally they rebelled against abusive officials or unbearable tax burdens, managing—as they had since colonial times—to alleviate temporarily the most intense demands and abuses. The most outstanding rebellion in this period occurred in the central highland province of Chimborazo, where in December 1871 Indians from Punín, Yaruquíes, and Cajabamba protested violently against rising taxation. Although the uprising eased tax burdens only briefly, it greatly alarmed members of white-mestizo society, reminding them of the potential danger of pushing disgruntled indigenous communities too far.

García Moreno's death by assassination in August 1875 brought an end to Catholic state building and marked the return of political turmoil, with conservative forces split and liberals not yet able to win state power. In the meantime, the political and economic rivalry between the coast and the highlands continued to build. In this atmosphere of intense regional and political polarization, a moderate leader such as Antonio Borrero (1875–1876) faced potential criticism from conservatives for suggesting reforms and possible rejection by liberals for not pushing reform along far or fast enough.[43] Others, like Ignacio de Ventimilla (1876–1883), promised to support radical liberal ideals but once in power proved to have dictatorial leanings.[44] Political upheaval had tangible results: though the economy was booming in the highlands and on the coast, road and railway construction came to a halt, and many public roads fell into disrepair.[45] By 1895 tensions were at a peak, and liberal forces were finally powerful enough (both politically and militarily) to overtake the national government.[46] For the next thirty years, from 1895 to 1925, liberals controlled the presidency; Congress, however, remained mixed with liberals and conservatives and was frequently the site of heated debate over liberal reforms. Given that Garcianismo had been the last period of orderly (if authoritarian) nation-state development, the conservative regime had a lingering impact on liberal projects. If on the one hand Garcian Catholic conservatism was anathema to secularizing liberals, on the other hand they had much in common with their conservative predecessor's educational and infrastructural projects. And, of course, they inherited the still-unresolved Indian problem.

Liberals, Indians, and the Nation

Liberal secularizing policies from 1895 to 1925 were in most ways opposed to García Moreno's Catholic unity. Whereas García Moreno had emphasized Catholicism as a unifying national force, liberals argued that Church and state had to be separated, and they presented the nation as a secular brotherhood. Many liberal reforms attacked the Church's social and economic power, made the Church dependent on the state, and promoted freedom of worship. Liberal reforms also replaced ecclesiastic control of education and marriage with secular institutions. These were not only strikes against a powerful national institution but attempts to ensure that the next generation of Ecuadorians would cultivate loyalties to the state rather than to the Church. The regional bases of the two regimes also differed: political power rested in the hands of highland landowners during Garcianismo, while coastal landowning and banking elites were the driving socioeconomic forces behind the liberal revolution.

Liberals claimed that they would regenerate the nation, saving it from the debilitating impact of religious and landowning authorities in the highlands (who were, conveniently, their greatest rivals for sociopolitical power). Indians featured prominently in liberal discourse, with reformers professing they would liberate highland Indians from their traditional oppressors. One aspect of this mission was evident when the state took over Church-owned haciendas in 1904.[47] The law allowed liberal reformers to claim that they had saved highland Indians from corrupt Church authorities while it gave the central state new political and financial power in rural areas. The abolition of *concertaje* (debt peonage) was, however, the most important liberal crusade against Indians' subjugation. Liberal rhetoric blamed hacendados for keeping Indians in an oppressed and semifeudal state, while identifying conciertos as good and honorable workers.[48] Coastal liberals argued that it was necessary to drag the highlands into modernity by eliminating the practice of debt peonage and replacing it with wage labor, which would in turn result in a more efficient indigenous workforce and encourage hacendados to adopt new technologies.[49] Such assertions also justified the liberal takeover of the central state, allowing liberals to argue that their regime aimed at finally making all citizens equal before the law, in contrast with previous regimes that had reinforced oppressive hierarchies and practices.

Yet highland haciendas were far from unchanging, and liberal reformers were not as progressive as they claimed to be. Although liberals identified concertaje with feudalism, hacendados often expanded production in order to take advantage of new markets, most recently new transportation routes created during Garcianismo. Moreover, in the early decades of the twentieth century, many hacendados of the north-central highlands were adopting modernized agricultural techniques or switching from grain to dairy production; both shifts lowered their labor needs and meant that concertaje was on the decline in portions of the highlands even before its 1918 abolition.[50] The elimination of Indian debt peonage was also not as fundamental to the liberal platform as many social reformers claimed. Besides the fact that it was twenty-three years into the liberal regime before imprisonment for debts was made illegal, concertaje was based on much more than hacendados' ability to send indigenous workers to prison for the debts they owed. Instead, highland estate owners secured indigenous labor through a complex system of obligations and rights, coercion and persuasion, cruelty and kindness. Though liberal legislators congratulated themselves on having eliminated concertaje, the 1918 law did not dismantle the system, which survived (under the name *huasipungaje* for the subsistence plots male workers received) until the 1964 agrarian reform law. The limitations of the "abolition" of concertaje were not lost on social critic Pio Jaramillo Alvarado, who noted how difficult it was to address the problem of interethnic exploitation on haciendas because "this form of slavery [concertaje] has been theoretically abolished. [Since] imprisonment for debt has been extinguished, concertaje has lost its greatest support! But is it true that this legal disposition is enough to extirpate this gangrene that has paralyzed ... agriculture?"[51]

Liberals' principal motive to eliminate imprisonment for debts on highland estates stemmed from coastal landowners' desire to gain access to indigenous laborers. Unlike the late eighteenth and early nineteenth centuries, when periods of economic expansion (or crisis) alternated between the highlands and the coast, in the late nineteenth century, coastal and highland estate owners experienced simultaneous growth, which led to conflicts over the acquisition of Indian workers. As historian Yves Saint-Geours aptly put it, "The Indian during this period is a [critical] factor in the struggles between highland hacenda-dos and large property owners on the coast."[52] Abolishing imprison-ment for debts also gave the central state authority to mediate disputes between hacendados and indigenous workers, strengthening state offi-cials' power over highland elites.[53]

Although based on opposed premises, Garcianismo and liberalism shared much common ground. One of the more obvious links between them was their commitment to national unification, beginning with the physical nation: construction of the Guayaquil–Quito railway, for example, began under García Moreno's rule and was completed dur-ing the liberal period. The railway was to do much more than simply improve transportation: its proponents hoped it would encourage peoples of all classes and regions to feel the presence of the state and to begin finally to think of themselves as belonging to the Ecuador-ian nation.[54] In general, both Garcianismo and liberalism attempted to unite the fragmented country and recreate it into a modern nation through the development of a strong central state. Both regimes, how-ever, failed to achieve a fundamental aspect of their goals because of their inability to resolve the problem of Indian difference within the nation.

Gender, Nation, and Indians

While an overview of nineteenth- and early twentieth-century state for-mation projects reveals how changes in Ecuador's Indian problem related to broader political, economic, and social transformations, questions still remain. A matter of special concern is how central government officials, regional authorities, and Indians themselves comprehended and acted on the intricate pattern of continuities and changes in nineteenth-century Indian-state relations. Given the uneven development of Indian-state relations, how did both state officials and Indian com-moners make sense of new and old themes regarding Indians' position in the emerging nation? Likewise, the specter of liberal individualism calls for deeper exploration. How did political leaders reconcile proclaimed egalitarian goals with practical reinforcement of racial difference in each era of nation making? To what extent did any of the ideals of liberal individualism penetrate indigenous communities or at least their negotiations with state officials as the nation took shape?

Gender analysis can be applied to explore, evaluate, and enunciate the changes in official political discourses about Indians from Independence through 1925; it also reveals the distinct relationships that indigenous men and women developed with the emerging state and the nation it claimed to represent. Gender offered a critical tool (though, certainly, not the only one) that state officials and indigenous peoples used to contend with the many challenges and contradictions involved in making Ecuador. Gender ideas were central to Indian-state relations because they had been essential to colonial Indian-state relations; moreover, both elite and indigenous peoples used gender as a fundamental component for structuring their own societies. It therefore stood to reason that gender concepts would prove important in the inter- and intraethnic struggles of nation-state formation, because they had been critical to maintaining social order for centuries. Whether reinforcing old concepts, or altering patriarchal precepts to fit new conditions, manipulating gender ideas was a natural, perhaps even unselfconscious, choice to make sense of the contradictory and unsettling changes that came with forging a nation.

There is a well-established precedent for asserting that gender was a central feature of nation-state formation. Phillip Corrigan and Derek Sayer identified patriarchal familial relations as "a major organizing metaphor for the state," and Anne McClintock has gone so far as to contend that "all nationalisms are gendered; all are invented; and all are dangerous."[55] Within Latin America, various scholars have found that gender analysis illuminates and alters our interpretation of how nations and nationalisms took shape. Where supposedly gender-neutral studies suggested that women as well as men benefited from liberal secularization policies, gender-sensitive investigations have often found the opposite, helping us to better understand the limits and contradictions of nineteenth-century liberalism.[56] Tensions between women and nation in Latin America can be seen from Independence forward, and they were predicated on a basic association between citizenship and patriarchy. Rebecca Earle and Elizabeth Dore, for example, have both demonstrated that patriarchal principles defined citizenship in nineteenth-century Colombian and Nicaraguan constitutions.[57] Nations were thus built on the powerful combined force of law and patriarchy. While this dynamic between gender and nation worked to elite men's benefit in most cases, it had a mixed impact on poor and nonwhite men. On the one hand, men like the artisans that Chambers studied in Arequipa, Peru, adapted elite-generated notions of honor to their own benefit, marking a democratization of honor that made it possible to assert their rights as citizens within the new nation.[58] On the other hand, politicians could use notions of male authority and paternalism to reconceptualize and reinforce ethnic hierarchies in the new republican setting. Both Rossana Barragán for Bolivia and Andrés Guerrero for Ecuador have indicated that gender ideas helped to reconcile the paradox of theoretically universal law codes coexisting with discriminatory regulations.[59]

Overall, various scholars have found that not only was gender central to nation-state formation, but patriarchy was in fact strengthened in the process. Chambers concluded that the democratization of honor in nineteenth-century Arequipa rested in part on women's subordination, and her findings reflect studies done in other regions as well.[60] Law as well as custom deepened patriarchal rights, particularly with regard to wives' legal status: as men gained new rights, women's powers were legally circumscribed, and wives especially were more clearly and fully subordinated within marriage.[61] Therefore, while poor and nonwhite men might in some circumstances be placed under the paternal power of white elite men, all men shared legally endorsed power over women. This aspect of republican patriarchy was one facet that distinguished it from colonial structures.[62] In all cases, whether an individual man's patriarchal powers were primarily strengthened or weakened, the process of nation making in Latin America *modernized* patriarchy.[63]

One important gap in the literature on gender and the nation pertains to the urban-rural divide. We certainly know more about middle-class and urban elite women and men's relationships to nation making than any other group, though our understanding of poorer urban dwellers' experiences has expanded significantly in recent years. Studies of gender and nation in the countryside, however, are fewer and typically less well developed. Important exceptions that combine the fields of gender and peasant studies for nation-state formation are Grandin's work on Guatemala and Mallon's work on Mexico and Peru. Grandin's examination of Indian-state relations has shown that indigenous elites' authority as patriarchs over their own families *and communities* was essential to their adaptation to political and economic transformations in the nineteenth century. Likewise, he has traced ways in which indigenous women's maintenance of outward signs of ethnic identity was critical to the urbanization and modernization of Mayan identity.[64] For Mexico and Peru, Mallon has argued that patriarchy was central not only to state formation from above, but also in the development of peasants' alternative nationalisms. She has proposed that gender ideologies, and patriarchy in particular, were on equal footing with class and ethnic hierarchies in "reproducing systems of domination."[65] Mallon, especially, has not only shown that gender was an important part of the history of nationalism but also suggests that nationalism cannot be seen as having only one meaning among peoples of different classes, ethnicities, and regions. Her discussion of gender further highlights ways in which subaltern peoples did not simply adopt elite nationalisms but rather reshaped them to address their own internal community relations, problems, ideologies, and goals.[66] Yet even these pioneering works tend to focus on Indians and peasants in leadership roles, and they offer little sense of peasant and indigenous commoners' experiences of and impact on nation making, given that Grandin's study focuses mainly on male indigenous elites, and Mallon's on peasant intermediaries.

One way to meet the challenge of filling gaps in the historical literature on gender, Indians, and the nation-state is by exploring the uneven and often contradictory processes of nation making in nineteenth-century Ecuador. Focusing this exploration on the countryside, and incorporating women as well as men, commoners as well as community leaders, when analyzing the relationship between indigenous peoples and the formative nation not only complements studies of Mexico, Peru, and Guatemala but also offers a new view of the overall process of state formation and nation making. Such an undertaking is particularly critical for Ecuador in order to understand indigenous women's paradoxical relationships to the rise of indigenous activist politics from the mid-twentieth century forward. Though the transformations in gendered interethnic politics in Ecuador were often irregular and incomplete, new sociopolitical conditions had taken shape by 1925 that made it possible for modern Indian-state relations to take root. This modernization of Indian-state relations in the making of Ecuador had significant, and divergent, effects on Indian men and women.

⇌ 2 ⇋

Making Ecuadorians?

Indian Child-Men and the Abolition of Tribute

[Tribute] made the *indígenas* a true minority that needed their interests and
rights watched over, with privileges and guardianship to protect them. . . .
Since that time this disgraced class has achieved next to nothing in culture:
the majority do not even know the national language in which our laws
are written: they are ignorant of the progress of civilization.

—José María Urvina[1]

President José María Urvina's evaluation of tribute, less than a year
after its abolition, was typical of early republican assessments that
blamed Spanish colonialism for both the unjust tax and for Indians'
marginalization within the nation. Urvina's statement also hinted at
the gendered underpinnings of the early nineteenth-century Indian
problem in Ecuador. Because Indians' childlike condition resulted from
the tribute system, the abolition of tribute (linchpin of colonial racial
politics) would bring them out of their perpetual minority status and
make them into men who could be civilized and eventually granted citizenship status. At the same time that politicians rhetorically endorsed
Indian manliness, however, both state officials and Indians themselves
continued to call on colonial-style racial paternalism in their interactions with each other. Interethnic paternalism was more than merely a
holdover from colonial times; it was also the product of early republican
political upheaval. In such uncertain times, Indian men were symboli-

cally and legally caught between past and present, between citizenship and subjection, between manliness and minority status.

The 1857 abolition of Indian tribute was a critical moment in Ecuadorian Indian-state relations, though not for making Indians equal to the rest of Ecuadorians, as legislators claimed when they discontinued this tax that, according to them, violated "constitutional precepts."[2] Because of its centrality to both nation making and indigenous history in the Andes, the abolition of tribute has been the focus of scholarly studies that have closely considered the tribute and post-tribute systems from state and indigenous perspectives. Researchers have shown that although statesmen were troubled by the ongoing collection of an ethnically distinct tax, indigenous peoples often preferred it over the host of new taxes and loss of land and leaders that came with abolition. Overall, Indians in these nations participated actively in the early processes of nation making, adapting to new republican initiatives, taking advantage of the dilemmas over the Indian problem, and setting limits on the changes that members of the central government could make.[3]

Information on gender dynamics, however, has been rather cursory in contrast with the depth of other findings, even though multilayered interethnic paternalisms were central to the colonial and early republican tribute systems. With Independence, national leaders sought to abolish tribute both to break away from the colonial past and to create a nation of liberal individuals who were equal before the law; these goals mandated overturning Indian men's colonial-era minority status in order to make men out of them. Concerns over tribute were so critical to national development that the dilemma constituted the first true national debate in Ecuadorian history. The contours, contradictions, and shortcomings of early nineteenth-century Indian discourses would in turn shape Indian-state relations for decades to come.

Gender, Indians, and Tribute in the Colonial Period

Gender ideas shaped and justified Spain's developing Indian policies from the very start, as when Juan Ginés de Sepúlveda (in his famous

1550 debate with Bartolomé de Las Casas) asserted that the Indians "are as inferior to the Spaniards as children are to adults, or women to men."[4] The Spanish crown acted on this premise by identifying Indians as perpetual minors who, although they gained certain rights of adulthood once they reached the age of majority, remained a legally subordinated group in need of the crown's protection and guidance.[5] The resulting system of two republics was deeply paternalistic, with the crown acting as a benevolent father figure promising to bring Indians to the true faith, protect their lands and interests, and provide them with access to justice. In return, the crown's Indian vassals owed their fatherly king loyalty, obedience, tribute, and periodic labor. Tribute was the cornerstone of the colonial system: to the Spanish rulers, Indian tribute was the "price that the native population had to pay for receiving the benefits of Spanish 'civilization,'" and as such, it continually reinforced Indians' minor legal status.[6] For Indians, paying tribute marked their legal right to land and their exemption from other taxes and military service.[7] Various officials were to ensure that the crown's paternal will was carried out in the colonies, including a Spanish administrator (*corregidor*), the *protector de indios* who represented Indians' interests in court, judges within the court system, the local priest, and even the local cacique. Although interethnic paternalism justified colonial exploitation, Indian men could use their minor status to call on the crown, through its representative judges, to "[look] out always for the welfare of the Indians."[8]

At the same time that the system of two republics legalized Indian men's perpetual minor status relative to Spaniards, it also quietly recognized their patriarchal authority within their own families. Tribute was collected from adult men only, based on the notion that men (including indigenous men) were the natural heads of households.[9] State recognition for Indian men's patriarchal authority was evident in early republican laws also, as when Simón Bolívar redistributed Indian communal lands to "the heads of Indian families," assuming these were men, when he first abolished tribute in 1821.[10] Deeply embedded gender assumptions within the system of two republics, and more specifically tribute collection, meant that when early nineteenth-century Ecuadorian statesmen debated and dismantled various aspects of the colonial system, they were forced to confront the gendered politics of interethnic rule.

There were republican as well as colonial reasons that gender was central to the debate over tribute. Early national leaders strongly identified the republic with manliness, as was evident when Simón Bolívar described Ferdinand VII as a "neglectful father"—suggesting that it was time for men of the colonies to assert their manly adulthood by breaking away from a paternal figure who had not fulfilled his obligations.[11] Once fully formed, the new republics would foster a sense of community and belonging among men; Bolívar, for example, opposed the tribute system because of its association with inequality before the law. He did not, however, extend individual rights and equality to the 50 percent of the population that was female. Bolívar did recognize women's contributions to Independence, stating that "even the fair sex . . . fought against the tyrants of San Carlos with valor divine." However, he opposed women's participation in republican politics because "a woman ought to be neutral in public business. Her family and her domestic duties are her first obligations."[12] Given this background, it was perhaps inevitable that gender would play a pivotal role in the debate over abolishing tribute in Ecuador, shaping not only legal disputes but also struggles between public and private authorities over who should represent Indians' or the nation's interests. Indian men added their voices to the debate by manipulating the contradictory state in which they found themselves.

Colonial Children or Republican Citizens?

At that same time that early republican leaders championed eliminating racial distinctions, they maintained many racial and social inequalities, always carefully highlighting the necessity of such actions. When Bolívar reintroduced tribute in 1828, under the name "personal contribution of indígenas," he emphasized that Indians themselves had requested that the tax be reinstated to maintain their exempt status from other obligations.[13] Such arguments were not unusual for The Liberator, who touted the ideals of republican, representative government while favoring life terms for some representatives and carefully differentiating between active citizens who could vote and hold office versus passive citizens who could not but who (supposedly) enjoyed equality before the law in all other ways.[14] Similar concepts were included in Ecuador's first national constitution in 1830, where it was stipulated that to be a citizen, one had to have property worth three hundred pesos, exercise a profession without being subject to another (such as a servant), and be literate. Those disqualified were mostly indigenous peoples and poor *castas* (peoples of mixed heritage).[15]

Critics of the personal contribution were quick to point out this contradiction between republican egalitarian ideals and racial distinctions that followed colonial legal practices. In 1856, minister of the Interior Francisco Icaza pointed out that "Our conscience over our bad proceedings has obliged us to disguise the ancient *tribute* with the name of contribution: we then proclaimed 'long live the Republic,' and we ... [are] proud and satisfied with our work, [in] the place of our conquerors."[16] In both 1831 and 1843, Congress attempted to resolve this early republican conundrum by establishing a head tax that adult Ecuadorian men of all races had to pay, declaring that since "indigenous peoples [pay] a personal tax, it is just to extend this to other classes within the State." In fact, many Indians would not have to pay the tax because it was not collected from men who earned fewer than one hundred pesos per year.[17] Attempts at creating universal contributions were short-lived, however, due to strong—even violent—protest against the new tax from a variety of socioeconomic groups. Although government officials viewed the tax as elevating Indians to the same level as non-Indians, poor whites and mestizos apparently interpreted it as lowering them to the same position as Indians. Guerrero has suggested that, in a republic where citizenship was based on racial domination, the tax robbed poor non-Indians of their citizen status, equating them instead with the "class of indigenes."[18] Some Indian peasants also resisted the universal tax, because it would undermine their distinct identity and put an end to the benefits they enjoyed with an indigenous head tax.[19]

Continuing to collect tribute also worked in the interests of Ecuadorian landed elites, who were consolidating their personal, political, and economic power in the early decades of the republic. Ethnically specific taxation was but one facet of the link between the state and elite interests. Slavery, vagrancy laws, and laws allowing imprisonment for debts all helped provide landed elites with increased power and sufficient labor, while limited voting rights guaranteed that only wealthy Ecuadorian men would have a voice in the government.[20] Consequently, despite the many presidential, congressional, and ministerial declarations calling for equality before the law, members of the national government, many of whom belonged to the landed elite and all of whom answered to it, had a vested interest in maintaining unequal rights and duties. It was therefore not only fiscal necessity, but also various class and race interests, that took precedence over political principles to ensure the continuation of the tribute system.

Even as they condemned the tribute system, state officials benefited from interracial paternalism in which Indians' childlike need for protection justified their unequal status in relation to whites and mestizos. The 1828 decree reinstating tribute, for example, identified Indians as *personas miserables* (miserable persons) who were exempt from paying court fees and fulfilling most other obligations to the state. It further indicated that local officials were responsible for "watch[ing] over their subordinates' conduct, in order to avoid excesses in drink and other excesses ... [and] represent to the government that which they consider useful and advantageous to the indigenous peoples, to their civilization and well being, and the conservation of their lands."[21] Placing Indians under such supervision suggested that they were unable to identify and defend their own interests, whether the matter at hand was protecting their lands from non-Indians or their own persons from excessive alcohol consumption. They therefore needed white-mestizo father figures to safeguard their rights and teach them civilization and self-restraint, and state officials were quick to lay claim to the role of paternal protectors. Elites also used these same notions, however, to justify beating and incarcerating Indians.[22]

Because paternalism justified the republican maintenance of the tribute system, each central government regime from 1828 to 1857 issued new (often redundant) laws asserting the need to protect and civilize the nation's Indians. When the 1833 Constitutional Congress stipulated regulations for the collection of tribute and the treatment of indigenous peoples, it declared that the law was necessary "in order to civilize indígenas and correct the abuses they experience." Legislators argued that although Indian men were required to pay a head tax, those who were behind in their payments should be persuaded with "gentle methods, without ever sequestering their tools or animals."[23] Two years later, Ecuador's National Convention reinforced most of the 1833 regulations, indicating that ongoing abuses against Indians had to be put to an end "so that this class, so important to society, is not oppressed in any way and enjoys the rights and guarantees that the constitution offers to Ecuadorians."[24] Throughout all the laws and decrees emanating from the central government, Indians themselves were defined as the "miserable" class that lived in ignorance and simplicity and therefore needed the state's paternal protection, because "they do not have the voice, or education, or knowledge of their rights to make them valid."[25]

In 1833, central government officials argued that in addition to oppressing Indians, the colonial system had also "reduced them to ignorance and coarseness." They therefore proposed building schools for Indian boys in every canton with significant indigenous populations (and for girls where practical). In addition to making Indian children aware of their rights by teaching them the constitution, and giving Indian boys greater potential to become citizens by learning Spanish, these schools were meant to provide civilizing moral instruction.[26] Proposals to educate Indians would be one of the consistent features of interethnic politics in decades to come, and paternalism remained a central process through which central-state officials defined and sought to solve the Indian problem. Yet educational initiatives show that interethnic paternalism evolved and changed in important ways after Independence. Unlike the colonial era when members of the republic of Indians were identified as perpetual children, central-state officials in the nineteenth century allegedly wished to eliminate interracial paternalism by abolishing tribute and expanding education. Republican discourses therefore classified Indians as inherently redeemable from their minority status, and some laws even went so far as to identify this as a national duty.[27] Thus, while it was greatly influenced by its colonial precursor, republican interethnic paternalism was distinct in its transitional nature and transformative intentions.

Concerns with family structure and its impact on the collection of tribute were likewise essential in this transitional phase of Indian-state relations. Elaborate and ever-evolving rules determined who had to pay tribute: in 1836, only sons with two indigenous parents had to pay it; previous laws had stipulated that a legitimate child's racial status followed that of the father, and an illegitimate child's status that of the mother.[28] The 1854 law reforming tribute, however, reinstated the distinction between legitimate and illegitimate children of mixed parentage.[29] This seems to have caused some confusion in the early years of the republic, and the minister of finance sent out a circular in 1836 clarifying that the children of a white man and an Indian woman, or a white woman and an Indian man, did not have to pay tribute, even if the parents' union was informal. Other laws and discussions of tribute collection were more pointedly focused on upholding indigenous patriarchal family structures, particularly with regard to questions over the extent to which contributors' wives (or children) were responsible for men's tribute payments. The 1835 National Convention, for example, ordered that "corregidores or collectors who imprison the wives or children of indigenous debtors will be punished."[30] With this statement the national government adhered to patriarchal sensibility that dependents should not be held responsible for the male head of household's shortcomings—although the very need to specify this indicated that wives and children of contributors were being jailed in practice.[31]

A more complicated question was whether indigenous widows were accountable for their dead husbands' taxes: legally, an Indian widow was not required to pay her husband's debts unless he left behind enough money and goods to cover them.[32] Though the law was designed to protect Indians, local officials could also use it in their conflicts with the central government. In 1840, tribute collector Nicolás Vascones of Riobamba referred to Indian widows to explain why he had not collected as much tribute money as expected. Vascones argued that his superiors should not enjoin him to collect money from "a miserable widow for the time that her husband was not alive. Imagine that an indigenous man died on the tenth of February; how could it be just to collect the third for the forty days that he lived [that year]?"[33] This defense manipulated multilayered paternalism—Vascones highlighted both his own fatherly concern for Indians and Indian men's responsibilities to their wives to protect himself from suspicion that reduced tribute collections might be the result of questionable actions.

Sometimes, especially during Urvina's rule in the 1850s, the state more forcefully supported indigenous patriarchy by identifying indigenous men as capable and responsible heads of households.[34] When Urvina addressed Congress in 1854, he argued that the position of protector of indigenous peoples should be abolished because the protectors were ineffective and sometimes even abusive of Indians. He also stated that the protectors were "opposed to our system of liberty and equality, because they prohibit a great many of our citizens from being able to negotiate and appear before a judge freely and without obstacles. … [Indigenous peoples] do not lack the talent and intelligence necessary to manage a small amount of money, as complicated and difficult calculations are not necessary, simple combinations suffice of which one is capable through the common sense that nature has provided in adequate doses."[35] Similarly, when Congress reformed tribute collection in 1854, they specified that Indians could enter into contracts, make decisions about land, and go to court without the intervention of protectors.[36] By emphasizing Indian men's capacity to act independently, central government officials of the 1850s reinforced Indian manhood in two ways: first, eliminating the paternal position of protector broke down one of the barriers that kept Indian men in a perpetual state of childhood vis-à-vis non-Indians. At the same time, the actual abilities that officials attributed to Indian men were all associated with responsibilities of male heads of household and reinforced Indian men's patriarchal power over their wives and children.

Still another way to support indigenous men's patriarchal authority was to claim that current practices and structures inhibited Indian men's ability to fulfill their patriarchal obligations toward their families. Consider Francisco Icaza's 1856 report as minister of the Interior:

> TRIBUTE is barbaric, precisely because it gets a hold on the most miserable and unfortunate class ... have you not seen upon arriving in our provinces, and between the scrub of our mountain chains, mountains of straw ... which appear to be guarded by wild animals? Well there lives the contributor with a family devoured by misery, hunger, nakedness, and cold; and there is where the minister of the law presents himself to tell him: the society of which you form a part, and in which you do not enjoy the least participation, requires half of your children's scarce bread, to sustain it ... and if they do not comply with this mandate, society will take them and jail them, without caring for the unhappy family that is going to perish.[37]

According to Icaza, the worst part of this emasculating scenario was that it was the state itself destroying the Indian family by collecting tribute. Only the abolition of tribute would allow the Indian man to resume his rightful and responsible position as a true and able head of the household.

Paradoxically, the same officials and laws that called on Indian patriarchy in the 1850s simultaneously reinforced that Indians were childlike. Even the 1854 tribute reform law identified Indians as personas miserables, deserving exemption from court and attorneys' fees, similar to previous laws and decrees.[38] The thread that tied these opposed perceptions of Indian men together was the impression of the Indian man as powerless. State officials sometimes recognized the Indian man as patriarch in his own home, but overall these representations of Indians before the abolition of tribute continually conjured up notions of an Indian man beleaguered and unable to change his own life, robbed even of his rightful manliness relative to his wife and children. Change could come only from above, and until tribute was abolished, central-state officials presented themselves as father figures who would protect Indians. Quito officials' criticisms of corregidores and other local authorities for treating Indians unfairly or cruelly are particularly revealing because they unearth underlying tensions between different levels of the state in early nineteenth-century Ecuador. In fact, the Ecuadorian state system fluctuated a great deal in the early to mid-nineteenth century, with overlapping authorities vying with each other for power. A closer examination of the principal tensions and protagonists in this process underscores how Indian-state relations were further complicated by governments that were diffuse, weak, and contradictory in the first decades following Independence.

Battles of the Patriarchs

Having identified Indians as child-men in need of protection and members of the central government as benevolent paternal figures, statesmen in Quito needed to be able to hold other patriarchs—particularly on the local level—accountable for indigenous suffering and interethnic strife from 1830 to 1857. Reform laws were replete with suggestions of failed paternalism in highland towns and villages. In addition to helping Quito politicians deny responsibility for racial inequalities, the accusations also justified the central state's interference in local matters and therefore dovetailed with the aims of state formation, though state makers in the early nineteenth century would not intervene in local matters as successfully as liberals would at the close of the century.

Statesmen frequently—though often indirectly—charged local officials with some of the worst offenses against indigenous peoples, and time and again they created new laws and policies to rectify the situation in provincial towns. Numerous decrees stated that corregidores could not collect more in tribute than the state mandated, and that *diezmeros* (tithe collectors) could not take more than one-tenth of an Indian's harvest, and never domestic animals in place of the harvest. Methods of collection also came under scrutiny: reminders that "gentle means" should be used to collect taxes from evasive Indians hinted that more forceful measures were being used. Other stipulations were more direct, establishing fines for officials who overcharged Indians and threatening to suspend officials who demanded payment or labor not sanctioned by the central government. An 1846 communication from the minister of the Interior went so far as to claim that Ecuadorian laws were not the cause of Indians' inequality and oppression; rather these dilemmas stemmed from the fact that the laws were not being upheld or made effective—a comment targeted at local officials.[39] Protectors of Indians were frequently the focus of attack: 1846 Minister of the Interior José Fernandez Salvador described protectors' powers over indigenous peoples as "arbitrary and excessive."[40] Ecuadorian law gave protectors a wide range of responsibilities and authority: they defended Indians in judicial matters, authorized their contracts and declarations, and oversaw the "exact and loyal observance of the law."[41] Urvina, however, proclaimed protectors unnecessary and ineffective, and he charged them with committing the worst offenses against Indians. Finally, the 1854 reform law abolished the position altogether.[42]

The struggle between the central government and the provinces, and between colonial legacies and republican goals, played out with redundant and conflicting authority figures at the local level. To see to the fair and efficient administration of local politics, the first national government in 1830 created a new local representative, known as the *teniente político*, or *teniente parroquial* (political or parochial lieutenants). These officials were meant to represent the central state at the local level and help the state develop a more direct relationship with Indians; to do so, they served as local police agents and as judges in minor disputes. These duties corresponded to what caciques and *gobernadores de indios* were already doing in their communities, and the central government had created the position with the aim of eventually replacing Indian leaders. Ultimately, because tenientes políticos were mestizos, this shift reinforced rather than weakened racial domination. It took time, however, for this transition to occur, and during the first half of the nineteenth century, tenientes políticos and caciques coexisted and performed overlapping functions. It was not until the 1850s that caciques lost their right to collect tribute, at which time those who maintained their political posts were newly defined as "state employees." Their revised duties focused on protecting order and morality in their communities and helping commoners "avoid drunken excesses."[43] Though the shift from caciques to tenientes políticos generally signaled a loss of Indian communal autonomy in the nineteenth century, many Indian commoners gained advantages from the period in which both authorities were officially sanctioned by the central government. Because caciques and tenientes políticos both presided over minor civil disputes, Indians who were unhappy with one authority's ruling could take their case to the other in the hope that this time they would win. These practices, before and after the abolition of tribute, point to Indians' ability to adapt to and take advantage of changing political structures.[44]

Private patriarchs, especially hacienda owners and priests, were also targets of the central government's search for villains in the early nineteenth century. Yet because of their influence and power, these provincial patriarchs held a contradictory position in central government discourse regarding Indians. On the one hand, religious officials were important protagonists in the quest to educate and civilize Indians, preparing them for incorporation into the nation. Therefore, when the economy was in dire straits, the National Convention of 1851 recognized that "religious houses deserve the special attention of legislators" and mandated that tribute did not have to be collected from conciertos who worked on estates owned by monasteries.[45] On the other hand, numerous laws and decrees associated priests with the worst abuses regarding the treatment of indigenous peoples. Priests were constantly being reminded that they could not use Indians as unpaid personal servants, must not require Indians to celebrate more than the four yearly religious festivals that the central government mandated, and were not supposed to force poor Indians to bury deceased loved ones with elaborate and expensive masses. The overall message was that priests could be a critical positive influence on indigenous societies only if they were kept under strict state supervision.

Even more complicated was the relationship between hacienda owners and the Indian problem. In the early nineteenth century, members of the central government acknowledged hacienda owners as legitimate paternal figures. This was apparent when a public prosecutor during Independence emphasized that Indians "who labor as contract servants on haciendas, [*are in a*] *condition much like that of children in families.*"[46] Though the republican government distinguished itself from the colonial state in many ways, it continued to legitimize hacendados' power to dictate indebted workers' behavior. Consider article 6 of the 1833 reform of the personal contribution of indígenas: "If any concierto or jornalero fails in his obligation to the property owner or *mayordomo* [steward] on the estate to which he belongs, he shall be brought under control with persuasion or other decent means; but if these are not enough, and he repeats his failures, he should be brought before the local judge so that he can have a double work penalty imposed or be arrested and placed in the public jail for a period not to exceed three days."[47] Laws that made it difficult or impossible for indebted workers to leave estates consolidated hacienda owners' socioeconomic positions while reducing many indigenous peoples to permanent resident labor on highland estates.[48] At the same time, hacienda owners posed the greatest challenge to tribute collectors because they had almost complete control over economic and social relations on their properties. It was not simply economic power that these estate owners wielded with the help of laws like that noted above but also interethnic paternal authority over the "Indian children" on their estates.[49]

Large landowners' reach extended beyond the boundaries of their own properties; they could make life more difficult for Indian peasants who lived near, but not on, their estates by blocking peasants from crossing their properties or charging fees to allow them access to pasturelands for grazing animals.[50] Hacendados' considerable local power also affected tax collection: in 1840, for example, the governor of Loja complained that hacienda owners frequently interfered with the collection of tribute from indigenous workers on their estates.[51] The central state, however, carefully respected hacendados' paternal authority on their properties. In 1843, the governor of Chimborazo sent a letter to the minister of finance to find out if action could be taken against Indians when hacienda owners and administrators hid contributors, hindered collection, or directly opposed collection agents. The reply to the letter was mixed: while local officials had the right to imprison Indian debtors, they would have to consult with estate owners before taking action against conciertos. This official communication related to both the problems with and the power of hacienda owners in early republican Ecuador.[52] Though the early republican state supported the expanding power of large estate owners, Quito authorities had to ensure the collection of the head tax that accounted for such a high percentage of government revenue. They also needed to find ways to prove (in theory, at least) that they were concerned with indigenous people's rights as well as those of estate owners. Over time, tensions rose between the Quito government and hacienda owners, as usual intensifying during Urvina's rule.

In 1854, highland hacendados lost their most important right under the republican system when article 51 of the tribute reform law specified that they could no longer force Indians to stay on estates and pay off their debts with labor. Instead, Indian workers had the right to liquidate their debts and leave estates.[53] In practice the law allowed a concierto, too poor to pay off the debt himself, to leave one hacienda for another if he could find another estate owner who would pay his debts. While this so-called seduction of Indians from one estate to another did not change conciertos' status, it did give them greater leverage to negotiate their treatment and the terms of labor on estates.[54] The article was a point of great contention, and congressmen came to loggerheads over it for a second time in 1856. Those who supported the change insisted that "the law has reconciled . . . landowners' interests with indigenous people's liberty." They also argued that reversing the law would deepen racial inequalities in the nation because then the Indian would be "the only disgraced debtor who is not allowed to liberate himself from his creditor by satisfying his debt." Opponents of article 51 viewed the situation quite differently, emphasizing that conciertos had explicitly agreed to pay off debts with work, and to allow them to fulfill their debts in any other way broke the terms of their (legally binding) labor contracts. In their view, the new law favored Indian debt workers as a special class rather than making them equal to non-Indians before the law. Opponents further alleged that this latest "preference" for Indians was another of "a thousand exemptions" enjoyed by a class that was already too much favored over other Ecuadorians, particularly in light of the fact that haciendas constituted all agricultural progress.[55] Such arguments were not new; hacendados and their political advocates had long contended that the liquidation of debts contradicted rather than advanced liberal individualism. When the Spanish Cortes first legalized the practice in the 1810s, hacienda owners complained that the law privileged Indians unfairly over other races. In hacendados' view, large estates were "the fundamental basis for public happiness," while Indian peasants who were willing to do no more than get by on subsistence agriculture did the patria no good at all.[56] If conciertos were allowed to liquidate their debts, worker insubordination would be rampant, leading to the ruin of haciendas and the destruction the economy as a whole.

Although central-state officials claimed to be interested in helping Indians advance toward incorporation into the political nation, actual government practices were often contradictory. At the same time that congressmen and presidents criticized local authorities for abusing Indians and failing to put protective laws into effect, they also mandated that these same officials—priests and corregidores in particular—be the individuals to make Indians aware of their rights. Granted, any local official discovered to have fallen short of his obligation to inform Indians of their rights would be fined. Yet in an era when the central government was already under considerable financial strain and local elites were extremely interdependent, it was highly unlikely that recalcitrant local authorities would be reported, let alone punished. Further, despite the central government's proclaimed mission to root out overtaxation, officials did not necessarily follow through in practice. Consider indigenous peasant complaints against *jefe político* José Manuel de la Guerra in Chimborazo (jefes políticos were political chiefs, the highest state officials in each canton). De la Guerra had allegedly overcharged Indians for tribute and threatened to jail them if they failed to meet his demands. Members of the Supreme Court, caught between a theoretical commitment to protect Indians and loyalty to the state's own agents, appear to have sided with de la Guerra and dismissed the case.[57] Even the 1854 law that freed conciertos from having to pay off their debts with labor fell short of taking away one of highland estate owners' most powerful tools for socioeconomic control: the ability to jail workers who fled their debts. The battles of the patriarchs, fought between various (mostly) white-mestizo authorities all claiming exclusive rights to father the Indian masses, remained a messy affair throughout the early nineteenth century. It also allowed many Indians to play up their status as child-men in the incipient nation as a means of advancing their own interests.

Indigenous Responses: Engaging State Patriarchy

In 1845, Indians in the civil parish of Calpi (Chimborazo) went to court against Ventura Mancheno and Carlos Zambrano, who controlled the hacienda San Juan.[58] Both the indigenous peasants and the hacendados claimed rightful control of a *páramo* (high altitude) property used for grazing animals. As in virtually all land disputes with non-Indians, the plaintiffs declared that this land had been put to communal use "since time immemorial"; also typical was their lawyer's stress on their status as *infelices indios* (unhappy Indians) to move the court to decide in his clients' favor. The descriptions and arguments in this case allow one to delve more deeply into the contradictory nature of gendered interethnic relations in the early nineteenth century. From the Indians' perspective, both their need for paternal protection from non-Indians and their patriarchal rights within their own families were being undermined. Their lawyer argued that the corregidor had failed to weigh carefully all evidence, including the indigenous community's documents, when he decided the dispute in favor of the hacendados. He further declared that Mancheno "thinks that he is by nature superior" to the Indians, making them work on the estate "without paying them even one *reál* for their work, nor that of their animals. [Hacienda officials] mistreat [the Indians] with lashes and blows, and chase their animals, all with the aim that they will help with the hacienda. They finally brought a complaint about this barbarous treatment to the corregidor of that location, but he has not brought justice to them."[59] The indigenous plaintiffs played on contradictory and uncertain republican interethnic relations in several ways in the case. They suggested that justice required state officials to fulfill their proclaimed duty to protect childlike indigenous peoples from abusive elites. Moreover, a particular point of contention in the case was that Zambrano at one time had jailed their women, undermining the Indian men's patriarchal authority over their own households. Finally, the plaintiffs charged Zambrano with attacks against their manly honor, which he robbed from them by beating them as if they were beholden to him rather than autonomous peasants with their own lands and families. Carlos Zambrano meanwhile referred to his Indian opponents as riotous and arrogant, accusing them of instigating violence and scandal, and of fabricating evidence. He reminded the court that the Indians' actions and claims should not be upheld in "a state where property rights are guaranteed."[60] It is not clear who won this case in the long run, and the surviving documents tell the story of alternating advantages and victories between the parties. Regardless of the final outcome, both the arguments and their (temporary) impact show that Indians and elites alike were quite skilled at exploiting the state's contradictory and gender-driven positions on interethnic relations.

Although this struggle over control of pastureland is especially rich and varied, it was not uncommon: indigenous peoples—especially men—were quick to act on legislation and regularly evoked their uncertain position in the emerging nation, usually applying (rather than rejecting) established rules of interethnic paternalism. Exactly how indigenous peoples engaged with evolving state policies and paternalisms, however, varied a great deal, particularly according to region. In the northern and southern highlands, where there were labor shortages, conciertos frequently took advantage of changing laws and national concerns in the early republic. In the central highlands, where labor was abundant, indigenous peasants rather than conciertos were most actively engaged with state developments, sometimes using legal means to pursue their interests, sometimes relying on violence (or the threat of violence) to influence the application of state policies. In the southern highlands around Cuenca, indigenous peoples frequently migrated to urban areas from the countryside; these movements, whether temporary or permanent, gave migrants increased interaction with and access to state authorities and lawyers, and therefore incentive to act on transformations in the national politics of interethnic paternalism.[61]

Individuals who had difficulty paying their tributes had various ways to evade the tax, particularly in an era when state officials debated its continuing collection. An 1836 government circular recognized this practice when the general accountant established an increased reward of four reales to anyone who captured Indians fleeing payment of the personal contribution, explaining that the previous one real reward had proved insufficient incentive to search out wayward Indians.[62] Even as Urvina fought to abolish tribute in the 1850s, he voiced his disapproval that Indians regularly created problems for the state when they changed jurisdiction to avoid tribute payment.[63] Other Indians sought relief from tribute payments by becoming conciertos and having hacendados meet their tribute requirements for them. In addition to meeting Indians' objective of relieving their burden to pay tribute, this tactic had two other critical consequences: Indian men submitted to a powerful patriarch, which placed them in the ultimate childlike position from state officials' perspective; further, their actions fueled the battles of patriarchs between the central state and local authorities that would continue to build in later decades.[64] Though the hacienda system was deeply exploitative, it did offer certain advantages to conciertos: because hacienda owners would pay the workers' tribute obligations, white estate owners and indigenous workers often allied against their common enemy: the tribute collector.[65] Owners themselves would prefer to avoid payment (or, at least, overpayment) and therefore protected Indians' interests, as was the case in 1847 when an hacienda owner went to court on behalf of his concierto Santos Siguachi, who had overpaid his tribute obligation because variations of his name appeared numerous times on tribute lists, rather than just once.[66]

Hacienda owners were not the only alternate patriarchs that Indian contributors could call on for assistance. Mark Van Aken noted that Indians of the early republican era frequently directed pleas to higher provincial or central government officials, because local authorities were unlikely to assist them.[67] Indians on the obraje Peguche (near Cuenca) did precisely this when they complained that their *patrón* (landlord or master) was a municipal judge whose connections kept his workers from seeking justice at the local level.[68] Indians from Chimborazo used different state agencies against each other when they used the court system to address what they deemed unfair collection of diezmos.[69] Indigenous peoples sometimes made indirect complaints against local authorities: a case in point comes from 1837, when Indians from the Riobamba area petitioned Congress to find out which public works requirements were legitimate.[70] The petition implies that Indians were suspicious that local officials were requiring more of them than the law mandated. Yet rather than directly charge local officials with wrongdoing, it was safer to couch their complaints within an informational request. In these cases, Indians defended their own interests by deftly pitting local and central-state father figures against each other.

Urvina's liberal reforms in the 1850s opened up a Pandora's box in some parts of the Ecuadorian highlands, particularly in the southern regions around Cuenca and Loja. In August 1855, the minister of the Interior reported that the governor of Loja had received a petition from indigenous peoples in Zaraguro, where they "implore[ed] the government's protection from the diezmeros of this province who, making a mockery of the repeated government rulings, have nevertheless continued to commit extortion against the unhappy class of indígenas."[71] The minister demanded that these indolent authorities be dealt with and the law strictly enforced, emphasizing the government's responsibility to intervene in favor of the miserable class of Indians. Evidently matters remained unresolved, because in June the next year the governor of Chimborazo reported to the minister of the Interior that the governor of Azuay had informed him of an indigenous uprising against the diezmero in the Loja region. He had requested that the Chimborazo governor send men to the southern Andes, certain that "the disorder will become more widespread."[72] Indigenous rebellions, though infrequent, often had a lingering impact on state officials and made them cautious when implementing new laws or collection procedures.[73] Moreover, in both violent and nonviolent interethnic confrontations, the divisions and mutual suspicion between regional and central paternal figures worked to Indians' advantage: they were able to call on the proclaimed benevolence of the central state to have their complaints taken seriously, or at least to forgive them when they engaged in illegal or violent actions.

Sometimes grievances against local authorities simultaneously played on Indian men's childlike need for protection and their manly honor and rights within the new republic. In 1831, Indians of San Andrés (Chimborazo) complained that Father Fernando Sanches had not only paid them insufficiently for services he demanded of them, but also beat them in public. Congress was still a few years away from passing legislation to declare humiliating whippings illegal, but the Indians' complaint certainly drew attention to a practice with which state officials were increasingly concerned.[74] At the same time these plaintiffs sought the state's paternal intervention against an abusive ecclesiastical father figure, they also sought to restore their manly dignity, which had been compromised with public beatings. Twenty-five years later, Gregorio Sambora, from the parish of Sumba (Azuay), took a similar approach when he charged his local priest, José María Arnijos, with various offenses, including harsh physical punishments. Sambora sought state intervention to advance the "well being of oppressed and miserable peoples," a plea that called on his continuing minority status. At the same time, he indicated that the priest's misdemeanors got in the way of his "individual liberty" and referred to laws in which it was the responsibility of jefes políticos to intervene on behalf of indigenous peoples.[75] In both instances, Indian men highlighted divergent features of their gendered status before the law. Sambora's case, though ultimately unsuccessful, offers an especially good example of an indigenous man ready to employ both aspects of his child-man status, referring to his individual rights at the same time that he called on paternalistic state officials to protect him from the abusive patriarchy of the priest.

Indian men could also draw on their paradoxical status in the early republic by simultaneously referring to their childlike relation with non-Indians and their patriarchal responsibilities within their own families. Consider Francisco Cumba, who fought in Independence: though his participation in the rebel cause made him eligible for exemption from tribute, his 1823 request to be free of the obligation also emphasized that "I have suffered many losses ... which result in danger to the life of my poor wife."[76] Cumba's masculinity was complex: having made a manly contribution to the nation, he had to present himself humbly before white-mestizo authorities to seek their assistance, which he needed to fulfill his patriarchal duty to provide for his wife. In a case from the 1850s, Indians of the village of Burga (Imbabura) used men's responsibility to support their families as part of their defense when they were charged with disrespecting the teniente parroquial. Though the pleas ultimately failed, the Indians' defense lawyer declared that the teniente had threatened "the fruits of the harvest which the unhappy Indians [infelices indios] cultivate in order to survive and meet the necessities of themselves and their families."[77] Although these two cases were quite different in many ways, in both the Indians involved deepened their pleas of misery by pointing to their own paternal obligations.[78]

Any study of nonliterate peoples raises questions about whose words appear on the written page. Was it Indians themselves who engaged with the language of the republican Indian dilemma, or did rural lawyers (tinterillos) and scribes put these words in their mouths?

Some cases suggest that a tinterillo must have been at work, as is evident in petitions for tribute exemption from the Cuenca region in the 1840s. In most of these cases, mestizo men sought relief from the tax burden based on new laws that exempted from tribute the offspring of all mixed unions. In one case an indigenous man pointed out that he owned sufficient property to earn release from the tax obligation.[79] The sudden appearance, regional specificity, and consistent pattern of these petitions from Cuenca hint that a tinterillo may have initiated them. Lawyers and scribes were skilled at precisely manipulating the Indian dilemma, and their words were likely often mixed into court records and Indian petitions.[80] Nevertheless, their clients had to be willing to follow this advice and therefore also had (or at least gained) an understanding of the changing atmosphere around interethnic paternalism. Indians' willingness to use the language given to them, combined with the actions they at times took, show that they were hardly pawns of tinterillos or scribes and were instead historical agents actively engaged with the political atmosphere in which they lived.

In sum, while indigenous peoples did not control how interethnic paternalism changed in the early nineteenth century, they did take advantage of the changes to forward their own concerns. Doing so meant co-opting and at times reshaping (or at least reinterpreting) new political ideas about the relationships among gender, family, and ethnicity. The state's fragmented and contradictory position on Indians meant that Indian men could choose whether to highlight their childlike need for protection or their patriarchal duties as they defended their rights, livelihood, and at times masculinity. Indigenous peoples were not, however, united in their views of early republican policies, as their responses to tribute reveal. If many Indian communities defended the tribute system, there were also numerous individuals who sought relief from and hated the tax burden. Yet whether they embraced or avoided tribute, they did so by taking advantage of central-state officials' theoretical concern with Indians' plight. This favorable political atmosphere would not, however, last for long.

Broken Promises? The Aftermath of Abolition

Ecuadorian statesmen unanimously regarded the abolition of tribute as a great accomplishment that would forge a nation of liberal individuals, yet the new law also raised questions regarding the extent to which the central state should still act as a paternal protector of the unhappy class of Indians in the nation. Minister of the Interior Antonio Mata defended his position that Indians needed ongoing protections in his 1858 report:

> It was reasoned that, with tribute extinguished, other exemptions should also cease. Thus various authorities and functionaries understood it, and [Indians had to] fill the ranks of the army ... the national guard ... pay judicial fees, sales taxes, and other contributions from which they were previously exempt.... [To obtain] the immediate and complete regeneration of the indigenous class, I recommend to you the necessity of conserving without alteration the protective laws for this miserable race. Three centuries of oppression and tyranny have ... taken from them almost all of the characteristics that distinguish man from brute ... the indigenous man ... is reduced to serve as the docile instrument of exploitation. ... Our institutions have sanctioned equality before the law without exception of the Indian; but who has not seen the immense difference which actually exists between [the Indian] and other citizens? ... the regeneration of the indigenous class is one of the most arduous undertakings ... [but it is] our redemptive work, to sanction dispositions more or less favorable to the indigenous peoples [by] ... Conserving the exemptions ... until they rise out of their state of abjection, misery, and helplessness in which they find themselves.[81]

Mata's argument captured the post-tribute paradox in which Indians were equal to non-Indians in theory but marginalized in practice. Indigenous peoples as well as central-state officials recognized that the tribute burden would be replaced with many additional taxes and obligations, and that it would likely eliminate the exemptions and protections Indians had previously enjoyed. In 1858, three hundred indigenous men and women in the civil parish of Calpi (Chimborazo) rose up violently and demanded the return of the tribute system in order to reestablish former exemptions and rights.[82] Though Congress did not restore tribute, the minister of the Interior ordered local government administrators to maintain Indian privileges temporarily, and he warned authorities against responding harshly when Indians resisted the new obligations.[83]

Members of the central government did not immediately remove Indians' privileges or protections, giving Indians a few more years to play on their contradictory status and seek sympathy from central-state officials. Supreme Court cases from 1858 underscore the ongoing paternal, protective thrust of the central-state's relationships with Indians. When Indians charged priest Manuel Yépes with various abuses, it was clear that they were using state officials as father figures to counteract the priest's failure to fulfill his paternal duty to them, noting that Yépes did not even know any Quichua.[84] Similarly, Indian peasants who had lashed out against the renter of the hacienda Taloa (near Ambato) while in the midst of a land dispute with him were quick to defend themselves by painting a bleak picture of the renter, José Paredes. Paredes, they claimed, had not only grievously mistreated them, but also arbitrarily and privately imprisoned them, infringing on their individual rights before the law. In particular, their defense attorney remarked, "It is an inhuman and ignorant principle that the indigenous class is considered outside of society ... as brutes over whom one can exercise all manner of domination."[85] In this tumultuous year following the abolition of tribute, Indians were most likely to use their continued contradictory status when facing criminal charges for acting violently, as Narciso Pulla did when he was charged with instigating a riot. His defense rested on the idea that "ferocious administrators oppressed the unhappy Indians" by mistreating and imprisoning them. He even claimed that the local jefe político obliged Indians to perform *trabajo subsidiario* duties without food.[86]

Gabriel García Moreno's rise to power in 1860 had a mixed impact on Indian-state relations: though the second phase of Garcianismo (from 1869 to 1875) was a period of rising tensions between Indians and state officials on almost all levels, historian Derek Williams has shown that central government officials from 1860 to 1868 often continued to intervene as Indians' paternal protectors, especially against local authorities. Likewise, he notes, the central state during this period did not attack Indian peasants' right to maintain communal lands.[87] For example, in the 1861 Ley de Regimen Político (Law of Political Rule), the central state obliged tenientes políticos to "protect the indígenas and miserable persons, taking care that they are not mistreated nor wronged."[88] Emphasizing local authorities' ongoing paternal duties to Indians in their jurisdictions both prolonged formal interethnic paternalism and, as Williams concluded, increased the central state's power in the provinces by holding local officials accountable to Quito.

It took even longer for local and provincial state officials to embrace Indians' newfound equal status with non-Indians than it did within the central state. One marker of this slow process is evidence that racial labels continued to carry great weight for local and provincial state officials in the decades following the abolition of tribute. For example, officials in the Chimborazo Superior Court continued to identify litigants by race throughout the 1870s and into the 1880s, only gradually letting go of ethnic labels in the majority of court cases.[89] Distinct central and regional government responses to "the Indian situation" were also apparent when Joaquín Pinto, public scribe for the superior court in Riobamba, wrote to the Supreme Court inquiring whether Indians had to pay legal fees in court cases. He pointed out that a recent decree did not denote any special status for Indians when discussing poverty exemptions, while in 1854 the state had proclaimed Indians impoverished and therefore exempt from court fees. Pinto explained, "until the present, the practice has been that Indians are not charged with this fee . . . [but] it seemed prudent to seek a resolution." Supreme Court judges reasoned that Indians would have to prove poverty in each individual case, because the abolition of tribute had put an end to automatic exemptions by making Indians equal to other citizens.[90] Similarly, when the governor of Loja inquired in 1870 whether Indians had to pay sales taxes or scribes' fees for sales contracts, the minister of the Interior responded in the affirmative, emphasizing the constitutional imperative of equality before the law.[91] Though the Supreme Court denied Indians' need for special treatment, these queries suggest that enduring perceptions of racial difference allowed at least some Indians to maintain exemptions they had enjoyed under the tribute system.

Abolition also undermined caciques' claims to local power, and references to these indigenous political leaders began to fade from judicial accounts by the mid 1870s.[92] Even caciques' appearances in most court records from the 1860s and 1870s were minimal: Indians might refer to themselves or others as caciques or Indian governors (either directly or through using the title "don" or "doña"), but such references primarily indicated status within Indian communities rather than judicial or decision-making power that the central government sanctioned.[93] Though the Ecuadorian political and judicial system no longer recognized caciques, Indians continued to use established community leaders to settle disputes when they could, rather than automatically resorting to the white-mestizo court system. This practice left Indians vulnerable to further litigation, but it saved them the cost of court fees that official disputes would bring.

By the 1870s the contradictions and shortcomings of abolition made it increasingly difficult for statesmen to imagine Indians as universal individuals who belonged to the nation. However, they were compelled to argue otherwise because the abolition of tribute was a key factor that made possible García Moreno's project to create a unified Catholic country. All state builders after 1857 would have to find ways to assert that they either had incorporated or were in the process of incorporating Indians into the nation on equal footing with whites and mestizos. Statesmen in the later Garcian era resolved this dilemma by again manipulating the language of patriarchy and paternalism, but with a new twist that blamed Indian men for their inferior status. The idea of Indian child-men, so intense during the early nineteenth-century attempts to abolish tribute, was an unresolved theme that would haunt the processes of nation-state building, permeating Ecuadorian Indian-state relations for the next seventy years and beyond.

⇒ 3 ⇐

Garcianismo

Patriarchy and Paradoxical Indian-State Relations

Woman has her duties, as well as her intimate joys, in the domestic sphere . . .
[in] all things related to religion, the fatherland, and her own family,
of which she is the core and principal center.
—Ambato Catholic Women's Group, 1878[1]

There is a deep-seated custom among the Indians, in which
a wife requires a dozen monthly blows from her husband as a token of
his affection for her.
—Defense attorney Alejandro Rivadeneira to the Supreme Court, 1874[2]

The Garcian state rarely focused on either the woman or Indian questions directly, and it did not in any official capacity recognize an Indian
problem or assign different rights according to race; given this official
refusal to acknowledge racial difference, sociologist Andrés Guerrero
remarked that late nineteenth-century Ecuadorian politics was dominated by a deafening silence on the subject of Indians' place within the
nation.[3] When impressions of women or Indians did appear in central
government documents, they justified García Moreno's withdrawal from
protective Indian policies after 1869. The above quotations evoke images
of very different household dynamics: the first presents the idyllic home,
emphasizing woman's domestic nature—without reference to her class
or race. In the second quote, marital relations are far from blissful, Indians are set apart from other Ecuadorians, and wives play a key role in

their own misery. The gender ideas behind these juxtaposed images of domesticity reflected and defended paradoxical relations between Indians and the state in late nineteenth-century Ecuador.

The central dilemma in Indian-state relations at this time was that, despite claims that Indians had achieved equality before the law after 1857, various state officials continued to treat Indians as inferior to whites and mestizos, and Garcian policies exacerbated indigenous peoples' problems. The central state's disengagement from the Indian question during this period resulted mainly from new challenges in addressing the specter of liberal individualism. Before the abolition of tribute, members of the central state could still imagine they were capable of truly re-creating Indian men into universal individuals who would be able to fulfill their manly duties to both their families and the nation. After 1857 this illusion was shattered, and though from 1861 to 1868 García Moreno prolonged interethnic paternalistic policies, these did not persist into his second phase of rule from 1869 to 1875. The overall impact of the Garcian era was that Indians' social and political marginalization remained unaddressed, while their economic situations typically deteriorated.

Because Garcian Indian-state relations rested on the idea that the abolition of tribute had made Indians equal to non-Indians before the law, ongoing and even increasing racial inequalities required rationalization. State officials used gender ideologies, especially two predominant images of Indians, to mask their roles in oppressing and marginalizing Indians. First, statesmen in the late nineteenth century (both during and after Garcianismo) continued to describe Indian men as perpetual children, passive before white-mestizo society, who fell short of meeting the qualifications for inclusion within the nation. At the same time a new image of Indians became important to nation-making discourse: the Indian man as brutally barbaric among his own people, especially toward his wife. This chapter's second epigraph captures this vision of Indians as inadequate father figures whose abusive behavior justified their marginalization within the nation. These paradoxical representations of Indian men as both submissive and violent served the same purpose: Indian men's failure to meet stated gender norms indirectly suggested that Indians failed to contribute significantly to the nation. Indian women garnered no benefit from the state's ostensible concern with indigenous domestic violence, because state officials classified them as contributors to, rather than simply victims of, an indigenous culture of domestic violence. In this sense, the two epigraphs are most meaningful when evaluated in relation to one another: it was the purported contrast between Indian and non-Indian gender norms that helped to rectify the contradictions between Indians' theoretical equality before the law and the exclusion and exploitation they experienced in practice.

Indian-state tensions increased over the course of Garcian rule, and because of the central government's silence on Indian matters, this friction played out mainly at the local and provincial levels. In addition to rising taxes and loss of land and recognition for local indigenous leaders, Garcian practices chipped away at Indian peasant life. Indigenous land tenure rights were vulnerable because state officials sometimes declared former Indian communal (or even private) lands *tierras baldías*—vacant lands the state owned and could sell. Indians were also more frequently the targets of vagrancy laws than non-Indians were, and they became the primary labor force for the numerous public works projects undertaken by the Garcian government.[4] This latter point was partly ironic, as the 1861 Ley de Regimen Municipal (Law of Municipal Rule) had outlawed using labor for payment of the *contribución subsidiaria*. It stipulated instead that all men between the ages of twenty-one and fifty had to pay the cash equivalent of four days' labor; seemingly, this alleviated the problem of having an exclusively Indian public labor force.[5] At the same time, however, local state officials were allowed to draft laborers forcibly for public works, and in the highlands most of these draftees were indigenous. Not only did these laws disadvantage indigenous peoples, but court trials from the period show that local state officials sometimes collected extra tax money to enrich themselves, or that they required men under twenty-one or over fifty to work for the state.[6] Indigenous economic crises of the period also stemmed from hacienda expansion, growth favoring large estate owners at the expense of Indian communities. All of these burdens and problems occurred under post-tribute claims of equality before the law, making pervasive racial inequalities more subtle and thus more difficult to contest, particularly by the late 1860s, when García Moreno backed away from his protectionist stance toward Indians.

Although Indians were largely absent from government discourses during the latter phase of Garcianismo, they remained involved in processes of state formation, particularly at the local level, to which Indian-state relations were relegated at the time. Indian men and women adapted as best they could to new insecurities, challenges, and changing resources in the post-tribute era. Using various strategies—from quiet accommodation to violent resistance—Indians fought to retain what land they could, struggled to make their new burdens to the government manageable, and ultimately played their part in defining the nation in practice if not in theory. Since gender ideologies remained central to the Indian problem, Indians too drew on gender ideas when interacting with state officials, though their manipulation of state-generated ideas did not necessarily mean endorsing them. Although indigenous peoples sometimes incorporated various state-sanctioned gender notions, at other times they rejected them or highlighted contradictions between theory and practice. Therefore, while state gender ideologies may not have reflected the reality of indigenous attitudes, characteristics, or behaviors, they did provide both state officials and Indians with resources to explain, negotiate, and evaluate the transformations in the politics of ethnicity that went hand in hand with nation making.

García Moreno, Catholicism, and the Politics of Patriarchy

From 1861 to 1875, Gabriel García Moreno combined classic nineteenth-century notions of progress with Catholic conservatism to control the central government and unite the divided country into *una sola familia*—a single family. Catholicism provided the foundation for state

morality and Garcian political ideology, as García Moreno acknowledged when he described in 1861 that his goals for his presidency were
"to re-establish moral authority without which order is no more than
suspension or weariness, and outside of which liberty is deceit and fan-
tasy; to moralize a country in the bloody battle of good against evil, of
honorable men against perverse ones, which has endured for half a century, and to moralize it through the energetic and efficient repression
of crime and through solid religious education of new generations."[7]
The Garcian state identified women—and some women identified
themselves—as pivotal actors in the maintenance of national morality. Domestic tranquility and feminine morality paralleled and reinforced the progressive agenda for economic development via exports
and nation building through centralization, Catholicism, education,
and improved infrastructure. As one scholar of the era put it: "Woman
has become the handsome mosaic of the national edifice: at the side of
piety, economic industry; at the side of modesty, delightful instruction;
all in the proper proportions."[8]

If woman was important to the culture of state building, however,
women were quite limited in their abilities to act on their own behalf.
Not only were all women denied the right to vote until 1929, but the
1860 civil code gave husbands control of all marital goods as well as the
responsibility to represent their wives' civil and financial interests. A wife
could act directly on her own behalf only with either her husband's—
or, in his absence, a judge's—authorization (permission which could
be revoked at any time). The explanation given for these limited female
rights in the public sphere in the 1860 civil code was that "the husband
is the master of conjugal society, and as such he freely administers his
wife's worldly goods."[9] In this particular patriarchal viewpoint women
could uphold the culture of the state while they were simultaneously
outside of the political nation; they therefore helped to define and augment their husbands' status and legal rights.[10] Men's public roles—in
the economy, and in Garcian politics—were based in large part on their
responsibilities as heads of households who acted on behalf of their
dependents. Women were to be obedient and protected, and although

they were supposed to remain firmly in the private sphere, their presence in the home was consequential in public matters.

Marriage was the cornerstone of Garcian patriarchy because it was both a civil contract and a sacrament; as such it helped to maintain social order and dovetailed nicely with Garcian Catholic morality.[11] Given its importance to the avowed moral mission of the state, the sanctity of marriage had to be legally secured, and the proper roles of husband and wife upheld. While the state did not allow the dissolution of marital bonds, couples with particular types of marital problems could seek a *divorcio* (permanent separation) from the Church and use civil courts to separate their goods; both options were based on Church- and state-sanctioned gender ideas. First, couples could seek separations only under specific circumstances, such as habitual mistreatment that put a wife or children in jeopardy, a husband's failure to provide food and clothing for his family, habitual drunkenness, or adultery.[12] Separations were largely, though not exclusively, a female prerogative since accepted grounds focused on women's need to have men provide for and protect them. Moreover, the 1860 civil code required a husband to sustain his wife after they were granted a divorcio—though he could retain control of his wife's goods if her infidelity was the cause of the separation.[13] Husbands involved in divorcios lost their manly rights to financial administration because of their own irresponsibility in the home—unless their wives had displayed unfeminine, immoral qualities by having an affair. Again, both requirements were filled with gender-rich moral standards through their emphasis on the male provider and the female homemaker. Moreover, separations were the domain of wealthy non-Indians: not only was it costly to use the court systems necessary to separate formally, but the separation laws themselves were founded on gender assumptions that were specific to elite whites and mestizos.

García Moreno also used his presidential power to protect the sanctity of marriage when he declared on May 5, 1869, that

CONSIDERING: That the penal code lacks punishments for a variety of offenses, especially those that destroy public morality; IT IS DECREED ... public concubinage of persons who could marry will be punished with two months imprisonment and two years of exile. If the guilty parties marry after the sentence is proclaimed they will not be subject to any penalty. Actual public concubinage between persons, at least one of whom is not able to marry, will be punished with at least one to two months in prison, [and] with six years of exile from the Republic for the person unable to marry.[14]

By placing the government squarely in the innermost sanctum of the private sphere, the bedroom, this decree blurred the line between public and private spheres, especially because the law itself was concerned with the impact of concubinage on wider society. It was not just private morality that was at stake, but the potentially dangerous impact that individuals' unseemly and sinful behavior might have on society at large and on the nation as a whole. Accordingly, most concubinage cases reaching the Supreme Court in Quito focused specifically on public aspects of alleged affairs: did the accused live openly as a couple, sharing a household and making their relationship known to others, even though they were not married? If the answer was no, the charges were usually dropped; if the answer was yes, the defendants were sentenced; if witnesses' testimonies were mixed, the case could be decided either way.[15] Other concerns and arguments might affect the severity of sentencing but not acquit the accused: a man's good reputation in business and other public transactions could only, at best, decrease the time he spent in prison, while references to a defendant's ignorance or *rusticidad* (rural nature or coarseness) rarely even reduced punishment.[16]

Making concubinage a criminal offense heightened the public and scandalous aspect of these relationships. Elias Laso, prosecuting attorney for the state, sometimes mentioned the shame these cases brought upon innocent wives: in one case, his argument for conviction centered on the tears shed by the defendant's wife; in another, he called for lenience from the judges to minimize a wife's anguish.[17] This image of the long-suffering wife, whether used to increase or lighten a defendant's penalty, was a powerful tool that played on long-standing white-mestizo patriarchal concepts that were also central to Garcian nation making. Because they rested on gendered notions of honor emphasizing female sexual purity, concubinage charges could bring disgrace upon a family, particularly a family of high status, even if they were unfounded. Once the accusation was made, this scandal could be alleviated only publicly, as when an edition of the national newspaper in March 1870 mentioned that the Supreme Court had dropped concubinage charges against Modesto Velástegui and Paula Cisneros.[18] From all angles, the decree making concubinage illegal was an important facet of the state's social control, and one that allowed it to publicize its commitment to eradicating immorality—whether or not cases were vehemently pursued in practice.[19]

In addition to what he deemed aberrant sexuality, García Moreno was greatly preoccupied with the deviant behaviors he associated with excessive use of alcohol. One of the most telling pieces of political literature on the dangers of drunkenness was an eight-segment opinion piece in the official national newspaper in 1875 titled "El demonio alcohol" ("The Demon Alcohol"), which stated that those who drink to excess "frequently lose the ability to reason and ordinarily remain in a violent and dangerous state."[20] Excessive drinkers were supposedly prone to criminal behavior, and one drunken murderer was depicted as having "a savage appearance, his eyes gleaming, his hair standing on end, his gestures menacing, his teeth gnashing; he spit on the faces of those present," after which the author went on to generalize that "alcoholic insanity is characterized by absolute brutality, and by stupidity."[21] In sum, alcohol abuse eliminated any natural moral inclinations in the excessive drinker to the extent that even the drinker's humanity was lost: the alcoholic supposedly had the "repulsive appearance of a filthy animal."[22] The presumed association between drink and brutality found its way into political policies, as when García Moreno endorsed higher taxes on alcoholic beverages in 1869 by referring several times to the moral depravity that alcohol induced.[23]

One of the moral problems most frequently raised in "El demonio alcohol" was the dissolution of the family, and more specifically, the drunken husband's failure to uphold his patriarchal duties. Rather than provide for his wife and children, this man spent his money on alcohol, and "his wife, suffering much as a consequence of this detestable custom, often leaves her [marital] domicile to seek refuge in her parents' house."[24] Rather than protect his wife and children, he beat them: "A certain individual, once he submitted to liquor … habitually abused his wife and son … [and] his family came to live in misery, which is ordinarily what happens when the head of the household surrenders to drunkenness."[25] This already tragic disdain for patriarchal authority could, the author asserted, result in even more formidable consequences, as when a husband's drunken stupor led him to murder his wife because he wrongly suspected her of infidelity.[26]

Whether the issue was marriage, sexuality, or alcohol consumption, the moral missions associated with Garcian state formation were founded on patriarchal concepts. Men and women's proper roles were clearly defined, and straying from them had serious legal and social consequences. Men's functions in public related to their powers and responsibilities as patriarchs in their homes; women's exclusion from public life was an extension of patriarchal protection. García Moreno was the ultimate father figure for the national family he was creating, and patriarchal values sanctioned his authoritarian power.[27] These concepts were far from racially neutral, and Indians strayed significantly from the prescribed patriarchal archetype according to state officials' descriptions, which waffled between discussions of Indians' childlike humility and vulnerability and assertions of their brutal savagery.

Indian Men as Helpless Children

Political and scholarly generalizations of Indian qualities in late nineteenth-century Ecuador frequently emphasized that Indians were naturally submissive, particularly in their relations with whites and mestizos. Juan León Mera—author of Ecuador's first novel and supporter of

Gabriel García Moreno's conservative regime in the 1860s and 1870s—wrote a school text depicting Ecuadorian law, society, and history in which he claimed, "Among Indians, humiliation, timidity, and guile are predominant [traits], acquired in their long and perverse servitude, from which also comes their notable air of sadness ... but they are [also] hardworking, active, long-suffering, and constant."[28] Though León Mera did not openly criticize indigenous attributes here, neither did he view Indians as equals to whites and mestizos in Ecuadorian society. Europeans, he asserted, were by nature "religious, honorable, generous, and lovers of their independence and liberty." Mestizos supposedly fell between the indigenous and European extremes, but "as they become more civilized they continue to shape themselves more and more in the likeness of [Europeans]."[29] He used similar distinctions in his discussion of Ecuadorian customs—Indians "exceed extreme simpleness in their rusticidad, and superstition holds great influence over them; those of European descent maintain Spanish customs ... [and] mestizos are more cultured than the Indians, but different than the Europeans."[30] Clearly, León Mera's evaluations of different groups' supposedly inherent traits reinforced rather than challenged racial hierarchies.

León Mera used this text and its racial profiles to construct a vision of the nation that instructed Ecuadorian youth of the time in the relative value of different members of society. When he asserted that mestizos were becoming more civilized by adopting European traits and discarding indigenous customs, he reinforced nineteenth-century notions of progress. European culture represented civilization and progress, and Indian (and other non-European) cultures represented barbarism and backwardness. Progressive elites hoped that by emulating European culture and embracing export-oriented economics, they would be able to duplicate European economic success and Garcian stability.[31] In their view, Ecuador's indigenous peasants inhibited cultural and economic progress because they maintained their own languages and customs, and they farmed subsistence plots rather than producing for the export market. Indians therefore had to assimilate European cultural standards in order for progress to occur. In the meantime, the traits

León Mera catalogued suggested how each group could be most useful in the national quest for progress. As moral, honorable men and lovers of liberty, men of European descent should lead the nation; as timid but hardworking and constant, Indians should serve as the backbone of labor in the quest for national economic success.

Indians' submissiveness not only differed from characteristics attributed to whites and mestizos, but it was also problematic. Indians' humility—combined with accusations of inherent dishonesty—could be used to defend employers' cruel treatment of Indian servants. James Orton's travel account elaborates: "Always humble and submissive to your face ... [the Indian] will do nothing unless he is treated as a slave. Treat him kindly, and you make him a thief; whip him, and he will rise up to thank you and be your humble servant. A certain curate could never trust his Indian to carry important letters until he had given him twenty five lashes."[32] Descriptions like this of course have multilayered biases because they were written by Westerners who viewed both indigenous peoples and whites in Latin America as backward on many levels. They are, however, particularly valuable for highlighting unofficial yet deeply embedded attitudes among privileged Ecuadorians toward nonprivileged members of their own society, because travelers regularly interacted with elite groups and reported on Ecuadorian life from their perspective. Here, Orton captures the elite view of Indians as figurative children in need of strict patriarchal discipline lest their dishonest tendencies get the best of them. Assertions of Indians' childlike nature therefore allowed elites to rationalize Indians' subordinate position within Ecuadorian society. Pedro Fermín Cevallos suggested that Indians' vulnerability before non-Indian society rested on their own lack of virility when he stated that Indians' "cowardice and humility are such that [they] allow themselves to be dominated even by the lowliest members of the other castes."[33] Even in his vulnerability, the Indian was not described as a victim, since his own shortcomings were to blame for how he was treated. Indians' childlike ignorance and dishonesty could even be used to explain why their testimony did not weigh equally with that of non-Indians in court. One defense attorney asserted, for example, that "if an obraje Indian overheard [a discussion of] geology ... he wouldn't know what they meant ... and would [simply] repeat what he had heard."[34] The lawyer used this analogy to suggest that Indian witnesses could not be trusted because they did not understand what they heard or observed, and in particular had no concept of how the law functioned. These diverse descriptions of Indians all maintained that racial inequalities in Ecuador were unavoidable: Indian men's inherent submissiveness and ignorance justified elite social and juridical dominance.

Given that Indians' timidity left them vulnerable to mistreatment, the central government sometimes—very carefully—defined Indians as a social sector in need of protection and guidance. In an 1870 letter to provincial governors, the minister of the Interior remarked that local political and judicial officials often abused their power over Indians by "compelling Indians to labor on private construction work against their will, and this scandal is so extreme that the aforementioned authorities oblige [Indians] into contracts that supply them with peons." In response, García Moreno declared that any government personnel discovered doing this would be subject to removal from office and would potentially face criminal charges.[35] These orders were cautiously worded so that they could not be misconstrued as calling for special treatment or protections for Indians—a critical point in the post-tribute era, when the central state insisted that the days of collective legal identity were over.

Another dubious quality that elites frequently associated with Indians was their supposed idleness or laziness, and they most commonly proposed education as the remedy for this problem. In his 1869 message to Congress, Gabriel García Moreno declared that Indians' lack of education explained their "ignorance and lack of honor[, which] are so frequently transmitted like a fatal inheritance, perpetuating the laziness and indolence with which we justly find fault, and from which the indigenous race, especially in the interior provinces, continues to be wretched, depraved, and miserable."[36] The solution was to found new primary schools that, by educating Indians, would help them raise themselves out of their abject positions. Technically, after 1861, literacy would also change Indian men's political status since it would make them eligible to vote.[37] The educational initiative did not proceed easily or smoothly, however. Just two years before García Moreno made declarations about the need for primary schools, the minister of the Interior admitted that "public education has only advanced slowly" because of idleness in rural villages. He went on to remark that rural schoolchildren "deserve to be called crowds of wretched beings who grow in indolence, without having their sublime destiny in the land known to them."[38] The submissive timidity which state officials attributed to Indians therefore placed indigenous peoples in the childlike position of being guided and protected to facilitate their advancement toward civilization. At the same time, identifying the indigenous idleness as one of the significant obstacles to educational goals again meant that Indians were held accountable for much of their own suffering.

Because the state associated submissiveness and vulnerability with women, statements that Indians were innately meek, long suffering, and in need of protection attributed to all Indians, men as well as women, a trait that was considered naturally feminine. This was evident in an 1892 statue depicting Sucre, one of Ecuador's Independence heroes, standing protectively over an Indian woman.[39] Indian women's assumed passivity may have fit into general ideas about intrinsic traits of men and women, but identifying Indian men as passive meant that they fell short of true manly qualities. This in turn helped to justify Indian men's political and social marginalization in the Garcian era and beyond, because the assumption quietly condoned employers and state officials who acted as patriarchs over childlike Indians. After all, if men were the proper authorities within the family, and Ecuador was una sola familia, it followed that the national family needed reliable patriarchs. Considering that Indian men were passive and ignorant, white-mestizo men had to take charge of the Ecuadorian household, sternly but fairly ruling over all women and Indians.

Indian Men as Undeserving Patriarchs

Though politicians and scholars of late nineteenth-century Ecuador considered highland Indians submissive in most ways, they sometimes stressed that Indians had violent characteristics as well, mainly in relation to their own families and peers. A Supreme Court case from 1874 offers an excellent example of how state officials evaluated this allegedly innate Indian brutality. Asencio López, an Indian man from Chimborazo, was charged with beating his wife, María Aguagallo, and mother-in-law, Rosa Aguagallo. Both the prosecution and defense used the trial as a platform from which to argue over Indian otherness and, ultimately, Indians' place in the Ecuadorian nation. Because of its valuable discussions of race and gender, the case warrants detailed attention and analysis.

Defense attorney Alejandro Rivadeneira admitted that López had committed the crimes of which he was accused, arguing that domestic violence was a natural—and unchangeable—part of indigenous life. He therefore requested the minimum sentence for López because of "Lopez's coarseness [rural character] ... which is *congenital*, with very few exceptions, to the indigenous class to which he belongs ... there is a deep-seated custom between the poor Indians, in which a wife *requires* a dozen monthly blows from her husband as a token of his affection for her: a peculiar way to show love!; but ... when a husband ... beats [his wife], he is driven by love, rather than by hate and vengeance."[40] Rivadeneira also called on racial stereotypes in his plea for lenience when he contended that his client failed to understand the severity of the crime he had committed. Since the attorney presented domestic violence as an inborn trait of this ethnically distinct group within Ecuadorian society, he claimed that such brutal displays of affection, while horrifying to non-Indians, should not be severely punished. He further argued that López could not understand the brutality of his actions because of his limited intelligence and drunken state at the time when the beatings occurred.[41] In essence, Rivadeneira's argument rested on the idea that the barbaric Indian could not be held responsible for his own actions because his very nature made civilized conduct virtually impossible. In this analysis, the Indian man was as much—if not more—of a victim as the Indian woman, because his wife instigated the crime by "requiring" violence as a sign of love and affection.

Prosecutor Elias Laso proposed similar ideas about white-mestizo civilization versus Indian barbarism, but he interpreted these differently than the defense:

> The judge should use all means at his disposal to contain the *savage* custom which unfortunately exists among our lower orders . . . of mistreating wives without taking into account the consideration that a man should have for a woman, not only because of religious or family obligations, but also *because it is characteristic of the rational mind. In a . . . free republic born in the century of enlightenment, and in a culture which guarantees individual rights to all within its territory . . . it is not impertinent to . . . request that you weigh heavily these offenses which deface the customs of a faithful people, renowned through other qualities for their gentle character.*[42]

Like Rivadeneira, Laso identified Indian domestic violence as endemic within Indian societies, but he did not recognize this as an inherent trait that absolved the Indian man from responsibility for his actions. Yet even within the prosecutor's harsher interpretation of Indian domestic violence, the indigenous woman was not the real victim of the crime. Instead, the more significant threat was that this example of barbaric behavior would reflect badly on the nation as a whole and on civilized white society in particular. Laso vehemently insisted that the government had to obliterate Indian domestic violence by rigorously punishing indigenous men charged with the crime.

The conflicts and continuities in the attorneys' arguments not only related to their roles in the case itself but also reflected broader ideas about European civilization and Indian barbarism. Here, however, barbarism had a tangible consequence with the disruption of the core unit of society—the family. This helps to explain why both the prosecutor and the defense attorney in Asencio López's case were largely indifferent to the plight of Indian women who were beaten by their husbands. The women's suffering was not unimportant to them, but it was less critical than their conviction that Indian domestic violence was an obstacle to Europeanized progress and modernization. Nevertheless, this concern did mean that, at least in theory, court officials had to commit themselves to stamping out domestic violence.

The impassioned arguments over civilization and barbarism made in this case were simultaneously deceptive and enlightening. Their deceptiveness stemmed in part from the contradictory position of state officials vis-à-vis patriarchal violence. First, issues of rhetoric versus practice stand out: though López was found guilty and given the two-year maximum prison term for his crime, most cases against indigenous men for domestic violence or sexual harassment went unpunished. More often, Indian men were freed either for insufficient evidence or on the grounds that women's injuries were not serious.[43] There were also contradictions in court officials' classification of domestic violence as a specifically Indian custom. Domestic violence was surely a problem, but not an exclusively Indian one, as laws and policies themselves suggested. Divorcio and the legal separation of goods, both outlets wealthy white-mestizo women were most likely to use, allowed abused wives to seek separations. Moreover, white elites themselves condoned interethnic patriarchal violence, as was evident in descriptions of how Indians had to be whipped to labor effectively.

The López case was also exceptional because Indian women rarely brought domestic violence cases to court. Indigenous women's reluctance to do so perhaps derived from court officials' leniency in these disputes, but the paucity of domestic violence cases also arose because Indian peasant women had other means through which they could address domestic problems. It is possible that women—both Indian and non-Indian—were more likely to bring cases against abusive husbands to ecclesiastical courts. In Gladys Moscoso's study on women and domestic violence in the nineteenth century, she mentions cases involving indigenous women and refers to cases where plaintiffs or defendants had indigenous names. What is not clear from this article is the extent to which indigenous women's complaints were more or less prevalent than those of non-Indian women's, if the nature of their grievances differed in any way, and what different patterns emerged in the countryside versus the city. Further research needs to be done to explore the cultural, regional, and class differences that shaped Ecuadorian women's experiences of domestic violence in the late nineteenth century.[44] Documentary evidence suggests that abused Indian women were more likely to abandon their homes temporarily, seek the protection of other men in their communities, or even leave their husbands to live with other men than to bring these cases to court.[45]

Although Asencio López's trial cannot be taken as a typical domestic violence case, its stereotypes regarding indigenous behavior, and the attorneys' dispute over how to interpret and respond to such conduct, mirrored contemporary elite ideas regarding Indian savagery. While Ecuadorian references to indigenous domestic violence were rare, United States official Friedrich Hassaurek's 1867 travel account pointed to deeply embedded assumptions about Indians: "The Indian is strongly attached to his wife, and very jealous, although he treats her cruelly; but the woman does not wish to be treated otherwise. If her husband should cease to beat her, she would be convinced that he ceased to love her."[46] Hassaurek (like Orton) formed this opinion based largely on elite views, and while his portrait of Indian marriages might not have reflected the reality of Indians' lives and attitudes, it echoed the prejudice of wealthy Ecuadorians. For historians of Indian-state relations, Hassaurek's statements on indigenous domestic violence suggest that Laso and Rivadeneira employed entrenched racial stereotypes when they formed their arguments.

Another critical way in which the López case illustrated broader ideas about aberrant Indian behavior was in its references to the link between intoxication and indigenous violence. Citing intoxication as a mitigating factor was a common defense strategy when Indian men were accused of violent crimes. As one lawyer proclaimed: "Our Indians surrender to intoxication and ignore the consequences . . . *thus one can logically deduce that a cerebral congestion develops.*"[47] Indian men were, seemingly, especially prone to alcoholism, which in turn made them violent. Pedro Fermín Cevallos, just after identifying Indians as timid and humble, continued his discussion of Indians by contending that "when they are drunk it is another thing altogether, and they become talkative and valiant, and they would resign themselves to dying rather than ceding to something they did not want." Indeed, when discussing indigenous dances related to the celebration of Corpus Christi in Quito, Fermín Cevallos referred to a level of drunkenness that "if it is not a palpable profanation of that which is most sacred, we do not know how to qualify it."[48] Thus drinking transformed the timid, humble, cowardly highland Indian into a bold and even vulgar character.[49] Widespread elite notions about drunken, violent Indians also helped whites and mestizos charged with beating up Indians, because lawyers could claim that the Indian plaintiffs were so drunk when the alleged crime occurred that they were confused about what truly happened.[50]

Elites used Indian drunkenness to make sense of rebellions as well as to explain intraethnic violence. When Indians of the central highland province of Chimborazo rebelled in December 1871, members of the central government identified intoxication as a root cause for the brutality of the event. In García Moreno's 1873 message to Congress, he stated that the revolt was "produced by drunkenness and vengeance, and marked with various acts of ferocious savagery."[51] Minister of the Interior Francisco Javier León concurred when he reported that "the rebels, stimulated by intoxication, committed repulsive excesses, killing and cruelly defiling the cadavers, burning and robbing not only in [Yaruquíes], but also in Punín, Cajabamba, and Sicalpa."[52] Drinking, it seems, unleashed a savagery that lay just under the surface of the otherwise socialized and docile highland Indians. These descriptions of the rebellion of course reflect elite views and fears rather than present an accurate portrayal of the event; in particular, the views allowed state officials to deny their own part in creating conditions for rebellion with policies that attacked peasant subsistence.[53]

Even "El demonio alcohol," while it made no explicit racial distinctions, described alcohol abuse in ways that led readers to conclude that Indians would be more vulnerable to the dangers of drunkenness than other members of Ecuadorian society. The national newspaper's elite readership would be especially likely to identify contrasts between moderate and heavy drinking with race and class divides in Ecuadorian society. According to the author, the moderate drinker remained a moral and dutiful patriarch who posed no threat to society. It was only the heavy drinker, the habitual drinker, who lost all rationality and lacked a moral compass.[54] According to this theory, some men were more vulnerable to heavy drinking than others, and if alcohol could "enslave the spirit of one who is devoted to good sentiments, there is even greater reason that it will produce this enslavement when such sentiments are weak, *by nature or by lack of education*, or when they are altogether absent due to an inborn moral monstrosity in which the dark passions are naturally greatly active."[55] The phrase "by nature or by lack of education" was highly suggestive since it alluded to characteristics frequently assigned to Indians within Ecuadorian society. Indians, with their coarse ways and ignorance, were at higher risk for chronic heavy drinking and all the violent behaviors that accompanied it. Because habitual intoxication and patriarchal irresponsibility were thought to go hand in hand, Indian men were again defined as aberrant, and as undeserving patriarchs.

Indian Engagement with Garcianismo

The central state's reticence on the Indian question meant that Indian accommodation to and conflict with the processes of state formation in post-tribute Ecuador typically took place in the local arena, and changes resulting from Indian-state interactions were often subtle and gradual. In general, the transfer of Indian-state relations from the central to the provincial or local state officials had a negative impact on Indians, because of Indians' increasing tax and labor obligations from the 1870s forward and large estate owners' domination of local politics. Local authorities' and attorneys' attitudes toward Indians could have further undermined Indians' hopes of successfully defending their interests in the later Garcian era: one defense attorney, for example, declared that an Indian plaintiff's witnesses "were interested in the case, and above all are indígenas without integrity, lacking good faith, and ignorant."[56] There were, however, ways in which provincial officials' reluctance to view Indians as equal to non-Indians could benefit indigenous peoples, such as with their ongoing exemption from court fees in some provinces. Similarly, some local authorities continued to think they had an obligation to protect, support, and represent indigenous peoples' rights and needs. Local authorities' attitudes and dilemmas were not lost on indigenous peoples: court cases from Chimborazo reveal that Indians actively manipulated the contradictory ideas about their status within the nation to protect their own interests during this period of heightened tensions with the state.

A particularly good example of Indians and local officials working in harmony comes from a dispute between Indians of the civil parish of Licán and hacienda owner Ygnacia Orosco (with her husband, Antonio Mosquera) over access to vital water resources. Indigenous peoples argued that not only did Orosco and Mosquera divert to hacienda crops water that should have gone to the villagers, but also the couple demanded work from Indians to which they had a right only if they allowed the peasants water rights. Several non-Indians testified on behalf of the plaintiffs, and the local priest, teniente político, and civil judges (along with the Indian governor) spoke several times in support of the Indian plaintiffs' petition. Non-Indians did not often defend Indian rights in this way, and local authorities may have done so for various reasons in this case. First, the conflict dated back to the early phase of Garcianismo, when the central government was more accommodating of Indian rights and demands; further, one suspects that non-Indians in the region, like Indians, were negatively affected by the hacendados' monopoly of water supplies. Finally, the case makes several references to 1839 agreements between the former hacienda owners and the inhabitants of Licán, promising access to water in return for some labor, and assuring that this agreement would be valid even if the hacienda were sold to someone else.[57] Though such support for indigenous concerns was rare from 1869 forward, the case offers an important reminder that changes occurred slowly at the local level, and the specific nature of Indian petitions played a role in determining whether local authorities would stand in the way of or advance indigenous interests.

Indigenous peoples did what they could to weather insecure times in the late 1860s and 1870s. Those who could afford to do so sought titles that would protect their land rights, typically for lands they claimed from time immemorial, but in a few cases seeking to gain "absolute proprietorship" to land identified as tierra baldía.[58] Others took the kind of action that villagers in Licán did, going to court to complain that large estate owners or local authorities had either taken their land or blocked their access to critical resources.[59] Cases against large landowners, however, usually failed due to hacendados' dominance of local political and judicial processes.[60] Without recourse against hacienda owners, most Indians were left to squabble with each other over remaining lands or to turn to haciendas for employment (whether temporary or permanent) to meet their subsistence needs. Indians often manipulated state-generated interethnic gender ideas to mitigate the negative impact of state formation. From the 1860s through the early 1890s, Indian men frequently employed elite ideas about their submissive, childlike nature to advance their own interests, calling on state authorities' paternal obligations to respond to their pleas. This strategy did work on occasion, mainly because of white-mestizo authorities' conflicting sentiments about Indians' status within Ecuadorian society.

Indian men played on enduring notions of their childlike status with numerous references to their misery and passivity, presenting these qualities as part of an inescapable condition of their rural lives, for which they deserved protection rather than punishment.[61] Not infrequently, indigenous plaintiffs and defendants emphasized their ongoing unequal status and the racism they faced, "imploring protection . . . [because] when it comes to our class, very few if any look at or respect us."[62] In an 1871 murder case, indigenous defendant José Ñaula was even more direct when he sought the court's mercy as a member of the unhappy class of Indians, arguing that only this sector of society was subject to the full rigor of the law.[63] This claim that whites and mestizos regularly received preferential treatment emphasized that, regardless of lawmakers' assertions, Indians were not equal to non-Indians before the law.[64] When appealing to regional or national courts, Indians might emphasize that such inequalities were mainly a problem in local-level politics, as did José Manuel Tenelema of Sicalpa when he questioned a local judge's integrity, stating that although those of his unhappy class had to put up with the hardships of others' ambitions and rash acts, "fortunately the laws of our fatherland offer remedies to cure the ills that result in the persecution of the tranquility of an *infeliz* [person of miserable legal status]."[65]

Indian men might also emphasize how policies or individuals undermined their ability to meet paternal, manly obligations. In an 1873 land dispute with a local hacendado, a group of Indian men insisted they needed access to former communal lands to pasture animals and to pay diezmos, *primicias* (first fruits of the harvest that went to the Church), and the contribución subsidiaria—all duties that fell on adult men, typically heads of households.[66] Compromised in their ability to provide for their families after the abolition of tribute, some Indian men claimed further harm to their paternal status when local authorities harmed Indian women: in the canton of Colta, in the midst of a complaint against the local teniente parroquial for fraud, José Miguel Ninabanda testified that the teniente also "forcefully beat his wife, who since then has been ill." Another Indian witness verified the beating.[67] As part of the unhappy class of Indians unable to protect his wife when she was beaten, Ninabanda perhaps hoped to reclaim his patriarchal standing in court. His accusation also stands in contrast with elite claims that Indian men were unconcerned with protecting the women and children under their patriarchal power.

As in other periods of Ecuadorian indigenous history, Indian litigants were unlikely to attack systems and laws on a grand scale; instead they worked within preexisting unequal and hierarchical systems to limit elite individuals' exploitative capacities. Doing so not only meant emphasizing their own childlike vulnerability but also entailed identifying opponents as malevolent patriarchs. Consider the lawsuit against José María Pacheco, teniente parroquial of Pangor, for fraud: several indigenous men testified that they had paid Pacheco to avoid working on the public road; he then sent them there anyway. Though Pacheco claimed to have collected the money for other, legitimate reasons, he was found guilty (and fled before he could be arrested). Some of the witnesses who agreed that Pacheco had failed to fulfill his paternal obligations were labeled *ciudadanos* (citizens)—a term rarely applied to Indians. Juan Naranjo, for example, was a ciudadano who told the court that he had heard from Indians about Pacheco's actions, after which he talked with Pacheco, telling him "to at least reduce the fines, looking upon these miserable ones with humanity."[68] Whereas Pacheco was charged with abusing indigenous peoples under his fatherly jurisdiction, in Columbe Indians filed a suit against tenientes Antonio Cárdenas and Camilo Biqui, and civil judge Carlos Sepada, for failing to protect them. When Roberto Burbano came to Columbe to gather workers for public highway construction, he went with Biqui to the hacienda of San Martin, where he forcibly took indígena Santos Guevara from his own home and beat him severely enough to cause a significant head wound. The three local officials were charged with failing to protect and seek justice for the indigenous victim.[69] What these local officials had in common was failing to fulfill their interethnic paternal duties.

Though less frequently than in the Urvina era, Indian men of the late nineteenth century did sometimes simultaneously emphasize both their childlike vulnerability and manly responsibilities as heads of households. This happened in the suit in which José Miguel Ninabanda complained that his wife had been beaten by teniente José María Pacheco. On the one hand, Ninabanda, like other plaintiffs, appealed to the court for protection as a vulnerable Indian, while on the other hand, he sought, as a good husband, to redress harm done to his wife. Another indigenous litigant, José Yllapa of Columbe, similarly asserted that teniente Agustín Lara acted against "the individual security of two men [*varones*], mistreating the wife of the first."[70] Besides referring to an assault on an Indian woman under his care, an Indian man might call on court officials for fatherly protection while clarifying that part of a local official's breach of conduct pertained to the way in which he ruptured the sanctity of the home, the Indian man's domain. When Roberto Burbano entered the hacienda San

Martin to gather indigenous workers for public highway construction, plaintiffs pointed out, "he arbitrarily entered the [workers'] houses on the hacienda," suggesting that Burbano had no right to cross the threshold of a man's home, even if that man was indigenous.[71] The case shows that court officials sometimes considered Indian men's patriarchal authority in their own homes more important than white-mestizos' patriarchal rights over Indians. Similarly, when Francisco Rodríguez pursued a complaint against the civil judge of Palmira, he declared "they broke [laws], attacking my rights, to the extreme of failing to respect the domestic home such that they... destroyed the place of my habitation."[72]

Local authorities took attacks on their paternal reputations seriously, since their status as good father figures (both in their own homes and in public) was central to their public honor. A slander case from Tigsán highlights this tension well. Vicente Aguirre, a judge in Tigsán, brought indígena Mercedes Pullayotan to court for damaging his reputation. Aguirre claimed that Pullayotan destroyed his "public reputation and honor as a *padre de familia* [male head of household]" when she called him "an old drunk and a livestock thief," also accusing him of confiscating land. Yet worse, Aguirre averred that Pullayotan had gone so far as to claim that he deflowered young women (*doncellas*) in his house. Witnesses verified Aguirre's claims, allowing him to restore his manly honor when Pullayotan was found guilty.[73] Though local officials' concern with their patriarchal honor was not discussed directly in other cases, it was part of the backdrop of indigenous grievances that made it possible for them to succeed.

Indian men were at the center of most negotiations and confrontations with state officials during the last few decades of the nineteenth century. Indian women were seemingly peripheral to the question of Indians' status because women were denied the vote and because the civil code had clearly outlined that all men, regardless of race or class, had significant economic and social power over their wives. Further, when highland hacienda owners, coastal elites, or state officials needed laborers, it was Indian men they sought. These factors all demonstrate that the Indian problem was specifically a question about the place of Indian *men* within the formative nation. However, the demands made of Indian men by coastal elites, highland hacendados, and the central state had a significant impact on Indian women's lives. State officials could take Indian men away from their communities to work on road construction, for example, only if Indian women were available to take over what was defined as men's work in their home communities. Yet many Indian women found it difficult to maintain family subsistence alone, and if a man's absence was lengthy or if conditions at home were especially difficult, an Indian woman might have to migrate—temporarily or permanently—to a sierra city in search of work.[74] Yet not all effects on women were negative, and it was in part these women's seeming insignificance in the eyes of state officials that at times made them central to family and community defense.

Indian women's participation in and importance to community defense had its roots in indigenous gender values, cultural norms, and peasant life; however, broader political and economic contexts also placed Indian women in pivotal positions to assist their loved ones and peers. For instance, Indian men's absences—whether for public works projects or temporary work on haciendas—changed Indian women's positions within and importance to their communities. When husbands were present, state legislation dictated that men would dominate disputes within their communities and with elites; only widows were allowed to defend their own economic and civil interests. But when Indian men had to leave to meet either their families' needs or state officials' demands, their wives became situational widows who, because their husbands were not able to represent them, could petition the court to represent their own interests in land disputes while their husbands were away.[75] Whether indigenous husbands left by choice or by force, their absence made women central players in the struggle to maintain local peasant autonomy. In effect, when outside forces drew men away from their homes, many indigenous communities were feminized.[76]

These circumstances sometimes made Indian women an important first line of defense of community or male interests. An excellent example comes from the civil parish of Baños (Tungurahua) in 1873, in which Indian María Laso complained that hacendado Manuel Toledo Onroi had wrongfully seized her husband (Ignacio Santa Cruz) and other indigenous men to work as conciertos for him. Laso pursued this case all the way to the Supreme Court, insisting that "none of [the indigenous men] owed him a centimo. Relentlessly pursued by demands and violent attacks . . . it is necessary to go to Quito and obtain a protective ruling from the Supreme Government."[77] The court ruled in her favor; once her husband and the other men were freed, they took over the case and successfully pursued further charges against Toledo Onroi. Laso's case demonstrates that Indian women's stability in their home communities sometimes made them critical links between Indian men and the court system. Without a woman at home who was ready to take matters into her own hands, the men whom Toledo Onroi forced into concertaje may never have found a way to bring their plight to the attention of the high government officials.

Some Indian women took initiative even when there were men available to start court proceedings, as an 1870 case from the civil parish of Punín demonstrates. Problems began when Francisco Mayacela, teniente parroquial of Yaruquíes, entered the Indian hamlet of San Francisco to search for two Indian men who had escaped work on road construction; his presence so irritated community members that the visit resulted in a violent confrontation between the outsiders and indigenous peasants. Though it was never directly acknowledged within the case, it is likely that Mayacela's connection to the hated trabajo subsidiario caused the peasants' ill feelings toward him. During the conflict, Mayacela severely wounded Catarino Guamán and Manuel and Juan Llangari. Paula León initiated the complaint against Mayacela for wounding these three men, who were so badly injured that they were unable to act on their own behalf in court.[78] After León began the case, court officials took it over, and Mayacela was convicted.

These data suggest that Indian women became critical actors against abusive authorities because of the demands that hacendados and local administrators made of Indian men. Women's protests were almost always on behalf of absent husbands or wounded male relatives, and they often stated clearly that they were pursuing cases only because men were unable to do so. Paula León's actions did complicate this pattern somewhat: there was likely a kinship tie between Paula León and the wounded Llangari brothers, given that other witnesses with the surname León were their cousins. Yet when Paula León initiated court proceedings against Mayacela, there were male relatives of the victims who could have done so themselves; León's role in this case therefore shows that Indian women would sometimes take action rather than wait for Indian men to decide to bring a grievance to court. The point should not, however, be taken too far: once León had initiated proceedings, she disappeared from the court record, and the majority of witnesses were indigenous men. In spite of direct action to defend their communities, Indian women avoided any affront to men's patriarchal rights and power.

In certain circumstances Indian men and women forged more equitable partnerships to defend community interests. This occasionally happened in court cases, such as one from Sibambe (canton Alausí) in which twelve indigenous men and twelve indigenous women sought to protect common lands from Felipe Bucheli. Though it was not directly stated, the twelve women and twelve men in the case probably were married and together represented the collective interests of women and men in the community.[79] Women's presence as men's partners was relatively rare in peaceful disputes, however, because indigenous communities and the state identified Indian men as heads of households who could and should represent their wives' and children's interests. Women's partnership with men against the state was instead most evident when indigenous communities rebelled against abusive officials or intolerable state demands, and references to both large and small uprisings typically referred to a relatively equal mix of male and female rebels.[80] The most outstanding example of this pattern of violent collaboration between Indian men and women in late nineteenth-century Ecuador occurred in the central highland province of Chimborazo: there, from December 18 to 24, 1871, thousands of Indian men

ECUADOR

TUNGURAHUA

Penipe

Guano
• Penipe

Guano ○

• Quimiag

Lican
San Juan ● • ⊛ Riobamba
• Yaruquies

Cajabamba ○ • Chambo

BOLIVAR
• Punin   Riobamba

Colta
• Licto
• Flores

○ Guamote

Guamote

○ Pallatanga

Pallatanga

Alausi

MORONA-
SANTIAGO

○ Alausi

GUAYAS

○ Chunchi

Chunchi

CHIMBORAZO

⊛   Provincial capital

○   Cantonal seat

∘   Civil parish

—·—   Provincial boundary

- - - -   Cantonal boundary

CAÑAR

0 ────────── 10 miles

0 ────────── 10 km

and women rose up against white-mestizo society. At approximately 4:00 p.m. on December 18, a group of Indians in the hamlet of Cacha (Yaruquíes parish) attacked and killed Rudecindo Rivera, a tithe collector who had entered their community. Indians mutilated Rivera's body, and the violence escalated and spread to Cajabamba, Sicalpa, and Punín. A young Indian man named Fernando Daquilema was purportedly crowned king and took over leadership of the rebellion. As the violence spread, rebels began to burn buildings in their wake and left some villages, including Punín, in ashes.[81]

The government response to the revolt was swift and exacting. On December 19, the governor of Chimborazo conscripted all men in Riobamba between the ages of sixteen and sixty to fight the Indian rebels, threatening severe punishment for anyone who failed to report for duty, because he would be jeopardizing all non-Indian inhabitants of the province should the uprising grow to even greater proportions.[82] García Moreno declared a state of emergency in Chimborazo province. Though the earliest attempts to terminate the rebellion failed for lack of manpower, by December 24 the assembled forces were large enough to stop the Indians, and the last outbursts occurred that day in the parish of Yaruquíes. Once whites and mestizos regained control in the area, the government responded harshly to the revolt: public officials immediately began to round up Indians they suspected of instigating and leading the revolt, and some leaders, including Daquilema, were executed. Though most of the fifty to sixty Indians tried were initially sentenced to death, either García Moreno or the governor of the province intervened and commuted many of their sentences to several years of either hard labor on public roads (in the case of men) or imprisonment (in the case of women).[83] By punishing Indian men with several years of labor on public works, the government accomplished two things: first, government leaders could claim to be acting as responsible patriarchs to Indians by treating them kindly. Second, sentencing men with labor on public roads promoted García Moreno's agenda for building up national infrastructure while punishing them with one of the very burdens against which they had rebelled.

In spite of the harsh punishments assigned to the fifty-two men and eighteen women whom government officials blamed for leading the uprising, Indians made several short-term gains through the rebellion. In early January 1872, Pío Cifuentes, a Yaruquíes official, requested that the government temporarily stop collecting the trabajo subsidiario in the area; other officials made similar requests to postpone tax collections.[84] Some state authorities, fearing further barbaric Indian violence, responded by proposing reforms. For example, the minister of the Interior sent a circular to all provincial governors in January 1872 prohibiting abuses in the collection of diezmos, primicias, and the trabajo subsidiario, having heard about cases where Indians were the victims of these corrupt practices.[85] The timing of these requests and decrees was more than coincidental, and it demonstrates how Indians near Riobamba used rebellion to secure relief from onerous tax burdens. Thus, while state officials regarded the Daquilema rebellion as evidence of the savagery lurking behind the submissive veneer of the highland Indian, for indigenous peoples—women as well as men—the action was part of a spectrum of strategies they used during the intense and mostly negative transformations in Indian-state relations during the late nineteenth century, resulting from policies that made subsistence harder to maintain and destabilized community structures.[86]

Walking the Garcian Tightrope

Identifying Indian men as childlike and subservient harked back to the paternalism of the colonial and early republican eras, though without the official structures or benefits that Indians had enjoyed under the old tribute system. Indicating that Indian men were irresponsible patriarchs in their own homes called into question their ability to be trustworthy in other ways, especially with regard to the political nation. State officials, however, had to make these claims carefully in the post-tribute era to avoid admitting to any kind of inequality among Ecuador's ethnic groups. Yet whether state officials identified Indian men as helpless children or cruel patriarchs, these exaggerated discussions of their supposedly inherent qualities helped to justify Indians' continuing (and even intensifying) marginalization in the nation, and they reinforced the idea that "better kinds of men" should run the country. In short, if Ecuador had failed to become a nation full of unencumbered universal individuals, it was not the fault of the state but rather of deviant Indian patriarchs.

Indigenous men and women who engaged with state officials, usually at the local and regional levels, were severely limited in their ability to address the problems they encountered in the aftermath of tribute, but they pursued available options with great skill and made the most of the late nineteenth-century politics of patriarchy in order to advance their interests whenever they could. This most often meant relying on lingering notions of Indians as childlike and vulnerable, but they did occasionally act on elite images of Indians as inherently violent, drunken, and barbaric—either through pleas their lawyers made or with their own violent actions. Thus members of the central state could justify or ignore the Indian problem through gender ideologies—but not make it disappear. Likewise, Indians could use gender ideas to alleviate individual or community problems temporarily—but, ultimately, they could not change elites' skewed ideas about them or bring an end to government policies that were detrimental to their well-being.

The period from 1860 to 1895 marked the second phase in Ecuador's transition from colony to republic (the first being the 1830–1857 tribute debate). Garcian policies set forth the first meaningful state-building project in Ecuador, and they provided a way of grappling with Indians' ongoing inferior status within the nation. García Moreno successfully managed the specter of liberal individualism through conservative manipulation of colonial religious ideals—albeit placed in a new republican setting and with a profoundly new state-making agenda. These solutions, however, were only temporary; it would not be possible to ignore the Indian dilemma long-term at the central government level. Yet it was not until the end of the century when liberal forces overtook the central government that modern Indian-state relations would be forged—in part as a reaction against nineteenth-century conservatism (including the negative images of Indian men), and in part founded on Garcian policies and gender ideas that began the process of creating that ever-elusive imagined community.

⇒ 4 ⇐
Liberalism

The Marriage of Democracy and Patriarchy?

Nothing is more painful than the condition of woman in our country,
where she is relegated to domestic tasks, incredibly limited in her sphere of
intellectual activity, and even more limited in circles where she could be
independently and honorably employed.
—Eloy Alfaro's Message to Congress, 1897[1]

The small property-owning indigene cares for his land with love . . .
the family happily collaborates on agricultural work, singing with hope.
—Pio Jaramillo Alvarado, 1922[2]

On the surface, liberal stances on Indians and women stood in opposition to earlier Garcian views. Where Garcianismo emphasized (white-
mestizo) marriage as harmonious, liberals identified it as enslaving
women. If Garcian officials labeled Indian men aberrant patriarchs, liberal reformers saw them as caring and honorable men. Yet if one con-
siders other issues, the two nation-making regimes were quite similar:
both associated women with the home, and both showed concern for
indigenous men's roles as heads of households. And, like state builders
from the 1850s to the 1870s, liberal reformers in the early twentieth
century failed to address adequately either racial or gender inequalities. Instead, liberal reforms for women and Indians mainly promoted
coastal liberals' political and economic goals against their competitors
rather than addressing women's or Indians' main needs. Further, even

though liberals scorned their conservative predecessors, liberalism built upon Garcian policies and accomplishments. For example, liberals could afford to develop a more optimistic view of Indians' place in the nation because García Moreno had already privatized communal lands and undermined caciques' positions in the nation-state. Not having to undertake such endeavors themselves meant that liberals could emphasize how they were intent on saving Indians from oppression, and they could more easily hide the underlying racism of their policies.

Despite similarities between liberalism and Garcianismo, liberal policies marked a critical new phase in nation making that laid the foundations for modern Indian-state relations and women's movements. Liberals' proclaimed concern over Indians' and women's situations gave the two groups new opportunities to employ nation-making discourses in a way that neither the Urvina nor Garcian regimes had. One can find the roots of Ecuadorian feminism in this era, when a group of (mainly middle-class) women adapted liberal rhetoric to improve their condition in society. Similarly, indigenous peoples seemed to regard liberal proclamations as an invitation to use central government policies for their own purposes, such as gaining better work conditions on haciendas or even reclaiming communal lands. The liberal period was thus one of mutual manipulation: liberals used the Indian and woman questions to increase state power, while women and Indians used the liberal state to promote their own interests. Neither feminists nor Indians, however, were terribly successful in getting liberals to expand their rather narrow reforms to address underlying gender and racial inequalities. Nor did either group fundamentally challenge liberal paradigms: instead, feminists' and Indians' demands invoked liberal discourse and ultimately reinforced the liberal project. In the long run, however, these failures were less important than the new dynamics that surfaced in the sociopolitics of nation making. Liberal statesmen honed language and laws to more neatly mask their part in perpetuating inequalities, and the central government gained power over a wider variety of regions and peoples within the nation. Even though Indians' and feminists' endeavors at the time did not reshape the contours of the nation, both groups would build on liberal-era lessons and embark on more significant challenges to the state later in the twentieth century.

Indian women were conspicuously absent from most of these encounters because liberal rhetoric and policies rarely acknowledged their predicament. When liberals discussed women's problems, they focused on issues that were important in the lives of middle-class white women, such as marriage laws, the right to work, and the right to control money. None of these topics captured the class- and race-based problems urgent to indigenous women. Likewise, liberal considerations of Indians were mainly concerned with Indian men's exploitation at the hands of highland elites, their rights as patriarchs in their own homes, and their potential incorporation within the nation. While Indian men and women shared concerns with class- and race-based exploitation, women remained on the barely visible periphery of the Indian problem, with liberals relegating them to the private sphere. Again, one can find compelling parallels with the Garcian era, when women also meant middle-class women and Indians usually meant Indian men. Yet the liberal period was not simply more of the same old marginalization for Indian women. Because Indian men gained new avenues for negotiating with the state, Indian women's fixed position relative to the central state meant that there was a widening gap between Indian men's and women's abilities to confront the state; this too would have significant consequences later in the twentieth century.

The Woman Question in the Liberal Period

Because liberal presidents and congressmen professed a desire to incorporate women into the modern nation, they proposed and passed laws that at first glance appeared to greatly alter women's roles within Ecuadorian society.[3] Liberal laws reconstituted marriage as a secular rather than religious institution, legalized divorce, encouraged women to work outside the home, and allowed wives to control money and goods that they brought into marriage. Each of these reforms, however, also strengthened the liberal state in one way or another. Civil marriage and divorce laws weakened the Church and increased the state's visibility and control in the most basic of societal unions. Decrees encouraging female participation in the workforce helped to overcome labor shortages resulting from economic growth and modernization. Allowing wives some control over money shed a positive light on the liberal state while allowing statesmen to congratulate themselves on having caught up with Western nations on matters concerning women's issues.

Marriage reform was a central aspect of liberals' treatment of the woman question, beginning with marriage laws passed in 1902 and 1910. The 1902 law established civil marriage and required couples to register their marriages with the state; it also allowed couples to divorce under certain circumstances, which led to debate in Congress. Senator Banderas made one of the most ardent (and lengthy) speeches against the law in September 1902:

> As a Catholic, I cannot contribute even the remotest cooperation with the creation of a law that my conscience tells me is anti-Catholic in all facets . . . marriage is considered a contract and a sacrament, it falls exclusively under the rule and authority of the ecclesiastical jurisdiction . . . radicals have tried to establish [a distinction] between the contract and sacrament of matrimony, considering one independent of the other, in order to conclude that marriage is a purely human contract, subject only to civil jurisdiction and that the Church has no reason to intervene . . . this ill-fated distinction [is false].[4]

In response, the law's proponents, most notably the well-known liberal senator Andrade Marín, identified civil marriage as a basic civil right that the government should not deny its citizens. To emphasize this point, senator Vela noted that even ultra-Catholic nations like Spain and Peru had civil marriage laws, and "none of these nations asserts that the law threatens ecclesiastical authority."[5] Advocates suggested that passing the law would secure Ecuador's place among modern Western nations, while rejecting it would throw the nation back into

the Middle Ages, when an all-powerful Church regularly denied individuals' natural rights.[6] The law's passage marked a victory for the liberal secular state, but limits to divorce in the 1902 law make clear that
even liberal reformers continued to be influenced by Catholic sensibili-
ties. The 1902 law permitted divorce only under specific circumstances,
such as infidelity, impotence, or a husband's attempt to prostitute his
wife or children; these conditions mirrored Catholic Church requirements for formal separations.[7]

Advocates and critics of civil marriage also debated its potential
effect on Ecuadorian society, and resistance to the law on this basis was
not always from the ranks of conservatives. Liberal senator Riofrío pronounced:

> [As one senator put it] 'I am a liberal ... but I declare that the project
> of Civil Marriage, sent here by the house of Deputies, is a monstros-
> ity and an absurdity.' ... We should not uproot the rocks that form
> the foundation of the social edifice, and that which we would [tear
> down] with this proposal would be not a single stone but an entire
> wall.... In effect, sirs, between law and social institutions there is
> a wall of separation, and between those institutions the one which
> forms the foundation stone, sustaining all else, is Christian mar-
> riage.[8]

Challengers argued that civil marriage would inhibit men from becoming useful members of the public sphere and keep women from obtaining the virtues necessary to build proper homes. Thus "neither would
the domestic home be maintained, nor could the Republic be considered
secure."[9] According to this view, "opening the doors to divorce, one also
opens the most appalling corruption; [divorce] degrades woman, who
is redeemed by Christian marriage; it deprives children of the sweet-
ness and caring of the home ... it annuls the rights of paternity, and
it destroys the family."[10] In response, defenders of the civil marriage
law argued that, if anything, the law was not comprehensive enough
in its protection of women. Senator Arauz pointed this out when argu-

ing that a man's as well as a woman's infidelity should be grounds for divorce, because otherwise the family would be dishonored and the home would become a kind of hell for women.[11]

The 1910 proposal to allow for divorce by mutual consent proved even more contentious. Liberals in congress, mainly from the central and southern highlands, supported civil marriage only as long as it correlated to Catholic teachings; many of them had voted for the 1902 law because its allowances for divorce paralleled Catholic grounds for separation. Granting couples the right to divorce, without requiring proof that one partner had broken the marriage contract, strayed too far from basic Catholic teachings about the sanctity of marriage.[12] Yet the 1910 congressional debates over civil marriage reveal that representatives were often at least as concerned with gender roles as they were with Catholic doctrine. Gallegos, a representative from Tungurahua province, proclaimed that he was trying to protect Ecuadorian women from abandonment by opposing the divorce law. He declared that "a husband has undeniable power over his wife, and when he tires of conjugal life, he obliges her to sign her own sentence of disgrace, perhaps of her dishonor, and what can she do?"[13] Other congressmen claimed that the law benefited only elite women—an accusation that the bill's supporters vehemently denied.[14] Advocates retaliated by claiming that the law would save women from domestic servitude: "It is necessary to abolish all forms of slavery, and among us there is still the slavery of woman who is shackled with indissoluble ties ... [and] prostrate before man. In order to recover her liberty and position, we must impose the law currently under discussion." In their view, divorce by mutual consent would liberate wives, allowing them to escape bad marriages without publicly shaming either marriage partner.[15]

If Congress ultimately embraced civil marriage, it was not without adamant complaints from conservative sectors within Ecuadorian society. In a series of manifestos written between 1902 and 1918, Ecuadorian bishops equated civil marriage with concubinage and charged that it went against the will of the majority of Ecuadorians, who were good Catholics. Like congressmen, the bishops focused on women's need for protection, claiming that today's daughter would be "tomorrow's mother: the day after tomorrow she will become the widow of her house. Mother, shamed by society! . . . A widow, but without the honor of mourning in her widowhood!" The dishonorable widow was the divorced woman, whom the bishops identified as the victim of civil marriage.[16] A group of married women in Quito and Cuenca voiced similar concerns when they pronounced that woman found civil marriage offensive, and that the new law prostituted her. Catholic writer Roberto Páez alleged that the law would put women at risk because a divorced woman would be unappealing to a prospective husband, and she would therefore have to live without a man's support.[17]

In short, both advocates and opponents of civil marriage proposed that they were acting in the best interests of married women, and probably many of them were sincerely concerned with women's plight. Even so, gender assumptions and ideologies provided statesmen with a platform on which to contest and negotiate the parameters of the modern (secular) nation-state. The claim to protect women also provided Church officials with tools to defend their influence within Ecuadorian society, power that was under attack from secularizing liberal leaders. These strongly divergent views reflected divisions among women themselves; middle-class and elite women had a mixed reaction to civil marriage laws, particularly articles relating to divorce. Though some voiced ardent opposition to the laws, others took advantage of new allowances for divorce in order to end unhappy marriages. For the latter group, the 1910 allowance for divorce by mutual consent enabled them to exit bad marriages without disgracing themselves or their families. Neither the 1902 allowances for divorce, nor the earlier rules for formal separations, gave them the opportunity to avoid shame in this way. Perhaps for that reason alone, I found no evidence of women going to court to obtain divorces in Chimborazo after the passage of the 1902 law, but several appeared in the provincial court records in 1912 and 1913. These newly divorced women may not have been as outspoken as their conservative counterparts, but their actions suggest that they agreed with lawmakers who viewed civil marriage and divorce as liberating.

Liberal references to traditional domesticity as a form of slavery also justified encouraging women to participate in the economy, especially in the workforce. Reforms included a decree to train and employ women as telegraph and postal workers (1895), various directives calling for female teachers (especially for girls' classes), and a 1911 law allowing married women to gain some (limited) control of money.[18] From the beginning of the liberal era, Alfaro identified these aims with the good of both Ecuadorian women and the state, arguing, "1st: That it is the responsibility of all governments to improve women's condition, providing them with the means [to obtain] honorable and decorous work. 2nd: That there are many places in public administration where married and single women can be satisfactorily employed."[19] Though Alfaro included married as well as unmarried women in his 1895 decree, liberal discussions of female participation in the workforce focused almost exclusively on single middle-class women and assumed that they would leave the public sphere once they married. Facing criticisms that women's education and work would destroy the family and thus the moral foundation of society, Alfaro responded:

And one cannot say . . . that these reforms in the education of woman do away with the poetry and tranquility of the home. On the contrary: an educated woman, a woman who possesses arts and industries, a woman who works and acquires experience through more immediate contact with real life, far from damaging the home, is a great auxiliary for the family and a valuable treasure for her husband, because, her soul is revived with realism, her ideas about fidelity and honor—her greatest patrimony—and therefore the education of children of such women will become more clear and perfect, more solid.[20]

Such assertions reveal liberal reformers' paradoxical stance regarding women and work. On the one hand, they challenged gender norms by encouraging female participation in the public sphere, while on the other hand, they carefully restricted what they defined as acceptable women's work so as not to challenge long-standing notions of female honor associated with sexual purity and domesticity.

Liberals' greatest challenge to previous ideas about marriage came with a 1911 law giving married women the ability to control some money. Specifically, the law stipulated that "the married woman can request the partial separation of goods, limited to all or part of those which are exclusively her own.... [She can then] freely administer that which she has taken away from her husband's power."[21] Some opponents of the law argued that since Ecuadorian women were deeply Catholic, if they gained control over money, they would merely dispose of the money in any way their priests commanded.[22] In this scenario, women simply traded one patriarch for another rather than achieving personal independence—an argument meant to appeal to liberal anticlericalism. One senator found the bill disturbing on an even more basic level: in his opinion, allowing wives to control money during marriage would turn the whole notion of marriage itself on its head, resulting in a society where "marriage would be constituted of two husbands, rather than man and wife."[23] As with civil marriage, opponents of the law argued that giving women control of money would disrupt social order, this time emphasizing that it threatened men's patriarchal authority.

Supporters of the 1911 law maintained that it would provide women with much-deserved individual liberty while protecting them from predatory men. Senator Vela from Tungurahua province, one of the bill's authors, even equated the law with national welfare:

It is well known that the family gives birth to society and from that to the Nation.... We who have opened the doors for woman to be a citizen, to have the same political and social rights as we have ... how can we not concede to her equality in the matter of civil rights? ... I have seen the need for woman to seek a door of escape in order to free herself from the cruelty of a husband without honor, without conscience, and who many times gets married because he is interested in a woman's goods ... [and] after a while, sunk in misery, he abandons her and lives in public concubinage, while … his own wife and her legitimate children, die in poverty.[24]

Vela's statement presents several subtle but crucial shifts in the gender underpinnings of nation-state making in Ecuador. The Garcian method for ensuring morality and familial stability centered on men acting as honorable and powerful patriarchs, threatening strict punishment for anyone who strayed from Catholic moral standards. Liberal reformers—concerned with many of the same threats to social order—instead proposed that women should be given leverage to recover their own moral and financial well-being. Notions of honor also stand out here: though a husband's honor still rested on his ability to provide for his family, now his motives in marriage also had to be pure from the start, and his rights as a husband were conditional. If he acted dishonorably, his wife could manage her own money or even divorce him. Finally, early twentieth-century liberals were the first statesmen to suggest that a woman belonged to the nation as an individual in her own right, not simply through her husband or sons. The "economic emancipation of the married woman," as liberal reformers called the 1911 law, may have been limited, but it gave women economic independence not previously enjoyed under national law.

Assumptions about proper gender roles did set limits on the 1911 law, however. The law's supporters adamantly assured their peers that control of goods was intended only for married women who were in unhappy unions, assuming that in good marriages, where wives were under the tutelage of responsible men, husbands would still control all marital possessions.[25] Furthermore, after the new legislation was passed, wives still had to file their intention through a public scribe to take advantage of their new rights, assuring that men continued to mediate women's economic destinies. If wives did not file, their husbands legally controlled all marital goods. Even when wives maintained control over money they brought into marriage, the law still allowed husbands to manage all money that the couple acquired after marriage. Therefore, while wealthier women might be able to use the law to support themselves and their children should they have the bad luck to marry irresponsible men, poor women still lacked sufficient means to ensure their own or their children's livelihood should their husbands prove unreliable.

Women's rights were a bone of contention not only between liberals and conservatives in Quito, but also between central and regional government officials. A Supreme Court case that took place shortly before the passage of the 1911 law offers an interesting example of the complexities of women's rights in the liberal period. In the suit, Vidal Pastor appealed a case that he had lost in the Riobamba superior court against Sebastiana Véjar. Apparently Pastor was renting the hacienda Pachanillay, having signed a contract with Véjar's husband, Victor Manuel Romo, a few years earlier. However, the hacienda technically belonged to Véjar, and she had recently established independent administrative control over it through a separation of goods from her husband. When she took control of the property, just before harvest time, she expelled Pastor from the estate. At the local court in Guano, a judge upheld Pastor's petition to retain control of the hacienda through the harvest, stating that previous legal contracts had to be honored. The superior court, however, found against him because it was Véjar's right to do with her property as she pleased, and since her name was not on the earlier contract, she was not bound by it. The Supreme Court upheld the superior court decision, and Pastor lost his harvest.[26] Though the 1911 law was not the source of this particular dispute, it reveals how the differing and often competing levels of the state complicated the enforcement of laws. Whether the new laws to redefine marriage and women's rights were meaningful therefore depended on the attitudes of state officials at every level of administration.[27]

The greatest challenge to prevailing gender norms came when the 1910 Congress debated female suffrage. Though champions of the reform argued that women who met the literacy requirement should have the right to vote, the proposal was too radical for most liberals. Representative Borjas Cordero from the coastal province of Guayas, the most vocal opponent of the proposal, thought that female suffrage would make a mockery of the democratic process, because "if there are men for whom voting is not possible, how can we permit a woman to do so?"[28] He also maintained that giving women the vote was contrary to their nature and would undermine good government, because "woman is under the direct power of man, such as her husband, her father, her brother, ... thus in a home where there are five or six daughters, all of them and their mother, will reflect the father's mode of thinking. And with what result? That the opinion of the father will be apparent in five or six or seven votes. This is nothing other than establishing corruption in the Legislation."[29] The opposition carried Congress, whose members clearly viewed political participation as a male prerogative; to break that association would be to undermine democracy and weaken the nation. It was not until almost twenty years later, in 1929, that Ecuador would become the first country in Latin America to grant women the right to vote in national elections. Even then, legislators gave women the vote not to advance their rights in society per se, but to bolster support for conservative forces. They, like their predecessors, assumed that women would vote as their husbands (and priests) instructed them.

Both liberal legislators and Church leaders accepted a common definition of woman that they used against each other. When liberals offered women new roles in the public sphere, they assumed that a woman's greatest social contribution, and her natural role, was to raise children.[30] Secular education, respectable work before marriage, and increased financial activity within marriage were all supposed to make women better able to raise children to be good citizens.[31] Catholic leaders manipulated similar gender ideologies that identified women with piety and motherhood to enlist middle- and upper-class women's help in the struggle against secular education and asked them to demand, as mothers, that their children be offered moral (Church-run) as well as secular education.[32] Though their views of what prepared women for motherhood differed, liberals and conservatives agreed that women had to be more nurturing, pious, emotional, and moral than men to fulfill their motherly duties properly. It was for this reason that reformers felt compelled to respond to their opponents' claims that their proposed changes would compromise women's virtue, insisting that the changes would make women even better mothers. In essence, liberals and conservatives agreed that women ultimately belonged in the private sphere, but they used differing interpretations of this role to express Church-state tensions in the liberal era.

This placed women in a precarious position vis-à-vis the nation: on the one hand, they were essential to national development as mothers, and liberal reformers in some ways even identified women as individuals with their own citizenship rights. On the other hand, women had to be excluded from the political domain of nation making: to include middle- and upper-class women in politics would highlight class and race differences that excluded poorer, especially non-white, Ecuadorian men. If liberals were going to co-opt men of all classes and races to support the liberal nation-making project, despite literacy requirements that kept most of them from voting, then women had to be excluded as well, even if they met legislated voting requirements. This was the mission behind Borjas Cordero's 1910 comment that female suffrage would make a mockery of democracy—it would undermine a sense of "democratic patriarchy" the state was attempting to create during the liberal period among men across class and race lines.

Even women who sought expanded rights carefully reinforced their supposedly natural womanly attributes and duties. Zoila Ugarte de Landívar, in the first edition of *La mujer*, assured men that female education would make women into better companions: "Female ignorance is counterproductive to man—on whom does he depend for his well being from the time that he is born until the time he dies but woman? . . . Woman asks for her part in life's happiness because she has her part in its pains . . . an intelligent man of good heart, therefore, would not be completely satisfied with a woman companion who was ignorant or bad, and one can be bad through ignorance."[33] To educate women would enhance their ability to tend to children and husbands, thus improving men's lives. An editorial note to the first issue of the journal quite directly connected women's education to social welfare. After remarking that women's situation had not greatly improved, in part because of men's resistance, the editor carefully added, "We do not want to say with this that woman will stop being the angel in the house as mother and wife, no; but we believe that her attentions should not be limited only to the narrow circle of family, as gifted as she is with intelligence and exquisite sensibility that can be made suitable to contribute efficiently to the betterment of society."[34]

Having assured men of their intention to remain angelic mothers molding the next generation of good citizens, women writing *La mujer* demanded not only better education, but also equal political and civil rights. Like their male liberal counterparts, these early Ecuadorian feminists identified their exclusion in civil matters and politics as a form of slavery.[35]

The impact of either feminists or women conservatives on liberal policies is difficult to gauge. Historian Martha Moscoso has pointed out that the women writing *La mujer* were actively buying into and making use of liberal discourses as a means of advancing their goals, rather than suggesting any fundamental departure from reforms that liberal men had already proposed.[36] In this sense they reinforced and strengthened, rather than challenged, liberal policies. They also made only those gains that dovetailed with liberal objectives, such as secularization, while their demands for equal political and civil rights were not achieved. Still, early feminists' demands show that liberal initiatives supporting women's education, work, and marriage rights did not come out of a vacuum, and that women themselves played a part in creating the context in which policies developed, even though they neither wrote the laws nor voted. The point need not be limited to feminists—many conservative women, in the name of defending traditional Catholic and family values, influenced lawmakers. Thus, although conservative women, feminists, and liberal reformers all insisted that women's natural domain was domestic, a number of Ecuador's middle- and upper-class women were knowledgeable about, concerned with, and actively participated in national political debates. In this way an important tension, or paradox, developed in which women were drawn into the politics of nationhood at the same time that dominant gender ideologies forced them to frame their interests and value as principally domestic.

Neither supporters nor opponents of these various reforms, including early feminists, referred to class divisions between women. Yet they all assumed that the label "woman," unless otherwise specified, referred to an idealized notion of white, middle-class or elite women. This is evident in debates over women and work, since all congressmen took it for granted that women did not normally work for wages, and that they had a choice about whether to enter the workforce. Only wealthier women were able to treat work as a choice; poor women (usually Indians or mestizas) had to work in order to support themselves and their families. Moreover, the gender divisions between public (male) and private (female) spheres, which liberals and conservatives alike promoted, did not even reflect the experiences of the many middle-class or elite women who were involved in one way or another with managing family businesses or estates. Debated notions of citizenship were equally weighted with class assumptions: typically, only middle- and upper-class women were literate; therefore the 1910 deliberation over female suffrage was quite pointedly a dispute whose aim was to decide whether women of means should gain this right. Such distinctions were typical, in Latin America and beyond, when legislators considered the question of female suffrage, but they had specific ramifications for Ecuadorian Indian-state relations. To statesmen of the time, the woman question remained separate from the Indian question. Ultimately, this barrier between women and Indians facilitated Indian men's access to liberal nation making at the same time that it severely limited Indian women's potential to engage with liberal initiatives. To elaborate on the divergent impact of liberalism on indigenous men and women requires an examination of liberal Indian policies.

Saving the Indian from 1895 to 1925

Like reforms aimed at women, liberal Indian policies addressed very real problems of oppression, but in a limited and contradictory way that always served the interests of the liberal state. Liberals focused the Indian question on education and concertaje, proposing that education would bring Indians out of ignorance and into the national fold, while eliminating concertaje would liberate them from centuries of oppression at the hands of highland authorities. Though building on gendered interethnic politics evident in the nineteenth century, liberal discourses masculinized Indian-state relations in ways that previous regimes had not.

The most widely agreed-on Indian reforms, and those put into effect the earliest, were educational. Advocates of these reforms assured moderates and conservatives that the entire nation would benefit from Indian education, because exposure to modern, enlightened ideas through education would finally bring Indians out of their backward and superstitious condition. More specifically, liberals had to convince their critics that education would make better workers of Indians, as president Leonidas Plaza promised in his 1905 address to Congress by emphasizing that "agricultural improvement should begin with the improvement of the operator."[37] To fulfill these promises, the mandatory nature of public primary schooling had to be carefully enforced. For this reason, the public education law of 1907 required parents or patrones to register all children between the ages of five and twelve with the local teniente político and penalized guardians who failed to send children over six years of age to school.[38]

Practical application of educational initiatives, however, fell far short of proclaimed goals. First, few primary education facilities were built in the rural areas where most indigenous peoples lived, suggesting that it was the concept rather than the application of Indian education that mattered most to reformers.[39] Even the theoretical foundation for Indian education was far from altruistic, as it was bound to the Church-state battle for social control within the nation. Finally, schools were arenas where Indians would be incorporated into the body of the nation through the obliteration of indigenous cultures and values. Agustín Cueva, a poet and politician from the southern highland province of Loja, essentially admitted to this in a 1915 article: "And, above all, [we need] schools, schools, and schools, which will replace the Quichua language with Spanish, which will bring the necessary and practical understandings to a race that has a peculiar psychology . . . to extract from them their confused and atavistic notions . . . and leave them with the spiritual pearls of contemporary progress."[40] Ultimately, liberal reformers were proposing that education would solve the Indian problem by eliminating indigenous customs and language through a process of acculturation. Educational reforms would consequently transform Indians while simultaneously extending the central state's reach far into all regions of the nation.

Having used Indian education to increase the liberal state's power relative to Church and local authorities, statesmen in the mid-1910s revisited a goal first outlined in 1895—eradicating the problem of debt peonage on highland estates. Though Alfaro had decreed reforms for concertaje in 1899, statesmen thereafter did little if anything to address what they deemed Indians' most burdensome oppression until after the secular government was securely established. Congressmen also debated the impact of drink on indigenous communities, the obligations Indians had to fund religious ceremonies, and indigenous land rights in certain regions of the nation. Concertaje, however, remained the cornerstone of varied liberal Indian reforms.[41] Abolishing debt peonage promised to release downtrodden Indians from exploitation and backwardness, allowing them to embrace modern civilization and contribute eagerly to the nation. Conveniently, it would also give central-state officials the power to mediate disputes between indigenous workers and highland estate owners, and it promised to increase indigenous migration to the coast for work.[42] To mask these aims, liberal supporters argued that the law was necessary in order to make Ecuador like other modern nations; maintain the proper separation between civil debt contracts and the criminal penalty of incarceration; and uphold individual liberty as "an inalienable human right." Opponents, too, framed their arguments carefully, claiming first that it was only the rare hacienda owner who abused contracts with his indigenous workers, and warning that the new law would result in Indian workers being able to flee debts without repercussions, potentially destabilizing the agricultural production on which the nation depended.[43]

All the proposed reforms, and especially the abolition of concertaje, presented intricate and often contradictory gender ideas regarding the interethnic politics of nation making. Similar to Urvina, early twentieth-century liberals viewed Indian men as childlike in their relations with non-Indians yet having great manly potential as patriarchs in their own homes and contributors to the nation. Tensions between state-sanctioned egalitarianism and (also state-sanctioned) interethnic paternalism resulted from this split view of Indian men; these were evident in an 1895 decree releasing Indians from the obligation to pay the *contribución territorial* (territorial contribution, or tax) and the trabajo subsidiario:

> CONSIDERING 1st that the disgraced condition of the Indian race should be alleviated by public officers; 2nd that the liberal Government has inaugurated Sir General don Eloy Alfaro, Supreme Chief of the Republic, who has the duty of protecting the descendents of the first inhabitants of the Ecuadorian territory; 3rd that in the campaign for national honor the Indians provided great services to the Liberator's army, thus demonstrating that they are disposed to adopt the practices of modern civilization.[44]

Here, Indians were childlike and backward as well as manly and modern—with the latter being a much more positive interpretation of Indian manliness than one finds in the nineteenth century, even in Urvina's regime. The difficulty over defining Indian men as either equal and unencumbered individuals in the nation or as a group with obvious need for paternal protection was also manifest in the 1897 constitution, which both asserted that all Ecuadorians "are guaranteed equality under the law" and maintained that "public officers should protect the Indian race, in order to improve their place in national life."[45] This conflict often worked to liberals' advantage because it justified reforming the highlands and increasing the presence of the central state in the countryside. As in earlier eras, discussions of Indian men most often focused on their childlike passivity and vulnerability, a view that allowed each nation-making regime to rationalize its policies regarding Indians.[46] Liberals, however, proposed that the root cause of Indians' childlike status was not of their own making as Garcian officials had argued, but that it resulted from centuries of oppression. In this, early twentieth-century liberals were similar to their 1850s counterparts, but again an important distinction can be made: whereas early- to mid-nineteenth-century statesmen blamed the Spanish colonial system for Indian exploitation and backwardness, liberals in the early 1900s held accountable highland priests and hacendados.

Liberals generally avoided references to barbaric brutality among Indians, and if they had to confront indigenous drunkenness or violence, they evaluated it quite differently from nineteenth-century statesmen. Agustín Cueva in particular dismissed ideas that Indians were either stupid or ferocious, stating instead that they were as capable of learning as anyone else, and that they tolerated their victimization quite tranquilly, without violence. Though he accepted other negative Indian traits as real, he did not think they were Indians' own fault. He maintained that if Indians were considered irreligious, it was because priests had abused them and failed to teach them the true doctrine of Christ. If they were thieves, it was because they lived with constant hunger; if they were eternal children, it was because they lived under tyranny; if they were indolent, it was because their situation gave them no incentive to be productive.[47] Liberal reformers thus classified Indian barbarism as a by-product of the abuses Indians faced at the hands of landowners and priests.

This reluctance to shed a negative light on Indians' character was not exclusive to liberals, however, as Ricardo Delgado Capeáns' discussion of Indian society and education showed. Though a conservative and ardent supporter of Catholicism's role in the nation, Delgado

Capeáns, like his sociopolitical adversary Cueva, emphasized Indians' inherent ability to learn and to improve, perfect, and civilize themselves. He proclaimed, "I do not see the reason for the contempt with which we look upon the indígena."[48] Like Cueva, he dismissed the idea that Indians were more prone to vices than non-Indians, and he made such statements as "If the Indian gets drunk, he gets drunk on the same pretexts as the civilized man."[49] Therefore, even as they argued against many of the changes that liberals were making, conservatives embraced the new Indian discourse that the liberals had set forth. This suggests that changing views of Indians had less to do with differences between conservative and liberal rule than it did with the modernization of nation making. The Garcian policy of relegating interethnic relations to local authorities was not a viable long-term solution because it left Indians on the margin of the nation while giving considerable power to local governments. For the modern nation-state to take shape, such a large population of its members had to be more clearly, if rhetorically, incorporated. It was also crucial that central-state officials gain greater control over local authorities—a goal readily advanced by the stated need to protect Indians from abusive elites.

This new and more positive impression of Indians was not without its limits. For one thing, only highland Indians were viewed as victims rather than perpetrators of backwardness; statesmen of the liberal era, like nineteenth-century scholars and politicians before them, identified indigenous peoples of the tropical lowlands as completely separated from civilization. Consider claims made in a Supreme Court case against a Shuar man for double homicide. The defendant is referred to as a *Jívaro*—a pejorative term whites and mestizos used for the Shuar. The defense attorney asserted: "The defendant is a jívaro, which is to say, a primitive man, a man who does not participate in our moral [order] . . . [the jívaros] live outside of society . . . how can we attribute bad intentions to a man who lives on the margin of civilized society? . . . it is impossible for the savage to distinguish between good and bad."[50] The defense therefore requested that the judges drop the charges against "this infant, this large child of civilization, this savage who is less man than brute."[51] The case makes clear that liberals saw some Indians as far from redeemable, though this view was limited to the small and dispersed lowland populations. At the local level, however, there remained a deep-rooted fear of uncontrolled Indian violence toward whites and mestizos. Take a Supreme Court murder trial in which Cuenca officials introduced the case to the court by writing that "the barbarous killing of Sir Manuel María Carrión Serrano, perpetrated by a gang of Indians[,] . . . caused horror in all of Cuenca society."[52]

In some instances, liberal assertions that Indians were childlike proved problematic, especially as they contradicted liberals' alleged goal to create a nation of liberal individuals rather than perpetuate racial difference. As was often the case, liberals blamed highland hacendados for the problem, declaring that Indian men's failure to achieve patriarchal maturity resulted from oppressive and backward conditions on haciendas. Of particular concern was Indian men's lack of authority over their own households, which liberal reformers like Agustín Cueva identified as a central feature of concertaje: "The servant, unlike the slave, lives separated from the master, he governs himself; but this liberty and independence are ironic, because . . . his economic life is circumscribed such that *neither is marriage spontaneous nor does the family belong to him*; he remains shackled to the land on which he has to live and die as a perpetual debtor, as an eternally forced laborer."[53] Hacendados' dominance of estate socioeconomic relations meant that they controlled not only conciertos, but also their wives and children. To Cueva, this was a crucial aspect of the concierto's lack of liberty: he was robbed of the right to rule his own household. While hacienda social relations were more complex than Cueva suggested, many liberal reformers shared Cueva's view and considered it their duty to promote Indian men's patriarchal rights within their homes.

Liberal reformers' conviction that Indian men were rightful heads of households influenced their proposals for improving Indians' lives. Indigenous women were almost entirely absent from liberal discussions of Indians' plight. One notable exception was Eloy Alfaro's 1899 reforms of concertaje, in which he stated that hacendados could not require conciertos' wives or children to work for them.[54] While this reference in theory addressed a form of exploitation that greatly concerned indigenous men and women, it was one of the hardest parts of the decree to enforce. To keep hacendados from requiring unpaid labor from conciertos' wives and children would require a level of constant supervision beyond the capacity of state officials. Even if state officials brought some hacienda owners to court for demanding unpaid labor from women and children, local judges were unlikely to penalize the owners.[55] Proposals for change based on the notion that men were natural heads of households, overlooking Indian women, continued when the liberal call to abolish concertaje peaked in the 1910s. Belisario Quevedo—a politician, sociologist, and liberal reformer—advised that Indians could be lifted out of debt peonage only if wages did not "fall below that which is necessary, indispensable, for the subsistence of the worker and his family."[56] Quevedo's proposition might well have met a positive reception among indigenous peoples, including women who would likely embrace a reform freeing them from the double burden of work and child care. However, Quevedo identified the worker as the male, patriarchal breadwinner for his family; even though women were already required to work on estates, he classified them as belonging to the private sphere of the home. Such associations, however, did not necessarily mean that liberal reformers were unconcerned with hardships that indigenous women and children experienced on estates.[57] Quevedo even suggested that hacendados' enslavement of Indian families often began with marriage itself, when an Indian man, unable to afford marriage, first became indebted to the hacienda owner on the estate where he grew up.[58] Recognition of the impact of concertaje on the entire Indian family was not entirely new, but it was certainly under closer government scrutiny than it had been previously.[59]

Other reformers did not directly discuss separate male and female spheres, but they assumed notions about proper gender roles when proposing social changes. In an essay on Indian education, Homero Viteri Lafronte and Pedro L. Nuñez emphasized that since agriculture was the basis for indigenous life, primary education in rural areas needed to focus on agricultural training. The authors did acknowledge that Indian women did not automatically fit into the private sphere: "The Indian woman generally does the same work on haciendas as the Indian man; we should not forget that for one reason or another the Indian woman can also be left as the head of the household, and, finally, we must remember the power that a mother or wife can exercise over her children or her husband."[60] From this statement alone, one might surmise that Viteri and Nuñez recognized and respected indigenous women not only as mothers, but also as workers. Yet when they mapped out a specific educational plan to teach young Indian boys and girls how to become good workers, their gender prejudices became evident. They proposed that Indian boys be educated primarily in agricultural techniques so that they would grow up to be good and knowledgeable agricultural workers. Indian girls, however, would learn domestic economics and hygiene, cooking, washing and ironing, sewing, and cheese making along with some minor agricultural training.[61] Therefore, even though they gave some recognition to Indian women's importance in the public sphere, Viteri Lafronte and Nuñez tacitly proposed that rural education would minimize Indian women's deviation from the dominant white-mestizo gender norm.

State officials and scholars used ideas about proper gender rules to include Indian men, symbolically, in the nation. If Indian men were not citizens who voted, they still belonged generally to the national community of men who participated in the public sphere and presided over their families. Importantly, their wives were relegated to the private sphere, regardless of whether they worked outside the home. To stress male egalitarianism, in spite of glaring socioeconomic inequalities, liberal leaders accentuated differences and inequalities between men and women. This was clear in the debate over female suffrage: allowing women to vote would make a mockery of democracy precisely because it would undermine the manliness of poor, nonwhite men, whom liberals were keen on redeeming. In essence, a common patriarchal connection would bind subordinate men to the liberal project and help to address the ever-present specter of liberal individualism by downplaying Indian men's childlike relationship to white-mestizo society. Therefore, liberals balanced references to Indian men's childlike passivity with allusions to their potential for masculine achievement in the public sphere. Indians' preconquest achievements, reformers argued, proved them capable of overcoming centuries of oppression and assimilating into the Ecuadorian nation.[62] Their encouragement did not go unheeded: Indian men regularly manipulated liberal rhetoric to suit their own ends, often in ways that were unanticipated by members of the central government.

Negotiating Liberalism from Below

Indigenous peoples combined tradition and innovation when interacting with state representatives in the liberal period, sometimes drawing on preexisting strategies while at other times altering tactics to take advantage of new policies. While often still referring to themselves as defenseless victims, Indian men were also likely—sometimes in the very same case—to remind court officials that "even though we are Indians, we know how to respect God and the law."[63] By combining declarations of their masculine rights and childlike vulnerability, Indian men reclaimed and transformed the ideologies behind the liberal state's approach to Indian-state relations.

Changing Indian strategies began on the eve of the liberal revolution. A good example comes from 1890, when Fabián Guamán, an indigenous man from Licán (Chimborazo), protested that teniente político Calisto Vinueza had arrested him illegally. Guamán's lawyer argued that a guilty verdict was necessary because "illegal actions cannot be justified by the custom [the defendant] cites, that in all civil parishes, since time immemorial, Indians have been obliged to serve in the post of alcaldes, because this custom, as ancient as it is, is contrary to the individual liberty guaranteed by the Constitution, which further prohibits the demand for forced labor from Ecuadorians."[64] The plaintiff's argument rested on simultaneously highlighting age-old injustices in local interethnic relations and constitutional rights guaranteed under liberal rule. Vinueza argued that he harbored no malice against Guamán, nor did he realize he had broken any law by arresting him; the superior court, however, found in Guamán's favor. Indian men in Bolívar province brought similar charges against a parish priest in 1892, alleging that the priest was "of the custom of making the indígenas of the parish serve him in his house for a week's time, against their will and without a contract." The priest, Manuel Rivadeneira, defended his well-established reputation and suggested that a local tinterillo had drummed up the charges among his (ostensibly content) Indians. Unlike the case against the teniente político in Licán, the superior court found in favor of the defense.[65] In another case, Indians in Licto (Chimborazo) complained that diezmero Antonio Mosquera abused his authority, pleading with the court for "your great and good favor on our unhappiness, [as we are] harassed [and] extorted" by tax collectors. The court found in Mosquera's favor because Indians had identified the whole tax system as corrupt, not just Mosquera's part in it.[66] Morality as well as individual liberty might have been at stake in struggles with local authorities, as when Teofilo Cabezas, the jefe político of Guano, faced charges for not only forcing Indians to work for him without pay but also leading the young men of Guano (hijos de familia) astray into gambling and drunkenness.[67]

Conflicts between Indian peasants and local authorities from the early 1890s draw attention to several ways in which Indian-state encounters were changing. Indigenous plaintiffs not only charged local authorities with abuse but identified systemic practices as unjust. They also stressed their rights as individuals in addition to highlighting their vulnerability as Indians. Local authorities attributed Indians' manipulation of elite debates to the influence of meddlesome tinterillos, foreshadowing complaints they would make regularly in the liberal period. Finally, these cases show that encounters between Indians and authorities in the highlands were undergoing changes even before liberals rose to state power. This suggests that developments in Indian-state relations grew out of the interplay between central and regional politics, rather than coming from central-state initiatives alone.

Other factors also point to the gradual rather than sudden transition in Indian-state relations in the provinces, particularly with regard to ethnic labeling. During and after the Garcian regime, the central government largely refused to address ethnic divisions, while ethnic labeling remained common at the provincial and local levels. Under liberal rule, ethnic labeling was reversed, reflecting nuanced but significant shifts in Indian-state relations. At the central-state level there were explicit, clear, and frequent allusions to Indians and their plight, followed by promises to tear down barriers that kept Indians from enjoying the benefits of liberal individualism. It was at the local level that interethnic labeling became cloudy, indicating the uneven impact of liberal policies. Some court cases lack any references to participants' ethnic identity, with only litigants' names suggesting that some or all of them had indigenous ancestry (which by itself did not necessarily mean they maintained indigenous customs). Other cases lacked ethnic labels but offered more tangible evidence of Indian identity, such as references to litigants or witnesses who did not know Spanish, or who were conciertos—both of which make it almost certain they were indigenous. But not all court cases attempted to sidestep the labels of "indígena" and "indio": Indians sometimes used the label to emphasize their miserable status, hoping to win the court's sympathy, while their opponents might use it to question indigenous petitioners' motives, knowledge, or reliability. Neither of these manipulations of Indian stereotypes was new, but their use was more overtly strategic than in earlier eras. Because court scribes no longer specified individuals' ethnicity when introducing civil and criminal conflicts, litigants drew attention to ethnic identity only when there was some particular advantage to be gained in doing so.

Indigenous peoples, already in the process of modifying how they interacted with state officials, were quick to take advantage of liberal rhetoric. For instance, they frequently called on liberals' proclaimed goal to save Indians from abusive highland authorities.[68] Even familiar references to Indians' miserable status or rusticity offered compelling reminders that state officials were supposed to protect and uplift oppressed Indians. At other times allusions were more explicit and developed, as when one lawyer pointedly reminded superior court judges that his clients "are miserable Indians from Guamote, destitute of fortune and serving as peons for señor Salvador F. Muñoz."[69] Indians thus continually reminded members of the state that they required special protection as long as they were not included in the nation on equal footing with non-Indians. Indian men also played on liberal suggestions that they were responsible patriarchs in their own families, going to court to defend their manly rights, dignity, and honor. When Pablo Quishpi was charged with injuring fellow Indians, he countered that his opponents had insulted him, calling him an *indio desnudo* (naked Indian), and therefore forced him to defend his honor.[70] An Indian man might also take insult if it his wife's reputation was smeared, as did César Quishpi when Ygnacia Calpiña purportedly called his wife a whore and accused him of prostituting her.[71] While this was not a new concern within Indian families, liberal imagery of Indian family life encouraged Indian men to assert their dignity as men and fathers of families.

Using liberal rhetoric to defend Indian manhood and dignity was even more critical in confrontations with local elites. In 1921, for example, Alfredo Costales brought a case to court against several Indian men whom he claimed accosted him in Riobamba for no apparent reason, dragging him to their home parish of Punín, where they meant to kill him. The defense lawyer responded that the plaintiff had provoked the Indian men by entering the area where they were gathered to drink *chicha* (corn beer, an indigenous drink) after selling goods in the Riobamba market. He further stated that the Indians had wanted to bring Costales before Punín authorities only to protest his involvement in the creation of the civil parish of Flores.[72] Unlike earlier descriptions of Indian drinking, the defense presented the Indian men's gathering over chicha as an acceptable form of male bonding and unwinding at the end of the day. Particularly interesting was the defense attorney's assertion that Costales had no right to interrupt such a gathering, suggesting that the Indian men took the intrusion as an offense to their masculinity. The Indian defendants also maintained—successfully, as it turned out—that they did not intend to harm Costales, but that they were exercising their right to seek justice against a white with whom they were disgruntled. These Indian men were thus able, under liberal rule, to assert that they were protecting their masculine rights on both personal and political grounds. In fact, they may have been using role reversal as a form of gendered interethnic justice. Costales complained that the Indian defendants had beaten him and taken articles of clothing from him, treatment that white-mestizos often used to humiliate Indians.

Some Indians in the liberal era responded to state officials' criticisms of hacendados to try to get the court to defend their communal land rights. Although Indians had often fought hacendados' attempts to take over communal lands in the 1860s and 1870s, these disputes tapered off in the last two decades of the nineteenth century because repeated failures gave Indians little hope of winning such cases. When liberal rhetoric offered Indians new hope that they could defend (perhaps even regain) communal lands, they again began to bring disputes against hacienda owners to court.[73] These liberal-era cases began to move away from previous community defense patterns, in which married men and widowers initiated and led most court disputes.[74] While the majority of men of liberal-period suits were married or widowed, single men also participated directly; single men's involvement suggests that political changes in Ecuador since the late nineteenth century were having a democratizing effect among the men of at least some Indian communities. Indian women, however, continued to be excluded from these actions unless they were widowed.

Although Indians' responses to liberal initiatives further strengthened the power of the central state in local politics, indigenous men (and sometimes women) did not necessarily respond in the manner that central government officials intended. Instead, Indians often appealed directly to higher officials, such as provincial governors, rather than local state representatives, and many were willing to pursue complaints to Quito if necessary.[75] For example, indigenous laborers on the hacienda Gatazo Hospital repeatedly complained to the governor of Chimborazo about their hacendados, until the governor finally ordered them to bring their petitions to the local authorities instead. His apparent exasperation with the Indians' complaints led him to guarantee the Indians that their local state representatives were obligated to listen to and act on their grievances.[76] Court appeals also made clear Indian skepticism that justice could be found with state officials close to home.[77] When Tomasa Tuqueres was charged with assault and other crimes, she sought her freedom not only as a poor, old Indian woman suffering from hunger and cold in jail, but also by insisting that local court proceedings against her had been irregular and unjust.[78] In another case, a defense lawyer complained that no interpreters had been provided for his Indian defendant and that the local authorities forced him into a confession.[79] Generally, liberal-era data show that Indians, through their lawyers, were quite skilled at interpreting liberal decrees and laws to suit their own needs. Clark, for example, found that Indians of the Alausí area used a clause in the 1897 constitution to their own ends. The constitution prohibited labor services that were not legally required or formalized by a contract; liberals' main aim with this prohibition was to stop Church officials from obtaining Indian laborers. Indians, however, used the law to protest their conscription for public works construction, by claiming that it violated their constitutionally guaranteed rights.[80] Therefore, even as indigenous peoples played on liberal discourse and strengthened the central state, they did so in ways that were unimagined by liberal nation makers.

Local elites—often the hacendados and priests whom the liberal state disparaged—generally greeted these Indian tactics with disdain and hostility, arguing that liberal policies resulted in Indians' preferential treatment rather than equality for all. One lawyer, defending an official charged with arbitrary arrest, stated, "I cannot comprehend, Esteemed Sir, how a tribunal as respectable as ... the superior court proved so hostile against an innocent [man], so susceptible to the rights of a poor indígena, such that we have seen various times that honorable men are reduced to prison."[81] By contrast, Indians were dishonorable and violent men who threatened public safety; or, at least, that was the claim many elites made to justify having injured or killed them.[82] Both public and private authorities in the highlands thought that Indians abused their new rights under the liberal regime, sometimes venting their frustrations when they referred to "the impunity that those of [the indigenous] race now enjoy."[83] As with cases in the early 1890s, local elites often blamed Indian men's renewed activism on greedy tinterillos.[84]

Yet while indigenous peoples drew on liberal discourses to defend their interests, their success rate was not much improved over earlier periods. Liberal rhetoric called on state officials to protect Indians from abuse, but in practice, court and state officials favored local authorities. Some of this had to do with the fact that many local officials continued to maintain close ties to elite families in their jurisdictions, making it almost impossible for Indians to address their problems. This helps to explain Indians' frequent appeals to provincial or national authorities, whom they hoped would be more receptive to their petitions. However, this was only occasionally the case. One of the many contradictions of liberal Indian-state relations was that, despite their proclaimed desire to improve Indians' lives, central-state officials' interests more often coincided with hacendados' or Church officials' causes than with Indians' needs or views. Indians' chances of success also depended on the nature of their disputes with elites. Conciertos complaining about abusive treatment at the hands of an hacendado were far more likely to achieve their goals than were peasants struggling with the same hacienda owner over land rights. In the first case, the liberal state officials could assert their power and paint themselves as righteous defenders of the Indian. In the second case, liberal leaders were liable to be wary of peasants' communal and subsistence tendencies, preferring hacendados' association with private property and the market economy. Despite significant obstacles and limitations, Indians apparently viewed the liberal state as more receptive than earlier regimes, since they regularly employed liberal discourse and policies. At the very least, they continually exposed liberal discourse as pretense, and some of them were able to achieve their goals. More importantly, indigenous peoples—especially men—adopted strategies in this period that they would use for decades to come, and that would eventually be more successful. It was the extent of their engagement with liberal ideas and policies, rather than their success rate alone, that marked the modernization of Indian-state relations.

Patriarchal Contradictions Modernized

Liberal gender strategies were more complex than those of Garcianismo had been: though seemingly champions of women's emancipation, liberal reformers proved time and time again that they were primarily interested in using new laws to undermine Church influence in

Ecuadorian society. Historian Martha Moscoso refers to the conflict between the proclaimed goals and limited impact of liberal gender reforms as part of an internal conflict over women's identities and roles with regard to wider sociopolitical and economic changes in the liberal era.[85] Like Garcian officials, liberals defined the nation—especially the political nation of citizens and real or potential voters—through the exclusion of women.[86] For this reason, even some of the most ardent champions of liberal reforms balked in 1910 at the thought of giving women the right to vote as long as there were still men denied this privilege. Though state-sanctioned gender ideologies misrepresented women's lives in many ways, they helped to justify the often contradictory relations between Indian men and the formative state and therefore reshaped Indian-state relations from both above and below.

Throughout the liberal period, social reforms focused on women or Indians tended to overlook the plight of Indian women. When liberal reformers did pay attention to Indian women, they were mostly concerned with restructuring economic and social conditions so that Indian women could come closer to meeting their ideal notion of womanhood, and they rarely considered grievances that Indian women might have about their own lives. Indian women therefore remained in the barely visible periphery of liberal debates because they were twice removed from the nation that liberal leaders sought to forge. Elite women were denied full citizenship only because they were women; Indian men were denied it (in theory) only because they were not literate. Indian women were doubly removed from potential citizenship, first because of their sex and second because most were illiterate. Therefore the liberal government did not need to concern itself too much with justifying Indian women's exclusion from participation in the political body. In their view, giving Indian women too much power vis-à-vis the state would even be dangerous, because it could undermine Indian men's patriarchal control of the family and therefore their association with men of other ethnic and class backgrounds. Given their emphasis on Indian men's dominance in the household, social reformers also assumed that any improvements in Indian men's status would automatically benefit their wives and children. The opposite, however, was often true: changes that either reinforced Indian men's patriarchal rights or improved their bargaining powers with white authorities often disturbed the balance of power between the men and women of Indian communities.

Although Indian women were rarely mentioned, they were important to the relationships between Indian men and the state. Garcianismo and liberalism, different in many ways, both used the symbol of the Indian woman as a tool to discuss the patriarchal implications of Indian backwardness. Indians, however, did not automatically accept state-sanctioned gender ideals or internalize elite stereotypes about Indian gender relations. To overcome the conspicuous absence of Indian women in the history of Ecuadorian Indian-state relations, it is necessary to examine local and regional data to elicit information on gender ideologies and practices within indigenous communities themselves. The internal gender dynamics of peasant communities and haciendas show that indigenous and state-sanctioned gender norms were distinct, and that central government patriarchies permeated indigenous communities only gradually and unevenly.

⇒ 5 ⇐

Alternative Patriarchy

Gender Relations among Indigenous Peasants

Her grandmother, Juana Chicaisa, told her that her husband had returned
from the festivities and . . . [because] it was clear that he had come back
drunk, hearing this news, she stayed in [her parents'] house without heading
back to her husband's house, for fear of being beaten there.
—Testimony from Manuela Tenemasa, 1870[1]

On February 25, 1870, Francisco Abendaño, teniente parroquial of
Tigsán, reported that Indian Matias Bravo had discovered the lifeless
body of Francisco Bravo in a hollow under the Pusillig bridge, where
he was placed after being beaten to death. Authorities suspected that
the deceased man's wife, Manuela Tenemasa, and her alleged lover,
José Ñaula, had killed Bravo, though both defendants initially denied
involvement in or knowledge about his death. Ñaula admitted that
his lifelong friendship with Bravo had ended when his friend married Tenemasa and became extremely jealous. Regarding his whereabouts on the night of February 24, he answered that after working on
the nearby hacienda Moyocancha, he stopped at the widow Curivilla's
house, where he passed the afternoon with other men getting drunk
on chicha. After this, he spent the evening with his mother and his two
brothers, sleeping until local officials arrived to question him the next
morning.[2] Manuela Tenemasa's initial testimony was more suggestive:
she explained that she had suffered in a bad marriage with a jealous
husband, which had led her into an "illicit friendship" with Ñaula.

Regarding her whereabouts on February 24 and 25, she claimed to have attended a party at the hacienda Moyocancha on February 24, returning to her parents' house around 3:00 p.m. When she learned that her husband had returned home drunk, and fearing that he might beat her, she decided to stay with her parents for the night, where officials arrived around noon the next day to inform her of her husband's death.[3]

Witnesses told a much more incriminating tale, forcing the defendants to change their story. José Ñaula's own brother, Pablo, told court officials that he heard his brother fighting with Francisco Bravo in their mother's house, though he could not hear what they were saying. He declared, however, that he clearly heard Tenemasa say "Let's kill him" several times in reference to Bravo. Other witnesses confirmed this shouting match, some of them adding that it was public knowledge that Tenemasa and Ñaula had lived in concubinage for years.[4] At this point, Manuela Tenemasa admitted she had gone to José Ñaula's house, but his mother had forced her to leave; she then encountered her drunken husband, who tried to beat her, when Ñaula came along, and in the midst of a struggle with her husband, the two of them accidentally killed him. Ñaula again tried to deny any part in Bravo's death, claiming that his own confession was the result of torture, that Tenemasa's confession must have been similarly coerced, and that his brother had lied.[5] In the end, both defendants confessed to killing Bravo accidentally, agreeing that Tenemasa had caused Bravo's death when she strangled him with his own scarf.

The defendants' attorneys did what they could to lighten the sentences, but with fellow villagers bearing witness against Ñaula and Tenemasa, the attorneys' arguments had little impact. Ñaula's attorney, for example, tried to prove that his client was physically incapable of killing Bravo, who was bigger and heavier than Ñaula—but witnesses claimed that Ñaula was at least as large, if not larger, than his opponent. Tenemasa's lawyer had slightly better luck asserting that Tenemasa could not have killed her husband due to her physical frailty and the sacred bonds of marriage.[6] In the end, Ñaula was found guilty of murder and condemned to death, while Tenemasa was proclaimed an accomplice to the crime and sentenced to six to eight years' imprisonment.

The tragic and extraordinary events surrounding Francisco Bravo's death offer a wealth of information on indigenous peasant life in the late nineteenth century, and they—along with information from other (typically briefer) court cases—underscore how indigenous gender ideas and practices differed from state views of gender relations. First, the criminal proceedings following Francisco Bravo's death indicate that Indian women were far from compliant members of the private sphere as state-generated gender norms suggested. In contrast to elite claims that Indian women required punishment as a sign of love, Manuela Tenemasa refused to accept an unhappy and violent marriage and took several measures to protect herself. Testimony in the case further reveals that indigenous women were active members of their communities—working, protecting their households and children, selling chicha to male peers, taking part in local festivities, and participating in crucial information networks. This case also offers clues about how distinct indigenous and state gender ideas shaped encounters between indigenous peoples and state officials, particularly regarding their views on women's capacity for violence. Though some of the community members of Pusillig deemed Manuela Tenemasa capable of murder, court officials clung to the idea that women were incapable of independent action, and too physically weak to murder a man, finding Tenemasa guilty only as an accomplice to murder despite her confession to a central role. Finally, indigenous participants in the case made their preference for their own gender and marriage standards clear: though the affair between Tenemasa and Ñaula was public knowledge, and it was central to the murder charge, the community members did not deem it a matter that required state intervention until violence was involved. They instead preferred to handle it within the public sphere of their own community, beyond the reach of the state, until outside intervention was unavoidable.

This chapter explores indigenous peasant gender ideas and practices, evaluating both their similarities to and differences from state-sanctioned gender models. Though Indian peasant villages were, like the state, patriarchal, the two gender systems diverged in many ways. Whether indigenous peasants upheld men's patriarchal rights or set limits on men's patriarchal powers in order to defend community standards, both stances developed from an understanding of gender relations that differed from the one proposed in the Ecuadorian civil code. In fact, gender relations, indigenous culture, and peasant autonomy were tightly intertwined and together shaped not only indigenous peasants' daily life but also their encounters with the state, including their resistance to white-mestizo threats to their self-rule. Socioeconomic and cultural conditions led Indian peasants to define patriarchy as a more fluid practice than state-sanctioned gender norms did. In particular, indigenous peasants evaluated the extent of a man's patriarchal authority along a continuum in which both men and women's generational rights and kinship ties also had to be taken into account. The alternative patriarchy exercised by Indian peasants, along with the importance of indigenous women's economic contributions to their families and communities, afforded Indian women greater capacity for action and independence than state officials typically recognized or condoned. This made Indian women central to the maintenance of community identity, functioning, and defense on a daily basis. Yet Indian peasants did not live in complete isolation from state-sanctioned gender ideas, and at times individual Indian men took advantage of the state's more rigid view of patriarchal powers in order to gain the upper hand in conflicts with indigenous women.

Marriage Standards among Indigenous Peasants

Marriage was extremely important within Indian communities, where unions directly affected the ownership of both private and communal lands; a well-made marriage could also create social ties between families and contribute to the smooth functioning of peasant autonomy more generally.[7] Husbands and wives had to conform as much as pos-

sible to specific marital standards to promote conjugal peace and coop-
eration that would help them meet their subsistence needs. The ramifications of keeping or breaking these standards reached much further
than individual household units, since marital discord could result in
disputes among extended family members over control of lands and
goods. In some cases, marital problems led to physical violence that
could disrupt social harmony by involving relatives or neighbors in the
couple's disputes. Marriage standards were also taken seriously because
conventions that encouraged conformity and harmony among family
members helped to maintain compliance with rules, harmony in social
relations, and order at the community level. In this sense, patriarchy
and marriage functioned similarly within indigenous communities as
they did on the central-state level, justifying unequal political, social,
and gender relations.[8]

Though indigenous peasants monitored marriages and moral standards, they sometimes allowed for premarital sex, especially if a young
couple intended to formalize the union later. A journalist criticized
this Indian practice in an 1871 issue of *El nacional*: "In villages where
Christian customs are widespread, monogamy is the general rule. But
the Indians live in concubinage before marrying, a practice which is
called *amañanza*, with the objective of studying each other's character . . . before making a permanent commitment."[9] Elites considered
such unions immoral, and they were even illegal at the time. Indians,
however, did not simply adopt the moral code that statesmen tried
to impose on them. One possible reason for this was practical: courtship and marriage cost money, and community members' acceptance
of temporary informal arrangements allowed young couples to avoid
these expenses until they were financially able to handle them.[10] These
unions might help to establish whether the young man and woman
were truly well suited for each other and ready to make a permanent
commitment; this could in turn help to prevent later intracommunity
strife, especially battles over land, which inevitably resulted from failed
marriages. Trial marriages could not provide any guarantees of long-
term compatibility and stability, however, especially for young women

who might be abandoned and left to raise children alone.[11] Rather than indicating immorality and disrespect for marriage, as the author in *El nacional* suggested, acceptance of premarital unions more likely grew out of Indians' respect and need for stable marriages through which subsistence production and sociocultural reproduction were more easily achieved.

Once established, indigenous marriages often centered on husbands' and wives' complementary rights and duties.[12] When asked about their profession by court officials, indigenous men usually responded that they were *agricultores* (farmers), whereas women would refer to some other aspect of their labors or simply say they were *de ocupación correspondente a su sexo* (of occupation corresponding to their sex). Indian women's labors were many and varied: they did contribute significantly to agricultural production, as well as cook, gather water, spin wool, make chicha, tend to children, and sell goods at local markets. Though men's labors were not limited to work in the fields, Indian communities more directly and consistently associated men with agriculture.[13] In spite of women's many contributions, without which household subsistence was impossible, men's association with agriculture was significant: since these communities were primarily devoted to agricultural production, women—more tenuously linked to farming—had a lower social status than men. Distinct gender roles in the household economy also affected men and women's physical mobility. Cooking and child rearing often confined women to the house even after the end of the day's agricultural labors, making it difficult for them to engage in separate leisure activities. Instead, Indian women socialized while working on certain tasks such as gathering water or spinning wool that could be performed as group activities. In contrast, men normally had a definite end to their workdays, at which time they could go elsewhere to socialize with other men over chicha. Though women occasionally joined men at these gatherings, social bonding over chicha was a predominantly male domain.[14] Because Indian societies regarded men as the primary agriculturalists and maintained that it was women's duty to remain in or close to the home to fulfill their duties there, complementary marital roles were ultimately unequal.[15]

Like gender complementarity, kinship and generational rights to land were central to Indian peasant social relations. Familial bonds—both nuclear and extended—were crucial points at which Andean notions of reciprocity and solidarity were practiced. Age and familial proximity determined one's rights and obligations regarding subsistence matters such as inheritance and mutual assistance. Generation also played a key role: not only did sons and daughters inherit more than grandchildren did, but older family members deserved respect and assistance. Marriage was therefore the key to creating and maintaining these reciprocal ties and thus social order.[16] In most ways, state law and community custom regarding familial rights to inherit, control, and bequeath land appear to have coincided. While both law and custom gave men greater control of land, Ecuadorian law clearly stated that neither sex nor primogeniture determined inheritance claims. Spouses and legitimate children of the deceased had the greatest inheritance rights, while those of illegitimate children and more distant relatives were less secure.[17]

Though many of these gender and generational dynamics centered on peasants' economic concerns, they also derived from Andean cultural practices and worldviews. Whereas Ecuadorian lawmakers treated the public and private, male and female domains as clearly separate categories, indigenous peoples interpreted men's and women's roles and rights as "conceptually distinct but flexible in practice."[18] Land tenure itself offers a good example: within indigenous cultural frameworks, the community recognized that while a man might own the products of land because he tilled it, if his wife had inherited it, she owned the land itself and maintained some decision-making power over it. Therefore ownership was not the exclusive domain of one spouse or the other; rather it depended on the context in which the land was being considered. Likewise, children or grandchildren might begin working land that they would later inherit, but as long as older relatives lived, they continued to manage it; this generational right and prestige was reflected through various daily and seasonal rituals centered on eating, drinking, and coca chewing.[19] Indigenous women were fundamental to the maintenance of cultural identity, especially because their duties making food and chicha for household and community consumption were daily reminders of Andean cultural roots.[20] Though these practices were economically oriented insofar as they helped to maintain agricultural production and secure subsistence, they simultaneously spoke of a fluid and organic view of social relations that were clearly indigenous and not simply based on peasant identity alone. For indigenous peasants, complementary gender roles and interdependence among kin infused economic interests with deeper meaning.

Indian husbands and wives generally accepted the limitations as well as the rights that came with community marriage rules, although conflict could erupt when one partner perceived that her or his mate had failed to fulfill required duties. If a wife did not prepare her husband's food promptly, was inattentive to other chores, or was too frequently absent from her home, her husband was likely to consider her a bad wife. Similarly, if a husband went out drinking too often, treated his wife harshly, did not provide sufficient economic support for the household, or abandoned his home, his wife would argue that he had broken an important marital agreement. Marital standards furnished disgruntled husbands and wives with sanctioned weapons of retaliation during times of conflict. As long as community members concurred with a husband's assessment of his wife's failures, he had several means of responding to a bad marriage: he could have an extramarital affair, expel his wife from their home for a short period, or temporarily abandon their home.[21] A husband could also punish his wife physically for failing to carry out her duties to him, provided that his grievances were well founded and he did not punish her too severely. Trying to determine how indigenous neighbors differentiated between fair versus harsh physical punishment is impossible with court records, but distinctions were evidently made. Plácido Musungando was not found guilty for beating his wife, Juana Chipantiza, for example, because community members emphasized that her injuries were not extreme, and Musungando had refrained from kicking her.[22] However, when Jacobo Morocho was charged with strangling his wife, Jesús Tenelema, his peers testified that it was likely that he had killed her, since he beat her frequently and cruelly.[23]

An unhappy wife had her own accepted ways of striking back at her husband: she might abandon her duties at home for a few days (usually staying with her parents or other relatives), or have an extramarital affair. Manuela Tenemasa twice emphasized that she had to protect herself from a violent husband, first by claiming that she hid at her parents' house to escape his drunken wrath, and later to explain how she and her lover had accidentally killed her husband in an attempt to protect her from further abuse.[24] Similarly, before Jesús Tenelema lost her struggle against domestic violence, she sought refuge in her parents' house, where she often went to escape her abusive husband.[25] If domestic violence was unbearable, a wife might turn to another male family member for help and protection: when Manuela Atampala's husband, Antonio Chatin, began beating her, her son from a previous marriage came to her defense, resulting in a skirmish that proved fatal for Chatin.[26] In a situation that threatened her financially and emotionally, rather than physically, a wife might act to guarantee whatever security she could. For example, when María Prudencia Quispi's husband had an affair and gave his mistress, Francisca Morocho, one of his cows, Quispi went to Morocho's land and took the cow back. It seems that even if she could not do anything to change her husband's behavior, Quispi was determined to protect the economy of her household unit by reclaiming the property that she considered rightfully hers.[27] If a woman was in grave danger or permanently abandoned, or her marriage had gone bad soon after it was established, a wife might leave her husband to live with another man. Her peers (both male and female) were likely to tolerate, though not officially sanction, this action if they thought her grievances against her husband were valid.

Many of these conflicts and reactions grew out of men's and women's differing interpretations of marital standards. Men might assume that they had the right to stay out all night or beat their wives, but their wives believed that these male privileges were limited and conditional. A wife might also think that if her husband did not always come home in the evening, she was not necessarily obliged to have a meal waiting for him or, indeed, be at home herself. Her husband, however, might think it was her duty to prepare his food regardless of his actions.[28] While both partners reacted to each other according to their distinct interpretations of a mutually accepted code of behavior, men were more likely to make the initial break from marital standards, with wives reacting to protect their marriages and livelihoods or, in the case of domestic violence, their lives. Usually, women retaliated to their husbands' actions by breaking similar codes of behavior, thus maintaining a kind of balance within marriage even when the fundamental rules of marriage had been broken.

Mary Weismantel's examination of the Ecuadorian highlands in the late twentieth century uncovered another form of wifely retribution in times of marital conflict. Rather than lash out against their husbands' abuses of patriarchal privileges by abandoning their own duties, Indian wives might instead punish their husbands by adhering very strictly to their own duties in the household. In particular, Weismantel observed cases when wives struck out against their husbands' all-night drinking bouts by overzealously fulfilling their food preparation duties. One young wife, angry that her husband had stayed out all night drinking while she had to return home with their children, had a large meal prepared for him when he finally came home. Weismantel observed that "the next day found [the husband] in an extremely delicate physical state, such that the three very elaborate meals [his wife] prepared for him, which he dutifully consumed, resulted in several hasty exits to the bushes outside. [His wife] appeared to enjoy cooking for him very much that day, smugly playing the virtuous wife in front of her in-laws, who watched with some amusement and did not interfere."[29] Weismantel explained that food is an especially powerful weapon because it is, even from a wife to a husband, considered a gift that cannot be refused without insult. This form of punishment for a husband's minor misdemeanors was therefore exceptionally effective because it left him with no basis for complaint. Because this type of female retaliation would not spark the kind of conflict or disagreement that other responses might, indigenous peasants would not consider it noteworthy in court proceedings. Thus anthropologists making field observations have access to information that historians, limited to written documentation, lack. It is impossible to ascertain whether this tactic was commonly used by Indian wives in the nineteenth century; even if similar punishments were used, specific customs would have varied in different towns or regions. It is likely, however, that Indian women of the past found comparable ways to use patriarchal notions to their own advantage within marriage, since such strategies would be universally accepted and highly effective methods of punishment.

Men's rights as heads of households, community acceptance of physical punishment for unruly wives, and male dominance of local politics all indicate that Indian peasant communities were organized according to patriarchal principles. State legislation that gave all husbands the right to represent their wives' economic interests further reinforced patriarchy within Indian villages; however, patriarchy took on a different form among indigenous peasants than it did in Ecuadorian legislation. Indigenous communities might not have valued Indian women's economic contributions as much as men's agricultural pursuits, but they did recognize them; this contrasts with state-generated views of women as passive and dependent. Furthermore, Indian communities' acceptance of premarital sex and other informal unions gave Indian women room in which to maneuver around (and within) patriarchal standards.

Once indigenous ideas about marriage and patriarchy are mapped out, it is possible to reconsider elite images of Indian men's supposedly inherent brutality. While male socializing over chicha could and often did lead to violence, this was not necessarily the brutal and irrational violence that elites labeled it. Instead, fights between men often broke out over tangible issues, frequently over women. Men might fight over possession of a woman if she was married to one man and having (or her husband suspected her of having) an affair with another. In other cases, a man would start a fight to protect his daughter, mother, or sister from a physically abusive husband. Men were also liable to fight over an insult against a female relative's virtue or strike back against another man's claim that they were prostituting women in their families.[30] In short, Indian men fought to protect their own and women's honor. The importance that indigenous peasants placed on gendered notions of honor stands in stark contrast to elite views of Indian men lacking either manly strength or paternal caring.[31]

The subject of indigenous domestic violence presents sensitive and complicated analytical issues. Many court officials claimed that domestic violence was the norm among Indians, and court records do suggest that in many Indian peasant communities, husbands had the right to punish their wives physically. But whereas court officers assumed that domestic violence was universally sanctioned among Indians, historical evidence reveals instead that Indian peasants tolerated domestic violence only within limits. If they thought a man had treated his wife unfairly, family members, neighbors, and community leaders would pressure a husband to change his behavior. If he refused to do so, his peers might allow his wife to abandon her home. Information on individual Indian husbands and wives further undermines the elite notion that all Indian men and women condoned domestic violence. First, one must question the elite assertion that domestic violence was ubiquitous. Second, court records show that Indian women did not submissively accept their husbands' abuse but instead used any means at their disposal to combat mistreatment. It was often women themselves, through their actions or pleas to other family and community members, who convinced their peers that their husbands had wrongfully beaten them. If matters were bad enough, these women were apt to leave their husbands altogether.[32] Though they may not have challenged the patriarchal principles per se, Indian women attempted to limit domestic violence whenever and however they could.

Why would indigenous women uphold community patriarchy at all? They probably did so out of a strong sense of solidarity with indigenous men based on shared experiences of oppression at the hands of non-Indian authorities, particularly because many state policies and practices undermined Indian manliness. Tenientes políticos and work bosses abused and belittled Indian men in forced labor projects; white-mestizo authorities and employers expected Indians to act submissively before them; and at times, local authorities humiliated Indian men as a form of punishment. In 1892 Francisco and Plácido Rea accused the local priest, Miguel Ribadeneira, for making Clara Angamarca (an Indian woman in his service) beat them when they refused to work for him.[33] Though the plaintiffs charged Ribadeneira with violating their constitutionally guaranteed liberty, their main grievance against the priest was that he had ordered an Indian *woman* to beat them—which Ribadeneira doubtless realized would humiliate the men. Angamarca, who resisted her role in this affair, was probably reluctant to take part in emasculating fellow community members. These dynamics help to explain why few indigenous women brought domestic violence problems to court: not only were state officials unlikely to punish Indian men for domestic violence, but non-Indian authorities represented merely a different and more rigid form of patriarchy. Instead, women chose Indian patriarchy over state-sanctioned patriarchy and considered marital problems a matter to be addressed within their communities. Indian women might, however, utilize state-generated paternalism to charge local authorities with abuse, as Josefa Tenelema did when she filed a criminal complaint against Aquilino Oleas, the president of the local municipal council, for beating her while she was pregnant. Tenelema charged that Oleas's abuse had caused her to miscarry and left her unable to work for a significant period of time. Her charges persuaded the court, and Oleas was sentenced to three months of prison and fined eight sucres.[34]

While state law and community custom often coincided, indigenous peasants (unlike the state) more readily recognized women's productive and public—as well as reproductive and private—capacities and importance. These dynamics sometimes gave Indian women greater powers within their communities than state laws condoned, and they served a few different purposes within peasant communities. Acceptance of informal unions allowed Indian women and men to work within the established order to address most of their interpersonal grievances. While community standards could not ward off outside threats to peasant autonomy, they could at least ensure a certain level of internal stability in the face of tremendous outside pressures and changes. Indian men and women's protection of indigenous patriarchy was likewise important to community defense because they protected Indians' dignity when white authorities were constantly trying to undermine it.

Morality as a Community Concern

The so-called private sphere was and is always a matter of public concern, as the Garcian concubinage law and liberal civil marriage legislation made clear. Yet Chimborazo's Indian peasants were absent from concubinage cases of the 1870s, and they did not petition for divorce as was their right under liberal marriage laws in the 1910s.[35] Rather than a single public sphere in contrast to the private one, there were numerous (and overlapping) public and private spheres in nineteenth- and early twentieth-century Ecuador. The first was the civil public sphere, consisting of the courts and other authorities, whose intervention indigenous peasants viewed with caution. Second, the indigenous community itself constituted a public space with norms that did not necessarily coincide with those of state officials; this community public sphere had its own set of sanctions applicable to domestic behavior. Then, there was the fact that the private sphere could manifest itself publicly, such as when family relationships could be invoked to strengthen one's case in either intra- or interethnic conflict. A truly private sphere did exist between husbands and wives, with community norms largely determining how couples negotiated (and even fought over) their relationships. Any one of these public or private sphere dynamics could escalate into violence that mandated judicial intervention.[36] Numerous public and private spheres made it possible for indigenous peasants to determine which public authorities had rightful jurisdiction over their private lives. More often than not, they chose the public arena of their own communities over the public sphere represented by state officials and central government laws. By ignoring Garcian and liberal attempts to intervene in and monitor intimate relationships, indigenous peoples set limits on the reach of the central government and therefore the parameters of the evolving nation-state. When Indians did, on occasion, bring morality issues to the court system, they usually stayed within a very limited realm of grievances to defend themselves against public slander.

Though indigenous peasants did not call on the Garcian concubinage law when two members of their own community lived together outside of marriage, they might do so if an illicit affair included an outsider. A case from the village of San Andrés (Chimborazo) illustrates this point well. In 1865, José María Ortiz brought Indians Rujerio Cajas and Santiago Carrillo to court for slandering his good reputation. Previously, Cajas and Carrillo had successfully accused Ortiz of living in sin with an Indian woman, Josefa Mariño. While court officials consistently referred to Cajas, Carrillo, and Mariño as Indians (indígenas), Ortiz was apparently a mestizo, since he was labeled as a ciudadano in the case. Later in the case, it became clear that Cajas and Carrillo were related to Josefa Mariño and were angered that Ortiz was living off land and goods Mariño's late father had left her, while the Indian men felt they had stronger claim to the land as kin of the deceased owner.[37] Ortiz claimed he had no personal relationship with Mariño and instead simply rented land from her (and her mother). His arguments, however, failed in both the immoral conduct case against him and in his slander accusation against Cajas and Carrillo. Here, Indians sought state intervention in interpersonal matters because José María Ortiz was an ethnic outsider who lacked the social and familial bonds with Indian peasants that were necessary for community-based solutions to interpersonal disputes.[38]

Indians likewise ignored liberal divorce laws. Despite the moderate but meaningful impact of divorce laws on whites and mestizos, particularly in large and liberal cities, there is no evidence that Chimborazo's indigenous peoples sought divorce by mutual consent. One reason for this phenomenon must certainly have been that divorce was costly, and Indians were

unlikely to undertake court expenses to end marriages officially. Moreover, many Indians may have deemed divorce unnecessary because community norms allowed them to separate and form new, informal unions.
While second unions could eventually lead to land disputes culminating
in expensive court cases, the cost was often divided among members of an
extended family rather than shouldered by one couple alone.

Indigenous peoples did sometimes bring moral concerns to the
courts through slander charges. Indian men typically went to court to
defend their reputation against charges of thievery, while Indian women
were most concerned when someone questioned their sexual propriety;
both kinds of complaints were linked to gender-specific duties.[39] Men's
association with agriculture meant that their entire reputations as men
and husbands were called into question if they were accused of thievery. Women's responsibilities for cooking and child rearing, along with
patriarchal principles of propriety, made their sexual conduct critical
for their reputations as women and wives. In effect, it was gendered
notions of honor that Indian peasants were willing to go to court to
defend.[40] But if community members held Indian women far more
responsible than Indian men for upholding moral standards, slanderous claims about a woman's sexual conduct were frequently targeted at
men just as much as they were at women. When a woman, especially
a married woman, was accused of being a whore, it was a reflection
not only of her own lack of self-control but also of her husband's (or
father's) inability to control her.[41] In other cases, husbands complained
that they had been accused of acting as pimps for their wives. A husband
was concerned with slander against his wife's good reputation, then,
because his honor was determined by her actions as well as his own.[42]
Slander charges do not, however, indicate that their peers considered
Indian women generally immoral, particularly since slanderous claims
were always vague rather than specific; insults were mutual rather than
one-sided, often escalating into fist fights between the two parties.[43]

The circumstances behind intra-indigenous slander cases imply
that plaintiffs were less concerned with the truth or falsehood of these
vague charges of immorality than they were with having lost status in

front of other members of the community. Indians were therefore using the public sphere of the white-mestizo court system to defend their reputations when they had failed to do so within the public sphere of the community. Since court cases were expensive and not lightly undertaken, these may have been plaintiffs' desperate attempts to regain status and respect in the eyes of their peers. The plaintiffs may well have been community members of high standing or greater wealth who felt they had more to protect (or lose) in these encounters or could better afford court fees as a means to try to save face. Even slander cases were not as numerous among Ecuador's indigenous peasants as they were among the urban and semiurban poor in Peru.[44] This suggests that, unlike plebeians in urban environments, indigenous peasants enjoyed both economic and ethnic connections to each other that provided them with meaningful avenues to protect, or regain, their honor. Distinctly indigenous gender ideologies meant that honor was a community concern, making it difficult for the state to intervene in this arena to assert social control.

Land as a Familial Right

Rights to land, its products, and animals were the economic mainstays of Indian peasant communities, and the post-tribute attacks on indigenous autonomy made community defense especially critical. Male initiative to safeguard communities partly resulted from state laws that put civil matters in men's hands, but it was also a by-product of indigenous patriarchy. Moreover, even though local indigenous governments lost much of their power to negotiate with white-mestizo authorities after tribute was abolished, they continued to play important roles within indigenous peasant communities, and by the nineteenth century, men dominated local indigenous governments. Together, these factors justified men's patriarchal powers in the home and in the wider community. Yet the limitations Indian women faced did not preclude their active participation—or even leadership roles—in community defense and land disputes. Besides those married women who pursued court proceedings independently while their husbands were absent from their communities, records show that single women, or women living in unofficial unions with men, also initiated civil actions.[45] Indigenous widows, however, were far more prominent in civil and economic matters than their single or married counterparts. Though widows were frequently embroiled in conflicts over land with fellow community members (often members of their own extended families), they also worked in conjunction with male peers to defend community land rights. For example, when indigenous peasants of Punín went to court in 1901 to complain that the religious order that owned the hacienda Tungurahuilla had wrongly claimed ownership of their communal pasturelands, six out of the thirty-six protagonists were widowed women. Though there were more men than widows involved, the men involved recognized the widows' right to participate in decisions and struggles affecting the community.[46] Although Indian women, even widows, had to maneuver carefully within patriarchal parameters set by their own communities and the state, Indian peasants' attitudes toward marriage and kinship allowed Indian women significant rights to land that would not have been granted to them under the civil code.

Indigenous women were sometimes involved in decisions regarding land tenure. Ecuadorian law did not allow married women to control land, but they could inherit, own, and bequeath land, and their husbands were supposed to act in their best interests when administering property.[47] Indians also typically followed inheritance patterns outlined in the civil code, which mandated that if an individual died intestate, his or her spouse and legitimate children inherited most goods, granting only limited inheritance rights to more distant relatives or children from informal unions.[48] Wills and inheritance disputes suggest that indigenous women had a strong sense of their decision-making power regarding land. In several cases indigenous men went to court to request the division of family lands after their wives had died, sometimes presenting their wives' wills as the basis on which court officials should divide lands and goods. Manuela Gadvay, an Indian woman from the civil parish of Chambo who died in 1878 after leaving a will, offers a good example. Notably, Gadvay's husband was still alive when she drafted her will, and her heirs proposed dividing property according to her wishes; Gadvay therefore did not have to be widowed to make decisions about property distribution. This power to dispose of property not only was based on her inheritance of land from her own family, but was also sanctioned within the community by her contributions to family subsistence. Gadvay's attitude about her rights as a co-owner of land that she bought with her husband early in their marriage is particularly interesting: she stated that while her husband should keep *his* half of land, she wanted *her* half of it to be distributed to other heirs.[49] Gadvay did not consider it her husband's sole right to make decisions about marital property, even if the government did.

Indigenous emphasis on kinship sometimes gave women the right to manage land in their own names, even though the law gave husbands the right to administer all marital property.[50] One particular civil case warrants in-depth discussion because it highlights the impact that indigenous gender and kinship ideas could have on widows in Indian peasant communities. In January 1890, Tomás Cavadiana initiated court proceedings to inventory and distribute family lands left behind by his wife, Vicenta Carguaitongo, who had died intestate five years earlier.[51] Cavadiana informed the court, "The interested persons in the [case] whom you should summon are: Juan Cavadiana, the only [surviving] son at the time of my wife's death, and the children of my [deceased] son Manuel Eucebio Cavadiana, Rafael, Rosa and Dolores, who are represented by their legitimate mother, Rosa Castro."[52] Cavadiana consistently referred to Castro as an independent participant in the case, at times accusing her and his son Juan of being in contempt of court when they failed to respond to the court's information requests.[53] Court officials followed suit, and at one point they asserted that Castro's involvement was "based on her own rights and those of her minor children"—a claim suggesting that Castro had an even stronger independent interest in the case than Cavadiana had mentioned.[54] The inventory specified that Castro's lands accounted for approximately 19 percent of the total value of all the property inventoried.[55] All these factors indicated that Castro had a seemingly secure claim to these parcels of land and to documentation ensuring her continuing right to them, at the very least while her children were of minor age.

Almost halfway through the court record, Rosa Castro's status in the case—and therefore her relationship to the Carguaitongo-Cavadiana family lands—changed drastically. When state officials delivered information to Rosa Castro and Juan Cavadiana in their hometown of Licto, the scribe reported that the officials had "informed Benigno Estrada, on behalf of his wife Rosa Castro, of the aforementioned decree and brief."[56] Apparently the court had not been previously aware of Estrada's existence, because from that point forward, they reported all case proceedings to him rather than to Castro herself. In fact, in all later communication, members of the court referred *only* to Benigno Estrada as a participant in the case without mentioning Rosa Castro at all.[57] Tomás and Juan Cavadiana at first continued to emphasize that Estrada's association with the case was only through Rosa Castro; however, after several instances in which court officials ignored her, the Cavadiana men also dropped her name from their communication with the court.[58] The decision on the division of lands at the closing of the proceedings stated, "The [court-appointed] divider awards these three pieces [of land] to the minor children Rafael and Dolores Cavadiana, the minor children of Eusebio Cavadiana and Rosa Castro, *for whom their stepfather, Benigno Estrada, will take the three pieces of land.*"[59] Though mentioned briefly, Rosa Castro had essentially disappeared from this case, having started as a vital participant with clear claim to land and ending as little more than a living ghost through whom others obtained it.

Rosa Castro's disappearance from this court case reflected her precarious legal position, leaving her to fall between the cracks separating indigenous and state patriarchies. The Ecuadorian civil code did not directly stipulate that widows who remarried would lose their right to control property directly, but it repeatedly stated that husbands had power over their wives' goods and interests, without making distinctions related to second marriages. One is hard-pressed to see this as an oversight, since other considerations with second marriages, such as guardianship of children, were discussed at length.[60] Therefore court officials in Riobamba who reported all proceedings to Castro's second husband were acting in accordance with Ecuadorian law. While state-sanctioned gender ideologies and the laws resulting from them explain why Castro eventually disappeared from this case, they cannot explain why Tomás Cavadiana initially considered Castro an independent actor in the proceedings. Cavadiana had to have known that Castro had remarried, because members of his family (including his son Juan) shared property boundaries with land that she had under her possession.[61] Cavadiana's actions therefore suggest that he acted in accordance with indigenous gender standards—not ignoring patriarchal privileges, but considering them in light of kinship and generational ties that led him to define widows' rights based not only on a woman's marital status but also on her relationship with her dead husband's family. Cavadiana at first ignored Castro's remarriage and second husband because it was she, and not Benigno Estrada, who had kinship ties to his family. Her former father-in-law respected her right, as his son's widow and grandchildren's mother, to maintain an active and independent role in the division of family lands. This insinuates that Indian women who remarried might have had flexible marital identities, being considered independent widows under some circumstances even though they would generally be regarded as married women who were subordinate to their new husbands in most ways.

The differences between state and indigenous views of widows' rights, however, are apparent only because court officials learned of Castro's remarriage. Without that discovery, state representatives—and historians—would be left to assume that Castro fit the legal definition of widowhood. Though one cannot know for certain, it is possible that these different gender ideologies shaped how Indians presented land tenure disputes in court. Cavadiana's silence over his former daughter-in-law's remarriage winks at us; it hints that other Indian widows might have maintained independent control of land even after remarrying. This opens new analytical possibilities for understanding gender and power within indigenous peasant communities, because widows did not necessarily have to choose entirely between the independence of widowhood and the economic security that a new husband might bring. Considering that indigenous widows' success at maintaining administrative rights over land depended on remaining silent about their remarriages, it could well be that many of the Indian widows one encounters in other court cases had also remarried.[62]

Women, Community, and Power

Indigenous women's relationship to land, their economic contributions to the household, and their place within kinship networks did more than give them leverage in marital relations. In many instances, women's work and social connections made them crucial to community cohesion, communication, and defense. Their importance to various community functions and rituals provided indigenous women with further means to advance their personal interests, maintain or even increase their status and power within the community, or emerge as pivotal players in the creation and maintenance of community solidarity.

Female labors facilitated communication networks both within and beyond indigenous women's home communities. Many female tasks—such as gathering water, spinning wool, and even some aspects of preparing food—were performed in the company of other women, making it possible for Indian women to incorporate socializing into work despite their general lack of clearly defined leisure time. These links with other women, however, were also important because of their relevance to intra- and intercommunity communications: not only were women likely to share information with each other about their own or other families, but women going to gather water or tend sheep might also be witnesses to a significant community event or help spread word of plans for broader community actions. The link between home, work, and networking could even extend beyond indigenous women's home communities. Many women sold wool or food that they prepared in their homes at local markets.[63] While they often traveled to markets close to home, some indigenous women traveled to more distant communities to sell goods.[64] Women who attended local markets were likely to bring home news of changes in other areas that could affect their own communities. Though men sometimes went to markets held in other communities as well, women might have been better able to get information from other community members because work and socializing were more commonly intertwined for them than they were for men.

The production and sale of chicha also connected women's supposedly domestic tasks to broader community networks and concerns. Rural *chicherías* (houses where chicha was sold) were, by nature, informal; Indians did not refer to stores or places of business where they went to buy chicha, but instead they would say that they knocked on the door and "visited" in a woman's home for a while, and only later would they mention that they paid the *chichera* for alcohol consumed during this visit.[65] Members of the local community would know which women made and sold chicha, but outsiders were unlikely to have such information unless they had well-established ties to a particular community. Though women of all marital statuses made and sold chicha, references to widowed chicheras were most common, and perhaps widows used chicha sales to compensate for economic strains they experienced after their husbands died. Selling chicha typically gave women increased economic power in their communities: not only did chicheras make money directly from sales, but men and women of the community often owed them money. These economic ties were primarily with men, since chicherías were most frequently spaces of male drinking and bonding (and fighting). Chicheras' position in relation to male drinking underscores one way that male behaviors affected women within a community differently: though chicheras themselves profited from instances when men drank heavily or frequently, these men's wives probably suffered because of their husbands' drinking: after all, money spent on chicha was money no longer available for family subsistence, and drinking and domestic violence often went hand in hand.

The women who ran chicherías also filled fundamental social roles within their communities. Although drinking was a ritual that often excluded women, chicheras presided over these gatherings, putting them in a position of relative power over male peers and increasing their social status within the community. Since information passed between members of the community who drank together, chicheras were also privy to a plethora of personal details about community members.[66] Finally, chicha was essential in community rituals; it was a central component of local celebrations such as Carnival, harvest times, or the commemoration for a local patron saint. Chicheras were therefore strongly associated with a ritual substance that was symbolic of community solidarity and ethnic identity. Yet these celebrations, officially denoting community solidarity, frequently erupted into violent outbursts, usually between male community members who fought over women.[67] In times when Indians had severe grievances toward white-mestizo authorities, however, chicha could lead to outwardly directed violence and even rebellion, rather than to intracommunity conflict. At those times, chicheras may have been well positioned to emerge as leaders in rebellions, given that these women were at the center of the rituals that preceded such actions. Their connections to intra- and intercommunity economies and communication, combined with their association with chicha, all indicate that although indigenous women may not have been equals to their male peers, they were vital and at times powerful members of their communities.

Just as state-generated gender ideas did not reflect indigenous women's contributions to their communities, they also did not acknowledge Indian women's capacity for aggressive, even violent, behavior. Court officials regularly held Indian men responsible for violence that broke out between men and women, even if witnesses testified that women had acted more violently than men.[68] Elite notions of female frailty favorably affected Indian women even when they were convicted of violent crimes: for example, court officials sentenced Manuela Tenemasa only as an accomplice in her husband's murder because of such assumptions. Their deeply embedded ideas about female weakness and passivity made it impossible for them to think of her as an instigator in the homicide. Sometimes Indian women never faced charges for their violent actions: when Gabriel Herrera, an indigenous man from the civil parish of Licto, was charged with beating and injuring Juan Chuto, witnesses testified that the men's mothers had been just as actively involved in the fight as the two men, yet the women were never accused of committing any crime.[69]

Similar to Indian men, Indian women often played on court officials' gender assumptions to advance their interests.[70] An Indian woman who faced criminal charges, for instance, might emphasize "I am a miserable Indian woman, and a widow" to evade or reduce the charges against her.[71] In a civil dispute, she might point out her female vulnerability if she encountered obstacles to her objectives, as did widows María and Manuela Chicaisa when seeking property titles in 1876. Once court officials realized that the women had petitioned the wrong authorities, they ordered them to begin their cases over again elsewhere. The two women, who had not previously mentioned their condition, immediately bemoaned their miserable status as old, frail widows; this convinced officials to let them simply transfer their petitions to the proper authorities, rather than beginning them anew and incurring further expenses.[72] This tactic was not always successful, and Indian women were often convicted of crimes or had to pay court costs even though they offered heart-wrenching renditions of their miserable plights as poor women. Yet the strategy was effective often enough to warrant its continued use, with each instance reinforcing white authorities' conviction that all Indian women were weak and passive.

State officials' stereotypes about Indian women also had community-wide consequences, particularly when relations between Indians and elites turned violent. Martha Moscoso observed that Indian women "could more easily act in a radical manner than men ... because of the surprise factor in the minds of the police, who considered women submissive and peaceful."[73] Rebellions—especially the Daquilema rebellion of 1871—marked the fulfillment of elite fears about Indian men's capacity for savagery, but Indian women's centrality to the uprisings was far harder for authorities to explain. They mostly made sense of it by identifying rebellion as a period when the so-called Indian masses overturned all the normal rules of conduct and morality. Because indigenous women's initiative in rebellions contradicted elite expectations for female passivity, authorities often attributed women with the worst atrocities committed during the Daquilema rebellion.

Associating Indian women with savagery in the 1871 uprising lasted well into the twentieth century, helping Alfredo Costales solve a dilemma in his historical account of the event. Costales was interested in uncovering the hidden history of Ecuadorian Indians and in finding heroes in their past. Yet he also assumed Indian rebellions were generally brutal, barbaric, and vengeful affairs in which Indian rebels killed all the whites they could find, going so far as to mutilate their bodies and drink chicha from the victims' skulls. Somehow, this assumption had to be reconciled with Costales' desire to identify the uprising as valiant and just. His solution was twofold: first, although he identified a few Indian men as heroic military leaders, he indicated that the masses of Indians went against their leaders' intentions by mutilating victims' bodies.[74] Second, he often attached the most outrageous behavior to Indian women, especially Manuela León, one of the leaders of the uprising, whom he claimed ordered the mutilation of white victims. Costales described León as a madwoman with an insatiable hunger for violent revenge:

> Manuela León, horribly macabre in her appearance, with a distorted face, bloodshot and vacant eyes ... disheveled, dirty, covered with dust and chicha, the corners of her mouth frothing with spit, yelling like a madwoman with a club and flag ... personifying the evil, the hatred and repugnance of the day. At times defiant, she staggered about and mocked the human beings who were crucified after being killed, with a stupidity that stemmed from ignorance. And as one who recently discovered a happy idea, full of vengeance, her sadism held back for years, she thought it best to dismember [the victims].[75]

This rendition of Indian women's actions during rebellion presents several problems, especially because Costales did not cite specific documents from which he drew his conclusions. He therefore either created these images or used elite descriptions of the rebellion, accepting them as fact. If elites consistently regarded Indian women as passive, then women's participation in the rebellion was even more irrational and aberrant than Indian men's. Because so few records on this rebellion remain intact, it is difficult to assess Indian women's actual roles within it. Neither the impression of Indian women as utterly submissive figures, nor the assertion of their especially savage roles in rebellions holds up under historical scrutiny. Indigenous women's land ownership and kinship ties, their access to communication networks, and their contributions to nonviolent community defense all indicate that they were consistently important participants in community life and defense. Women's roles in rebellion were therefore an extension of their normal community functions to unusual circumstances rather than being entirely out of character.

Undermining Indian Women

Although Indian women made vital contributions to family and community life in Ecuador throughout the period under study, the masculinization of Indian-state relations, beginning with the abolition of Indian tribute in 1857 and culminating in the democratic patriarchy envisioned by the liberal state, ultimately undermined not only Indian women's capacity for community defense but also their status relative to their male peers. While the struggle for peasant autonomy often got Indian men to limit their patriarchal rights in order to protect their communities, at other times, state-generated patriarchy left Indian women more vulnerable in land disputes than Indian men usually were.

Indian women were peripheral to both state and community politics, and while this sometimes meant they were valuable in community defense, it could also make it difficult for Indian women to confront authorities. The discrepancy between Indian men's and women's abilities to oppose state authorities is evident in two cases from the 1870s against Nicolás Novillo, the teniente político of the civil parish of Cebadas. In 1872, Indians

Juana and María Misachi charged Novillo, along with mestizos Pedro and Juan Zavala, with confiscating and destroying their property. The Misachi sisters, both single and recently orphaned, complained that Novillo and the Zavalas had unjustly taken property from them as payment for a debt their deceased father had owed the men since the 1860s.[76] According to the sisters, Novillo brought "Indian traitors" to the house and confiscated goods, destroying anything that he did not want or could not carry.[77] He also threatened to auction off their property, leaving them "begging bread from others."[78] The Misachi sisters maintained that their father had paid the debt in 1864 "twice over, with abuses and extortion," but Novillo and the Zavalas eluded conviction by submitting documentation that the debt was still outstanding. Community members did not strongly support the sisters' claims, further justifying the defendants' position. Novillo would not be as fortunate later in the 1870s when Pedro Aucansela brought him to court on similar charges. Aucansela told the court that Novillo took his horse and nine of his sheep on the assumption that he owed a debt to fellow Indian Pascual Yaguarsungo, son-in-law to Novillo's close friend José Mishqui.[79] Furthermore, though Novillo gave the sheep to Yaguarsungo, he kept the horse for himself. Novillo was hard-pressed to justify his actions, since he had personally benefited from Aucansela's losses. Novillo's defense was also weakened when many community members testified on Aucansela's behalf—something they were unwilling to do for the Misachi sisters. In the end, Novillo was convicted for abuse of authority.[80]

Being orphans and single women made it hard for Juana and María Misachi to promote their cause against Novillo. If their father had still been alive, he may have been able to disprove the claims made by Novillo and the Zavalas. Or, if the two women had been older and married, their husbands might have been able to muster up community support against Novillo, just as Aucansela, as an adult male member of the community, had been able to do. Their case probably would have been stronger even if they had been older and widowed, since age (regardless of gender) commanded a certain amount of respect within Indian communities. In this case, it appears that state and indigenous patriarchies reinforced each other to the Misachi sisters' disadvantage, because neither gender system strongly supported young single women's property claims.

At other times, state-sanctioned patriarchy more clearly undermined indigenous women's positions, above all when Indian men applied the state's strict interpretation of patriarchal privileges in order to sabotage the land rights that Indian women normally enjoyed in peasant communities. Disgruntled Indian men could, for example, call on white-mestizo morality to subvert Indian women's claims to land. Consider an 1888 land dispute between Indians in Licto: Julián Chicaisa and Antonio Guamán (on behalf of his wife, María Chicaisa) protested Gregoria Conduri's possession and sale of land that they claimed was rightfully theirs. At the root of this disagreement was the fact that Conduri had lived for many years with the plaintiffs' father, José Chicaisa, even though his legitimate wife had still been alive. Apparently, José Chicaisa and Gregoria Conduri had treated each other as true husband and wife, and they also had children together. Chicaisa even gave her "possession of everything pertaining to a conjugal relationship."[81] While José Chicaisa was still alive, he could, as the family patriarch, protect Conduri's (and her children's) land rights at the expense of children from his first relationship. He could not, however, protect his second family from the grave. Chicaisa and Guamán won their case against Conduri because court officials would not recognize the land rights of an adulteress, whereas indigenous community members may well have supported land rights for both sets of children because of their kinship ties. This decision affected not only Conduri herself but also her surviving son and grandchildren, who were left with no land when she died in 1892.[82]

Even legally married Indian women faced potential problems as the nation-state took shape. Although indigenous peasants usually recognized and supported women's inherited land rights, a crafty Indian man could argue that a woman did not really have a right to these lands because her husband administered them. In 1901, Manuel Tene and Mauricio Caiza—both from the indigenous hamlet of Cacha—each claimed the right to several parcels of land. Caiza was acting on behalf of his wife, María Susana

Chiliquinga, who had inherited the land from her mother. Tene maintained that he had inherited these lands through his half-brother, who had died without leaving other heirs; he also asserted that he was actively farming the land. Tene and Caiza each produced documentation (wills) and witnesses to support their arguments, but in the end, Tene won the case. Apparently, what persuaded the judges to decide in Tene's favor was his argument that Chiliquinga never had material possession of these lands herself. When explaining the reason for their verdict, the court officials referred to several points in the proceedings—each reference mentioned that Mauricio Caiza, and not his wife María Susana Chiliquinga, claimed these lands.[83] The legal restraints working against the married couple were clear: Caiza, as the legal administrator of conjugal goods, had to represent his wife in court; at the same time, his control over conjugal goods undermined his wife's case and therefore compromised their family's subsistence.

The cases above show instances when the state could strengthen Indian men's preexisting patriarchal rights. Indian men could, however, also use the state to seek control of lands that were not yet under their domain as patriarchs. In particular, young Indian men occasionally used the state's preference for male land ownership to overcome their communities' emphasis on generational or kinship rights to land. Under normal circumstances, when individuals did not seek the intervention of the state, men and women could inherit land equally. Whenever possible, land went to the next closest generation of kin, even if that meant that a widow or daughter inherited property instead of a son or grandson. Women of Indian peasant communities also gained a certain amount of respect with age, even though they were not able to take part directly in indigenous government. A young man's patriarchal rights were therefore limited by community custom, and he could subvert this pattern only by using the state's more consistent preference for men's rights over the rights of women. Specifically, there were cases when younger Indian men emphasized male privilege in court to wrest land from Indian widows whose kinship and generational rights to control land would normally have taken precedence over the men's patriarchal interests in their communities. Two cases from late nineteenth-century Chimborazo offer striking examples of this strategy.

In 1878 widow Ignacia Cuenca appealed a local judge's decision to allot a parcel of land, which she considered her own, to Salvador Vinlasaca. Though neither party initially mentioned it, one of the witnesses indicated that Vinlasaca, as widower to Soledad Laso, was Cuenca's son-in-law, and the two had worked the land together for eight years before engaging in a legal battle over ownership of the property.[84] Cuenca called on witnesses to testify that she had "possessed the land peacefully for more than seventy years, without anyone's contradiction," and that she had generously allowed her daughters Soledad and María to use some of the land that belonged to her. Witnesses professed that they not only agreed with Cuenca's claims, but had seen her working the land with their own eyes.[85] Vinlasaca's evaluation of the conflict was, of course, quite different. First, he declared that he had documentation proving he purchased part of the land from Cuenca's daughter María; second, he contended that Cuenca "had not presented any title with which to prove that she was the owner of the land in question, the testimony of witnesses is not sufficient proof ... [and] folio fifteen clearly shows that in 1839 teniente Antonio Orozco awarded three solares of the land [known as] Salantotoras to Gerónimo Laso, *documentation that clearly shows that the land did not belong to the plaintiff but rather to her husband, Gerónimo Laso.*"[86] Vinlasaca concluded by drawing the court's attention to the seven witnesses who had testified that he had possessed the disputed land for over twelve years—assuring the court that his witnesses (unlike his mother-in-law's) were impartial observers in the case.

Cuenca's lawyer responded immediately and adamantly. After criticizing the local judge because he "rashly and scandalously denied [her] right," he attacked each aspect of Vinlasaca's argument. He contended that Vinlasaca's slick tinterillo had misrepresented the land sales of the 1860s, emphasizing that only public documents provided valid proof of sale, whereas Vinlasaca's papers were from a private and thus invalid sale. Finally, he stated that Cuenca's witnesses had proven that Vinlasaca had not worked the land for ten uninterrupted years as the law mandated in order for him to claim it as his own.[87] Despite her best efforts—and those of her own slick tinterillo and his elaborate arguments to the court—the judges decided against Cuenca, emphasizing that Vinlasaca was in possession of the land and had produced more witnesses for the court.[88]

In a similar case, members of the Cabay family in the civil parish of Calpi initiated court proceedings against widow Josefa Acalo in 1883, with their attorney, Dario Gonzalez, telling the court, "On February 21[,] 1881, Pedro Quisnancela sold us ... land named Quisnanshi.... The seller had established judicial possession as an heir [to the land], and with said title he made the land transfer through public documentation. Suddenly, Josefa Acalo, surprising the civil Judge of the parish of Calpi, took effective possession [of the land], causing my clients grave injury."[89] And so began an embittered struggle over land that involved documentation issues, family conflict, gender discrepancies, generational questions, and legal nuances. Josefa Acalo's attorney, Antonio del Pino, argued that she had a twofold right to the land because she both inherited it from her parents and had active possession of it. Del Pino further emphasized that Pedro Quisnancela did not have "the right to transfer what did not yet belong to him." Quisnancela, however, maintained that his grandmother, Rosa Guillcasunta, had bequeathed him the land in the seventh clause of her will; del Pino demanded that Quisnancela produce Rosa Guillcasunta's will to settle the matter.[90] The situation became more confusing when the plaintiffs claimed to have submitted the will, but because they did so during national holidays, Acalo's lawyer had not seen it. Regardless of del Pino's insistence, the will was never again produced for the court, though another document submitted in the case referred to it in passing.[91] Moreover, it turned out that older members of the Cabay family had informally purchased the land from Quisnancela over twenty years earlier, and it was only in the 1880s that they formalized the sale with documentation. Del Pino made a last-ditch plea for the court to consider that "While parents are alive, their children cannot take control of their goods," but his client lost her case. The judges gave preference to the documentation that was submitted formally to them and awarded the land to the Cabay family.[92]

In these two cases, similar to the one in which Rosa Castro was involved, widows' land claims were undermined; yet these latter quarrels offer instances when the struggle to define gender rights was between community members rather than between Indians and court officials. In each of the cases above, Indian men asserted their right to own and control land with arguments that more clearly reflected state than indigenous patriarchy. Josefa Acalo's son was less confrontational when he did so, because he did not directly contradict either inheritance laws or community customs when he carefully assured the court that his dead grandmother had proclaimed his ownership of this land in her will. Still, without clear evidence of this, his community would have favored his mother's inheritance claim over his, so he was emphasizing the state's preference for male control of land—which he further reinforced by acquiring a statement from the civil judge in Calpi that the land was his. With the case between Salvador Vinlasaca and Ignacia Cuenca, not only did Vinlasaca fail to produce proper documentation, but his argument focused on his right to control land as the male head of the household. He asserted this patriarchal power over the interests of a woman who had closer kinship ties to the deceased landowner, and whose stronger claim to inherit the land was recognized by Indian communities and the state. By declaring his legitimate ownership of the land as the only living adult male heir, Vinlasaca was in direct conflict with community practice. He even misrepresented lawmakers' intentions, since the law allowed women, especially widows, to own property even if they could not always control it.

Local state officials' own gender ideas and attitudes also helped the men gain control of land. Vinlasaca's overstatement, like Pedro Quisnancela's strategies, succeeded because it invoked the gender division between private and public spheres that was far more prevalent among state officials than it was among Indian peasants. An incident from Josefa Acalo's case offers a clear reminder of court officials' preoccupation with patriarchal protocol. At one point in this case, Juana Cabay petitioned the court to act on her own behalf in the proceedings while her husband was unavailable to represent her. Although this request was in accordance with national law, Cabay had to bring several witnesses to court, and court officials debated her request at length, before she was allowed to participate in the proceedings. Her husband, Manuel Ati, immediately ratified Juana Cabay's decisions when he returned; apparently he did not question the validity of her direct involvement in the case, even though court officials had been uncertain about it.[93] The record of these procedures indicates that the gap between Indian peasant customs and state laws was further widened by many local and regional judges' and lawyers' rigid patriarchal convictions. These local state administrators were key players in evolving Indian-state relations because they routinely interacted with Indian men and women, and they had power to interpret laws generated in Quito when they enforced them.[94]

The question then becomes, Why did the men in the cases here use state-sanctioned gender ideologies to undermine widows' interests, while Tomás Cavadiana supported indigenous gender norms regarding Rosa Castro? The answer lies in generational considerations. Tomás Cavadiana enjoyed a secure position when he petitioned the court to divide his deceased wife's lands. As an older member of his community and as the widower of the former property owner, he had little to lose by respecting his daughter-in-law's rights as an indigenous widow and nothing to gain by pointing out that Castro had remarried. Salvador Vinlasaca and Pedro Quisnancela's position in their communities was quite different: they were both younger men struggling over land with older, more established widows in their communities, and their relative youth weakened their claims. They therefore called on the state's more consistent preference for male control of land regardless of age. In essence, they used state gender ideology as a tool to gain access to lands that were not yet under their domain as patriarchs. Indian men's willingness to make use of patriarchal legislation, however, was not necessarily an indication that they accepted white-mestizo patriarchy more generally. Their actions could have been based on economic need: post-tribute state policies made land tenure insecure, and Indians were often left to squabble with each other over remaining arable lands. Indians, men and women alike, used what means were available to them to protect and bolster their land rights, and state policies and ideologies gave men clear advantages in these contests.

Alternative Patriarchy and Its Limits

Although they were meant to maintain community coherence and provide for the smooth functioning of household production, indigenous gender rules could guarantee neither familial nor community harmony. Husbands and wives often disagreed on the extent of a man's authority; families frequently fought over the division of lands; individuals periodically undercut each other's reputations in order to augment their own status. While these conflicts offer proof of the boundaries of community conventions, they also uncover distinctly indigenous gender ideas. Cases of discord reveal Indians' overall acceptance of informal unions, respect for women's economic functions, and reverence for kinship relations that all denote a different set of gender principles than those that state officials encouraged. Indigenous peoples often showed a strong preference for their own gender system over state-sanctioned gender norms. Indian women might struggle with their husbands' abuse of authority, but they rarely brought these problems to court. Individuals might attack each other's reputations, but they did not allow the state to dictate standards of personal conduct and instead defined such standards within their own communities. Indian women might not have had the same rights over economic decision making as Indian men had, but even Indian patriarchs would defend women's rights before state officials in certain circumstances.

This alternative patriarchy, derived from a combination of peasant production and indigenous cultural values, should not, however, be overstated. Indigenous men maintained the right to control their wives and children in myriad ways. Indigenous communities, as well as the state, helped reinforce the idea that men, as household providers, should have power to decide on most economic and civil matters for their families. Indian men's control also—very importantly—included the power to punish, a right that indigenous patriarchal norms and community members reinforced. Therefore, the smooth function of the family economy and community social relations was founded on women's subservience to men in many circumstances. Patriarchy was thus a tool that the men of Indian communities, similar to the men who made up the central state, used to maintain social order.

Indigenous and state patriarchies did not function in isolation from each other, however. Indian women might be active members of their communities, earning status through their labor, kin, and land, but they knew to present themselves as helpless and weak before state officials. Elite impressions of female passivity also added to the element of surprise when Indian women acted violently, particularly in rebellions. Individual Indian men manipulated the state's more rigid interpretation of patriarchal rights and powers to challenge older widows' rights within their communities. The infiltration of state gender norms into indigenous peasant communities was, though important, uneven. It is true that nation-state formation masculinized Indian-state relations, and state-sanctioned gender ideas could undermine Indian women's rights. Yet the rising power and presence of the state did not appear to alter indigenous gender norms and practices in a fundamental way. Instead, Indian peasants lived with competing gender norms that sometimes reinforced each other and sometimes conflicted. In the end, a distinctly indigenous gender system survived, even if weakened by the rising power of the state.

⇒ 6 ⇐

Family Matters

Gender and Social Control on Haciendas

[Conciertos'] *condition is much like that of children in families.*
—Supreme Tribunal in Quito, 1820[1]

The servant, unlike the slave, lives separated from the master,
he governs himself; but this liberty and independence are ironic,
because ... his economic life is circumscribed such that *neither
is marriage spontaneous nor does the family belong to him.*
—Agustín Cueva, 1915[2]

Nineteenth-century scholars and statesmen frequently identified conciertos' position on estates as the most childlike position in which indigenous men could find themselves. This made the debt peonage system a major national concern, because the very nature of socioeconomic relationships between hacendados and peons conflicted with the central-state goal of achieving equality before the law. Particularly during liberal regimes of the 1850s and early 1900s, central-state officials ardently identified concertaje as an atrocity against liberty and individualism; according to these statesmen, the concierto and his family lived in misery so absolute that it even explained Indians' descent into barbarism. While these views of highland haciendas offer valuable evidence of Indians' problematic status vis-à-vis liberal individualism, they also suggest that hacendados also were not adequate liberal individuals because of their active promotion of familial and corporate labor relations on estates. In doing so, liberals contended, estate owners perpetuated unequal race relations that made it impossible to real-ize the goal of establishing equality before the law.

Liberal critics of concertaje got it both right and wrong. Hacienda life subjected indebted workers to the will of the hacendado, an authority who (in theory at least) had complete control of all that happened on the estate. Likewise, conciertos were bound to a group-based and ethnically specific identity without the advantages that Indian peasants enjoyed regarding their collective identity and autonomy. Certainly conciertos' options were quite limited, especially from the late 1860s through 1918: if they tried to escape their debts or get out of their contracts, they could be punished or even jailed; if they tried to address abuse, they were unlikely to succeed because local authorities and hacienda owners frequently collaborated with each other. Yet concertaje also offered Indians certain advantages: owners paid their debts to others and often guarded their interests in court, and some conciertos received subsistence plots of land (*huasipungos*), allowing them to maintain a semblance of peasant autonomy within a system of dependent labor.

Both nineteenth-century state officials and the historians who stud-ied them recognized that, whether conciertos contested or tolerated it, an hacendado's authority rested on paternalism. But just as it was more than a vague or generalized paternalism that shaped Indian-state relations, scrutiny of gender ideologies on haciendas reveals that they were nuanced, historically dynamic, and complex. If conciertos were perpetual children in their relations with estate owners, the system simultaneously suggested that indigenous male workers functioned as heads of households in ways that one does not find within self-contained indigenous peasant commu-nities. The boundaries of a concierto's patriarchal authority are difficult to gauge precisely, partly because the topic appears in historical records only when contested. Indian masculinity on haciendas is also open to multiple interpretations because hacienda paternalism itself was multifaceted and deeply contradictory, and even indigenous men's rights as heads of house-holds might ultimately benefit the estate owner. It does appear, however, that Indian men expected the hacienda system to support at least some aspects of indigenous patriarchy. Conciertos' ability to defend their own manly authority most likely followed other patterns of negotiation with hacendados: labor shortages made it easier for Indian men to assert masculine rights, while labor abundance made it difficult. Indian women, however, were consistently disadvantaged within the hacienda hierarchy and in relation to their male peers. Women's deeper marginalization and exploitation meant that the transition from life in peasant communities to haciendas was quite different, and much harder, for them than it was for Indian men.

These multiple hacienda paternalisms were a matter of national concern, particularly at times when tensions between hacendados and central government officials ran high, such as in the Independence period and during the liberal regimes of the 1850s and early 1900s. In these periods, conciertos gained new leverage to challenge hacendados' fatherly authority and reinforce their own manliness. Conciertos most commonly questioned landowners' paternal legitimacy by indicating that hacendados had acted cruelly rather than kindly toward workers. When doing so, indigenous men often called on state paternalism to counterbalance hacendados' cruelty, but they sometimes asserted their masculine rights by demanding their own liberty rather than pleading for the state's paternal protection. Less frequent, but equally telling, were times when conciertos complained that hacendados had overstepped their patriarchal power by interfering with the function of indigenous families, a domain that indigenous men proposed fell under their authority.

The dynamics among Indian men, the state, and highland landowners suggest the need to reevaluate hacienda paternalism and its impact on indebted workers. First, hacienda paternalism was far from simple or one-sided and was instead a complex, multilayered, and deeply contradictory construction. Furthermore, hacendado-Indian relations were not enclosed or isolated from broader national and historical phenomena; rather, they were intertwined with the historical development of the nation-state. Ironically, the centrality of concertaje to nationalist discourse often made it possible for indigenous debt workers to exploit national Indian policies more successfully than their counterparts in peasant villages. Finally, the depth of indigenous women's exploitation on haciendas affected more than interpersonal or even interethnic relations on highland estates: constraints on Indian women were part of the larger web of masculinization of Indian-state relations that came with nation-state formation.

Gender on highland haciendas is illuminated by both the internal patterns of life and labor on large estates and the broader sociopolitical contexts in which hacendados and conciertos maneuvered. Internal structures of the hacienda system—its hierarchy and labor patterns—revolved around a paradoxical set of gender ideologies. These gender norms, however, had differential impacts on the indigenous men and women who lived and worked on highland estates. Finally, conflicts between conciertos and hacendados reveal how male Indian workers engaged with interethnic discourses of nation making to advance their own (individual or collective) interests.

Hacienda Hierarchy

The formal labor hierarchy was an essential component of hacienda life, denoting the chain of command and levels of power and specifying the duties and rights that an individual had within the hacienda system. This hierarchy not only helped maintain productivity but also underscored the parent-child relationship between owners and workers. All hacendados were the ultimate authorities on their estates, making the most important financial decisions and ruling social relations through their manipulation of the hacienda's lower orders. The extent to which the owner would handle daily operations depended on the size and the location of the property: hacendados with smaller properties or those distant from cities usually lived on them most of the year, whereas owners of larger estates, or those closer to cities, were far less likely to spend much time on their rural properties. In all cases, however, the owners' roles on estates were social and familial rather than purely economic: in particular, hacendados' success at ruling social relations rested on adequately presenting themselves as benevolent parental figures. They meted out justice and even intervened on behalf of their conciertos when the latter were embroiled in criminal cases.[3] Women of the hacienda class wielded power, though their position was not as clear as that of male estate owners, given men's legal right to manage their wives' property. Only widows had formal power over their estates, and theirs was an interesting position: they exercised masculine power, yet social pressures mandated that they display feminine qualities of gentleness and morality. More commonly, elite women influenced hacienda life as wives of estate owners—a function that was important to establishing the estate as a large family. Though their roles were often unofficial, these wives were more consistently and directly linked to the normally male hierarchy than any other women on the hacienda. An owner's wife managed the hacienda house, oversaw the maintenance and distribution of all domestic labor, and sometimes distributed loans to conciertos (chiefly for courtship and marriage). Some wives may even have had other direct, if informal, input in running haciendas, especially if the land came from their families.

On the next tier of hacienda hierarchy were *mayordomos* (hacienda administrators or stewards), who were usually mestizos hired from the local area, charged with managing hacienda work and production.[4] Since mayordomos most often punished slow or disobedient workers, conciertos frequently associated them rather than owners with unfair conditions on estates. A mayordomo therefore helped an hacendado maintain his reputation as a benevolent father figure, even though the hacendado might have ordered punishments carried out by his administrator.[5] Tensions between mayordomos and conciertos were also based on race: as mestizos, mayordomos enjoyed more rights and authority in Ecuadorian society than Indians did; ethnic distinctions therefore bolstered mayordomos' power and authority on haciendas. More generally, mestizo mayordomos attempted to "distance themselves from their indigenous roots and claim a white identity," further aggravating their relations with indigenous workers.[6] Mayordomos were not always cast in such a negative light, however, and sometimes their roles as middlemen put them in workers' favor, as when they distributed money to conciertos on the hacendado's behalf.[7]

Just as the mayordomo supported an hacendado by handling administrative duties, a *mayoral* (overseer) assisted the mayordomo by assigning chores and gathering workers for specific duties. Factors that might qualify a concierto to become a mayoral were years of experience on the estate, a record of good conduct, or knowledge of Spanish. In return for helping to keep the hacienda running smoothly, these overseers had greater access to both goods and cash than other conciertos. In spite of these advantages, conciertos sometimes resisted becoming mayorales because the position could potentially put them in conflict with other indigenous laborers.[8] This reluctance suggests that hacendados were not entirely successful in orienting their laborers to vertical rather than lateral reciprocity. Although hacienda owners successfully created a dependent labor force, indigenous workers also relied on each other for economic and social support; men chosen as mayorales feared they might lose these horizontal ties if their peers resented them.

Male indigenous laborers were at the bottom of the formal hacienda hierarchy and usually labored from early in the morning until about three or four in the afternoon, six days per week.[9] While all conciertos were tied through debt to the hacienda owner, only the Indians who received a huasipungo were *indios propios*, or permanent laborers with greater official rights and obligations than other hacienda workers. After mayorales, indios propios had the greatest right to cash and goods from the patrón, because of which they were paid only about half as much as workers brought in from surrounding communities.[10] Conciertos regularly solicited loans known as *suplidos*, which functioned as part of their earnings, helping them to achieve a higher standard of living than their salaries and subsistence plots could support. At the same time, suplidos benefited the estate owner: goods loaned were usually low-quality products that could not be sold at market, and every suplido increased a concierto's obligations to the owner.[11] Other loans, *socorros*, came on a scheduled basis, usually at harvest time; these generally consisted of clothing, food, or animals, and they symbolized the goods patrones owed to conciertos in return for their labor and loyalty.[12] Both types of loans reinforced an estate owner's role as benevolent patriarch who saw to the well-being of the indigenous workers under his care. Socorros were especially important symbols of hacienda paternalism: because these loans typically consisted of basic necessities, they identified the hacendado as a fatherly provider and underscored the concierto's inability to meet his own family's needs.

Overall, the hacienda system involved a complex series of negotiations between conciertos and hacendados. In many ways the hacienda owner's power was supreme: conciertos belonged to him (or her), and he could even transfer them to a new patrón if he sold the property.[13] Indigenous workers also sank into childlike dependence on the hacendado each time they sought loans and assistance submissively in order to make ends meet. Hacendados' patriarchal powers further restricted conciertos' autonomy and mobility, though workers were not prohibited from leaving the hacienda and might regularly visit nearby towns. Sometimes conciertos had no choice but to leave the estate, if the owner required them to work for a period on other properties they owned or as domestic servants in their urban homes.[14] At the same time, however, the hacienda system provided conciertos with meaningful if limited powers. By treating suplidos as regular earnings, conciertos constantly negotiated their income with patrones, and they maintained a certain level of subsistence autonomy and peasant identity through their huasipungos.[15] Moreover, workers required an estate owner to live up to his (sometimes her) proclaimed role as a benevolent parental figure. Finally, conciertos' childlike position on the estate was not absolute, as anthropologist Barry Lyons's analysis of masculinity among hacienda workers shows. Lyons found that through marriage, fiesta sponsorship, and rising reputation among fellow workers, "men could aspire to [a] mode of mature masculinity and to the position of authority within the hacienda community associated with it." This authority was generational in its nature; elders taught respect to juniors, and they collaborated with hacienda administrators to punish wayward youths. The inclusion of a subset of conciertos in the realm of masculine authority on the hacienda reinforced an hacendado's role as the ultimate paternal figure on the property.[16] Even before accounting for indigenous women's roles on the estate, then, one sees the ways in which gender, along with race, shaped hacienda life. Though the broader rules of paternalism clearly undermined indigenous masculinity, the finer points of the gender structures sometimes upheld conciertos' manliness. This becomes even clearer when one examines Indian men's and women's different experiences of the hacienda system.

Marriage, Work, and Gender on Haciendas

Although Indian women were absent from official hacienda hierarchy, their presence was of great consequence in the hacienda system. Marriage cemented formal socioeconomic ties between estate owners and indigenous workers, and women's work contributed, directly and indirectly, to hacienda productivity. Perhaps most important, women's subordination on haciendas helped to define and reinforce indigenous masculinity in a socioeconomic system that in other ways undermined it.

Marriage served the central function of cementing the ties of unequal reciprocity between male workers and hacendados. Since marriages were important celebrations in which all hacienda residents participated, conciertos needed money to fulfill their social obligation to entertain fellow workers on the wedding day. Even before this celebration, Indian men needed money to offer their fiancées and future in-laws gifts during the courtship process. To meet courtship and wedding costs, a young Indian man would go to the hacendado—or, on many haciendas, the hacendado's wife—and request a loan. This was often a young man's first debt to the hacendado under his own, rather than his father's, account.[17] After the marriage had taken place, both the rituals and emergencies of family life made further loans necessary. A concierto's economic and social obligations deepened with each birth, sickness, and death in his family because he sought medical care or Church services for these events. Loan requests were also linked to family needs such as clothing, food in times of difficulty, and animals to supplement family subsistence.[18] Though it was costly, conciertos also benefited from marriage. First, it was only through marriage that a concierto could obtain a huasipungo and begin to engage in subsistence agriculture.[19] Second, though a married worker had high debts, the loans helped him achieve a better standard of living than he could attain as a single man. Even the nature of the debt itself changed over time: Guerrero found that many conciertos borrowed large sums of money in the early years of their marriages, but they were later able to use their children's labor to stabilize and perhaps even lower their debts.[20] Marriage and the acquisition of a huasipungo also marked Indian men's ascent to patriarchal power over women and children. Conciertos represented their families quite literally on estates: even if an Indian woman worked or sought credit, she always did so in her husband's name, because all labor and loans were listed under his account.[21] This, along with her lack of pay for work she performed on the estate, placed her in a position of doubled dependence: she relied on her husband, who was in turn ruled by the hacendado.

Women's labor was essential to both household and hacienda production.[22] On some large haciendas, there were even two sets of mayorales; one gathered men for work, and the other gathered women.[23] Women had to provide domestic labor in the hacienda house on a rotating basis—cooking, cleaning, washing clothes, and so forth. On many haciendas, women also fetched water, combed and spun wool, pastured animals, and milked cows.[24] At harvest time, an observer would find women alongside men in the fields, and indigenous women made chicha for the harvest celebration—though hacendados provided the corn to make it and distributed the finished product to their workers. These various tasks were quite similar to, often exactly the same as, indigenous women's work in peasant communities. Indigenous women labored, however, in a very different socioeconomic context on haciendas than they did in peasant communities. The distinct nature of hacienda patriarchy obscured indigenous women's contributions to estate productivity, and as a result, women's standing was quite low in both the hacienda community and concierto households.

Most indigenous women's duties on haciendas were connected to their husbands' concierto status, as was evident at harvest time when families worked together in the fields and women followed behind male harvesters to glean leftover grains from the main harvest.[25] Hacendados benefited a great deal from women's unpaid labors. When conciertos fulfilled the rotating position of *vaquero* and had to tend to the hacienda's cattle, their wives did much of the work, milking the cows every day under the supervision of another concierto, the *lechero*.[26] Conciertos' wives or older children also had to pasture hacienda livestock, even though the official duty was assigned through the male laborer. Similarly, *huasicamas* had to perform a number of duties in the hacienda house, and their wives were expected to serve alongside them. From conciertos' perspective, their wives' most important function was to support family subsistence. Not only did women and children often farm the huasipungo and pasture animals while a concierto worked on the estate, but they sometimes helped him finish work more quickly so that he could then devote time to subsistence production.[27] If a family could not subsist from the huasipungo, an Indian woman might work as a cook for a mestizo family in the local town. Both men and women sometimes traveled to help relatives on other haciendas in return for which they received goods. A concierto might even be able to migrate for seasonal work on coastal cacao estates, leaving his wife and children to take over his duties on the hacienda and huasipungo during his absence.[28] Yet when Indian women took over their husbands' labors on the estate, they were concealed within hacienda hierarchy because any work they did was attributed to their husbands' account. This contrasted with the greater independence that male migration might bring to a woman living in a peasant community, where she could control land and partake directly in civil matters during her husband's absence.

Indian women's exclusion from the official hacienda hierarchy meant that hacendados were able to gain extra labor value through women's work, whether because women and children worked on the hacienda without pay, or because their work on huasipungos allowed owners to get more work out of conciertos.[29] In short, it was economically advantageous for owners to designate Indian women as informal laborers who simply helped conciertos fulfill their duties, because the hacendados paid far less than the value of labor indigenous families provided for them.[30] In a study of northern Peruvian haciendas, anthropologist Carmen Diana Deere suggests that the intriguing question is why male workers "allowed their household's standard of living to be less than it might have been if they had struggled against the exploitation of female labor." She posits peasant patriarchy helps to explain this: male workers thought "it was perfectly justifiable that women should serve men, [therefore] it was 'natural' that women should serve the landlord as well."[31] In highland Ecuador, peasants' patriarchal concepts must have also carried over to life on large estates, reinforcing at least some aspects of hacienda patriarchy. The extent of this overlap, however, was not always clear. For example, although conciertos at times protested the fact that their wives worked without pay, this was not a universal grievance (at least, not in the nineteenth century). I suspect that conciertos lived within a contradictory conceptual framework: they would have liked to have their wives earn money to help with family subsistence, but at the same time they wished to maintain their wives in a dependent state to define their own patriarchal authority.

While hacienda and indigenous patriarchies were predicated on similar assumptions, their impact on indigenous women and men was quite different. For indigenous women, the consequences of hacienda patriarchy were consistent and dire, particularly when contrasted with their experiences in peasant communities. Whereas in peasant communities, patriarchy was limited by women's kinship, generational, and land rights, on haciendas, these balancing factors were absent. Kinship remained meaningful among conciertos, but it was secondary to the vertical ties with the hacendado; furthermore, land was distributed only to married adult men. Lacking both land and formal recognition within the hacienda system, indigenous women on estates lived under the triple patriarchy of peasant, hacienda, and state ideologies aimed at their subordination. For indigenous men, the experience was more mixed, and their position in hacienda patriarchy was ambivalent. Indian men's childlike position on estates made even their control of households conditional and limited. Hacendados determined when and how indigenous households took shape by controlling loans and the distribution of huasipungos, and they could get extra labor power from a concierto's wife and children. Yet while these factors undermined Indian manliness, other aspects of the hacienda system reinforced indigenous patriarchy. The most important assumption tying together different features of hacienda life was the assumption that Indian men were the natural and exclusive heads of households, as was evident in hacienda record books and huasipungo distribution. Although hacendados assumed that wives and children would help conciertos with work, these duties were mostly implicit and did not directly impinge on a concierto's decision-making power in the household. In sum, the hacendado was the great father providing for all indigenous workers on the estate, but he (or she) delegated lesser paternal authority to conciertos, through whom all of the land, goods, and money were distributed.

The extent to which this patriarchal system penetrated indigenous women and men's personal relationships is difficult to gauge exactly, but women's capacity to defend their interests was not as strong as it was in peasant communities. Not everything changed: in most cases indigenous wives probably used similar strategies against their husbands' drinking or violence on haciendas as they did in peasant communities. There is even evidence that hacendados sometimes punished husbands who beat their wives, although they might simultaneously punish women for (in their view) contributing to domestic violence through insubordination. Therefore, even though an Indian woman might use the hacendado as an alternate patriarch who could lessen her suffering, from the owner's perspective, these interventions were aimed mainly at controlling laborers rather than protecting women. Yet even if women on haciendas used many of the same tactics to confront marital discord that indigenous peasant women did, the hacienda system put them at a disadvantage in ways they would not have experienced in peasant communities. For example, gender complementarity of hacienda labor did not provide indigenous women with the leverage or negotiating power that one finds in peasant communities, because women were alienated from the means of production on estates.[32] In general, Indian women's lack of formal status or rights meant that they had fewer weapons at their disposal than their peasant counterparts in their confrontations with Indian men. I suspect that these losses limited women's ability to enforce their own visions of proper gender roles and obligations on estates. Even the production and sale of chicha afforded women less power on haciendas than it did in indigenous peasant communities. In particular, chicheras' symbolic roles as transmitters of sociocultural identity and solidarity did not survive the shift from peasant to hacienda life. Although Indian women continued to make and dispense chicha regularly, on the most important ceremonial occasions hacendados provided women with the materials necessary to make chicha and served it themselves. In doing so, estate owners appropriated Indian women's cultural value at critical moments in ritual and production cycles.[33]

Effects of the hacienda system on widows seem to have varied. Similar to women in Indian peasant communities, indigenous widows on haciendas were responsible for their deceased husbands' debts.[34] Though rare, widows occasionally appeared in hacienda record books under their own names. After Rosa Yubailla's husband died in 1871, she was listed in the hacienda record as a shepherd (*ovejera*) and in a later record as a *concierta* along with Tomasa Pomache. Even though Pomache's marital status was not recorded, she also must have been a widow, considering the rigidity of hacienda patriarchal structures.[35] Court cases from the period also suggest that hacendados might occasionally have allowed indigenous widows to remain on huasipungos. A criminal case, for example, revealed that the defendant, Manuel Llangari, lived on the hacienda Palacio with his mother, an ovejera. There was no specific mention of the mother's marital status, but if Llangari's father had been alive, Llangari would have referred to living on his father's land.[36] In another case, Felipe Guillca of the hacienda Gulag mentioned that his sister-in-law had property on the hacienda also.[37] Data pertaining to widows' relationships to land on haciendas provide no consistent patterns, though it appears that a widow received land only at the owner's whim rather than as a systematic right, and it probably happened infrequently. All widowed workers were likely to remarry quickly, as it would be close to impossible for them to meet both hacienda work demands and subsistence needs without a partner. But a widowed concierto's relationship to the hacienda and land did not change when he remarried, whereas a widow who remarried would disappear from hacienda records because all her labors and needs would once again be registered through her second husband. This stands in contrast to widows' land rights in indigenous peasant communities and suggests that indigenous widows' ability to blur the lines of patriarchy was severely limited on haciendas.

In general, while both indigenous men and women on estates were exploited and dependent, women's subordination was more complete than men's and served to compensate men for their own exploitation.[38]

For men, marriage raised their status to heads of households who wielded at least a modicum of patriarchal power; for women, marriage symbolized deepening dependence on their male peers as well as on the hacendado. For men, land and loans supplemented income and made subsistence possible; for women, male control of land, goods, and cash left them with little recourse in marital conflicts. Indigenous men's and women's differential experiences on estates imply that hacienda structure depended as much on gender domination as it did on racial domination.[39]

Hacendados' Use of Religion and Morality

Religion provided patrones with a particularly useful tool for social control because numerous occasions—whether yearly events or everyday occurrences—presented them with opportunities to identify themselves as guardians of estate morality. Priests of course were essential in this quest because they preached the importance of obedience, ran masses, and organized religious celebrations; nevertheless, the estate owner remained the ultimate authority in moral matters.[40] As with other aspects of hacienda life, estate owners' manipulation of morality categorized Indian men as both perpetual children in relation to the estate owner and patriarchal authorities within their own homes.

Carnival was the most important religious celebration on haciendas in Chimborazo,[41] and hacendados used it to reassert hierarchy and social reciprocity, as Carola Lentz's description of the festivities shows:

> The Friday of the week prior to Carnival, families met at the call of the overseer on the path to the hacienda house, for the giving of the *camari* [a gift, in a hierarchical context]. In the patio, they kept a respectful distance from the steps where the patrón was seated.... Upon being named by the overseer ... the head of the family had to step out of the line, kneel before the patrón, and [hand his gift to] the overseer, naming what he was giving. The gift was personal and public—not everyone gave the same thing—and was visible both to the other families and to the patrón; the hope was that the gift

would guarantee favorable relations for the coming year. Then, the overseer presented the camaris that had been collected to the steward, who, in turn, gave them to the patrón, thus following in detail the steps of the hierarchy of command. The hacendado, after receiving the camaris, gave out cane alcohol and chicha . . . as a symbol of his wish to maintain the (asymmetric) relations of reciprocity.[42]

Such rituals reinforced hacienda hierarchy and relations of unequal reciprocity by having conciertos' gifts make their way to the hacendado through the tiers of hacienda hierarchy. The fact that the hacendado was both separated from the initial offerings yet was present to account for each personal gift also suggested that even when he was not physically present on the hacienda, workers still owed him their labor and allegiance. Though not deeply analyzed in Lentz's work, gender dynamics were central to the ritual she described. Having only male heads of household present gifts to the hacendado marked women's exclusion from the official hacienda hierarchy, and it emphasized indigenous men's authority over their homes. Even if members of the hacienda community assumed that Indian men worked for the hacendado and Indian women worked for the owner's wife, Carnival celebrations stressed that female lines of authority were informal and therefore secondary to the male chain of command, since all men on the hacienda had authority over their wives and children.

Lentz also discussed the custom in which young men dressed up as women or widows during Carnival and paraded around "begging for alms."[43] This custom may have been used as a way to clarify the normal power structure of gender relations by mocking them: by playing with sexual identity and reversing it, young men may have highlighted the authority over women that they would eventually enjoy.[44] It is also possible that they were expressing their own dependent and subservient position relative to the hacendado. Finally, it could be that young men, rather than mature indios propios, dressed up as women because they had not yet gained full access to male rights on the hacienda. In any of these cases, young men used images of women, via cross-dressing, to symbolize submissiveness in a way that all members of the hacienda community would recognize. This is not to say that the participants or observers busied themselves analyzing the deeper implications of ritual cross-dressing. Instead, Carnival was a periodic celebration when participants let off steam and enjoyed themselves. Ultimately, they did so in ways that reinforced rather than weakened the system, and cross-dressing served this purpose, upholding both interethnic and gender domination.

Just as it was central to hacienda structure more generally, marriage was critical when hacendados used morality to control workers. Hacendados, mayordomos, *doctrineros*,[45] and priests all took part in regulating indigenous workers' marriages, and they frequently intervened in marital disputes or punished workers for immoral acts. Extramarital affairs, domestic violence, and children's disobedience were all disruptions for which hacienda and religious authorities could punish indigenous residents. As noted earlier, in the case of domestic violence, an abused wife might be punished along with her husband if an estate authority decided that she had acted disrespectfully toward him.[46] Hacendados sometimes even forced couples to marry. Consider Gregoria Guamán, who had lived with her husband, Modesto Remache, for over twenty years on an hacienda owned by Miguel María Gonzalez.[47] At one point Remache fled his debts, leaving his wife behind. After he had been gone for some time, Guamán entered into an "illicit relationship" with widower Antonio Ambi, another resident worker on the hacienda. Gonzalez, still her patrón, considered this relationship a bad or evil condition (*viendo que estaban en mal estado*), and he forced the couple to marry. Since Guamán had no idea if her husband was still alive, Gonzalez himself solicited information on Remache and obtained a death certificate from officials in the civil parish of Sicalpa, where community members testified that Remache had fallen into a river and must have drowned, though his body was never found. Once Remache's death certificate was in hand, Guamán and Ambi married. A year later, court officials discovered that Remache was still alive, and Guamán faced criminal charges for double matrimony.[48] Owner Miguel María Gonzalez's actions in this case offer an extreme example of how hacendados used marital and family conflict as a means of maintaining control over both male and female laborers on their haciendas. Dictating morality also allowed hacendados to keep Indian women in formal relationships of dependence on male workers: when Gonzales forced Guamán to remarry, he placed her, after a brief period in which she had an uncertain status, back under the formal rule of a male hacienda worker.

Guamán's case uncovers critical differences between gender relations on haciendas versus those in Indian peasant communities. Initially, Gregoria Guamán responded to her abandonment just as an Indian peasant woman would, by entering into an unofficial union with another man. If she had lived in a peasant community, it would not be necessary to take further action, because abandonment or abuse provided acceptable reason for a woman to establish a new relationship. But on haciendas an Indian woman's response to abandonment or abuse was subject to the will and moral authority of an hacendado, who required her to remain within the bounds of legal, Catholic marriage. Although the hacendado's moral authority was over male as well as female laborers, Indian women were particularly vulnerable because hacienda structure identified them as appendages of male workers.

Given the structure of hacienda labor relations, the rules of morality were relative to one's position in the estate's hierarchy. Though hacendados held conciertos accountable for a strict set of moral regulations, there were virtually no limits on their own sexual conduct. Mayordomos (perhaps even mayorales) were also able to bend the rules of morality in their interactions with indigenous laborers. Indian women, who had only informal ties to hacienda hierarchy, and who linked Indian men to hacendados in bonds of unequal reciprocity via marriage, were therefore targets of sexual harassment and abuse at the hands of hacienda administrators. Such actions displayed hacendados' and administrators' dominance over Indian men as well as women on the estate.[49] Conciertos may have been allowed to rule over and represent women within their own homes, but hacienda owners and employees could sexually abuse Indian women to remind Indian men of their lowly position on the estates. Hacienda owners' and administrators' sexual abuse of indigenous women symbolized the ethnic domination of these white-mestizo authority figures over indigenous workers more generally.[50]

Hacienda Conflicts

Although indigenous workers generally accepted hacienda paternalism, hacendado-concierto relations were not always smooth. Struggles often focused on contested patriarchy in a way that was similar to indigenous peasants' marital disputes: conciertos and hacendados disagreed on how to interpret their familial arrangement rather than denying the validity of the unequal relationship more generally. Conciertos might accuse an hacendado of either failing to uphold his own patriarchal duties or inhibiting indigenous workers' patriarchal powers, sometimes emphasizing both. Estate owners would claim that they met or even surpassed their parental obligations while presenting conciertos as untrustworthy children. Indigenous women did not appear often in court clashes between estate owners and workers, but on occasion their voices can be heard, mostly reinforcing the hacienda's gender system. Regional and historical contexts also mattered a great deal in these cases. Conciertos were far more likely to bring suits against hacendados in favorable political climates, such as in the Independence period or during the liberal regimes of the 1850s or 1900s. Likewise, more conciertos from the north-central or southern highlands brought cases to court than those in the labor-abundant central highlands.

Conciertos routinely referred to hacendados as abusive patriarchs who cared only for the profits they could garner from their poor workers. In doing so, they confirmed general patterns of interethnic paternalism, both on haciendas and in Indian-state relations. Not only did Indian workers claim they were treated poorly and punished harshly, but some of them, like Lauriano Quispi and Pedro Coque, declared that "our ultimate disgrace has been to be reduced to being concierto[s] for don Eusebio Miño, a powerful man in this small community... this inhumane patrón has enriched himself at the cost of the sweat of our labor."[51] Rudicindo Sulca made a similar accusation when he sought to liquidate his debts to Mariano Bermudes in order to "seek another *amo* who will look upon me with human caring."[52] The protector general of 1816 summed up this perspective well in a communication criticizing hacendados' abuse of

Indian workers: "It has been observed that [Indians] suffer oppression and injustices at the hands of their amos, administrators, mayordomos, and other servants [on the estate] . . . they make the Indians work from four or five in the morning until nine or ten that day . . . they give them twice the number of tasks that they could [reasonably] complete . . . [and] punish them, not allowing them to rest until the work is finished."[53] Conciertos' pleas were often effective, partly because laws emphasized estate owners' paternal obligations. In an 1833 case, judges freed Juan Crisanto Morales from imprisonment for stealing because the law dictated that servants, like women and children, should be punished privately (which Morales already had been) rather than penalized publicly. Even though the early republican political atmosphere was more advantageous to estate owners than to Indian workers (who had lost their guaranteed right to liquidate debts), the Supreme Court upheld this argument and even allowed the concierto to liquidate his debts and move to work on another hacienda so that his amo could not seek vengeance against him for the court case.[54] A concierto was also likely to play directly on political interethnic paternalism, calling on court officials to "look upon me as a father" and save him from the estate owner's brutality.[55]

Hacendados responded by justifying their extensive paternal power, and they warned what would happen if Indians were not kept under their close watch and guidance. Because interethnic paternalism was central to concertaje, estate owners were adamant in their assertions that they had scrupulously fulfilled their duties as benevolent father figures. Martín Chiriboga, owner of the obraje San Juan, captured typical arguments when he stated that he had "never mistreated a single Indian," and that his concierto Luis Paca had lied about being abused.[56] Hacendados generally identified Indians as "mental and spiritual infants requiring the protection, discipline, and moral teachings of a 'buen patrón.'"[57] This contrast between the benevolent patrón and the unreliable, childlike Indian were evident when don Antonio Jijón of Otavalo attested, "The Indian Pedro Campo, having been my concierto to whom I gave socorros, paid his tributes, and did not prove unkind in any way . . . [should] fulfill his obligation, using work to make up the twenty pesos and six reales which he still owes on his bill. If the opposite happens ... all the Indians will take the same advantage and not a single concierto will remain ... the Indians [will go] to the valleys where they will cause themselves many losses and death."[58] Hacendados thus argued that Indian workers were incapable of caring for themselves, because they were given to "drunkenness, lewdness, and other vices," while in contrast, estate owners made essential contributions to the economy, and their control over indigenous workers benefited broader society. In essence, if Indians were left to their own devices, they might destroy the nation, whereas hacendados advanced national interests.[59]

Female hacienda owners appeared less often than men in these disputes, but when they did, their position required them to make nuanced gender arguments. In 1814, hacendada Francisca Jijón not only referred to her parental obligations toward her indigenous workers, but also emphasized that her character and her inherent female gentleness kept her from mistreating her Indian servants. She claimed that the Indians on her estate were trying to take advantage of her vulnerability as a widowed woman, and that they could not prove any of their allegations.[60] Rather than allowing her sex to undermine her parental power on her estate, Jijón reinforced it by calling on notions of her gentle maternalism at the same time that she sought male judges' patriarchal protection by referring to her female vulnerability. To advance her cause, she touted herself as an honorable widow, got several of her indigenous workers to testify that she treated them kindly, and charged that fellow female hacienda owner doña María de los Reyes was trying to take all of "her Indians."[61] Though she used all the right kinds of arguments, they failed because court officials judged that even if she treated her indigenous workers fairly, it was their legal right to liquidate their debts and move to another estate.[62]

In addition to calling into question estate owners' legitimacy, conciertos presented themselves as protectors intervening to defend their own charges against mistreatment from the malevolent patriarchy of the estate owner.[63] Indian men were, in this view, prevented from being the good providers, to the detriment of their dependents.[64] One complaint that Indian men raised in several different altercations was that their wives and children were forced to work, without pay, on their behalf. As Juan Tiauanquisa of the obraje and hacienda San Yldefonso put it, "Sir, children are obligated to help with their parents' work, and when it passes that they are separated to do work with women . . . neither can sons help fathers nor fathers help sons."[65] Tiauanquisa's evaluation of family labor on estates suggests that at least some Indian men thought it was important that they have official say in where and how their wives and children would work. Other conciertos promoted themselves as concerned patriarchs when they protested that their wives or children had been unjustly fined or punished in their place. They proclaimed that a son "cannot be made to satisfy his father's debt through his own work."[66] Another concierto protested that his wife had been imprisoned after he had left the hacienda: "It is irregular to make a wife suffer in her husband's place, even if he is guilty."[67] Conciertos who highlighted their manly responsibilities were doing several things at once. First, they broadened their complaints of abuse, emphasizing that it was a whole family, not just one individual, who suffered under the estate owner. They also played on state officials' proclaimed desire to make it possible for Indian men to act as good patriarchal providers and protectors. Finally, they asserted that the home belonged to them, reinforcing their own masculine authority and dignity within a labor system that exploited and made children of them.

Two cases are fascinating for their treatment of what it meant for a concierto to have his wife forced to work without pay. As Eusebio Minango indicated in a complaint against Francisco Carcelén, "my amo has beaten me for the slightest thing, for having done my work without [the assistance of] my wife, as is the custom, *without giving them even the minimum salary for the work that these women do*; this has occurred not only once, but various times."[68] Roque Culimba and José Gavilima stressed the negative impact of their wives' work on their own well-being when they stated that the hacendada "makes our wives work every day without ceasing, *without giving them any time to make us a small meal to placate our hunger, and thus we go to bed at night . . . [husbands] don't even have anyone to give us a drink of water.*"[69] On the one hand, these two cases suggest that Indian men were concerned with their wives' right to be paid for work they did, and not all conciertos accepted that women's work was rightfully informal and unremunerated. On the other hand, the conciertos' authority was also at stake: having their wives serve them food was a sign of deference, the loss of which subverted their dignity as well as leaving them hungry.[70] Their anger over how estate owners treated their wives was therefore neither a simple act of support for indigenous women nor a mere defense of indigenous patriarchy, but a complex combination of both assertions at once. That Culimba and Gavilima's complaint was against a female hacendada raises another intriguing possibility: perhaps these conciertos were especially concerned with protecting their masculine pride because they answered to a woman? In other words, it is possible that Indian men would tolerate losing some of their patriarchal authority to a powerful landowning *man* but found it far more humiliating to have a woman assume that power.

Emerging scholarship on the nineteenth and twentieth centuries supports an argument that indigenous masculinity was interwoven in both the hacienda system and concierto resistance. Derek Williams found that Imbabura conciertos in the 1850s and 1860s questioned the extent of hacienda owners' paternal powers and often complained that hacienda paternalism interfered with family relations in their own households.[71] In 1930, indigenous workers on strike in Cayambe included provisions on women's labor when they presented a list of demands to authorities. They insisted that women should be paid twenty centavos daily for their early morning work as dairy maids, without obligation to perform labor later in the day. The petition also stated that if a woman performed less strenuous labor than a man on the estate, she should be paid thirty centavos per day.[72] As with early nineteenth-century references to women and work, these demands spoke to men's solidarity with women while also highlighting the value that conciertos placed on their positions as heads of households. Conciertos supported indigenous women by demanding that they be paid for the work they did, and it is likely that women would welcome not only the compensation for their work on the estate, but also having their labor burdens reduced. However, taking women out of the hacienda workforce after early morning hours also reinforced that women belonged in the home while men worked to provide for their families. Similarly, the stipulation that women's work should be paid left open the likelihood that any work women did was "less strenuous" and therefore deserved only three-quarters of the forty centavos that male workers earned each day. The tensions evident here between indigenous patriarchal authority on the one hand and indigenous men and women's shared concerns on the other can be seen even in the language that indigenous workers used to describe conflicts with hacendados. In interviews with former hacienda workers in Pangor, anthropologist Barry Lyons found a strong correlation between masculinity and resistance on highland estates. Lyons recounts that although these Quichua speakers lacked an exact word for "resistance," they most often used the term *cariyana* to describe times when workers challenged the estate owners' authority. He explains that the term "cariyana" means, essentially, "to act like a man," suggesting that estate workers strongly associated resistance with masculinity. Interestingly, even when women challenged estate owners, their actions were described as belonging to a masculine domain.[73] Women's resistance to hacienda owners was not necessarily frowned on, however, even though they were acting in a male fashion. Because the arrangements between hacendados and conciertos were themselves fraught with contradictions, particularly with regard to indigenous masculinity, the paradox expanded to affect concierto-hacendado conflicts also.

Indigenous women only rarely appeared in legal disputes between hacendados and conciertos. In 1832, widow Manuela Yucasa took Francisco Carcelén to court, because when she remarried and left the estate, he refused to let her take her minor sons and some of their livestock. Yucasa's pleas were typical insofar as she emphasized her status as a miserable Indian and her misfortune to have worked for an amo devoid of natural human feeling. She apparently won her case.[74] Two years later, indigenous women on the hacienda Peguche petitioned the court for their husbands' release after the estate renter, Antonio Estebes Mora, had the men jailed. The women claimed that he treated all the indigenous workers terribly, and since he was too well connected in the local arena for them to seek justice there, they turned first to the governor of Imbabura province for help, then to the Supreme Court.[75] In another case, María Yuquilema was included along with male petitioners seeking liquidation of debts in 1867.[76] Indigenous women's absence from most cases highlights their marginalization on highland haciendas. Yet the times when they did participate directly suggest that, despite their weak position on estates, indigenous women were not necessarily powerless or unimportant in confrontations with landowners. Widows might find ways to protect their interests, and wives sought justice for husbands when the latter could not do so for themselves. Even Yuquilema's silent presence in a request to liquidate debts hints that either she was a widow who had a debt in her own name, or indigenous men supported her as a peer, valuing their shared experiences with a woman over their privileges as men. Without further details, however, it is impossible to tell exactly why Yuquilema's name appears alongside those of indigenous men. Most evidence for the above situations comes from 1800 to 1860; conciertos brought hacendados to court less frequently from 1868 to 1895. Indigenous laborers' silence probably resulted from the central government's support of hacienda expansion and definition of Indians (especially Indian men) as uncivilized barbarians who were incapable of contributing to the modern nation. Indigenous hacienda workers of the north-central sierra had little to gain by bringing grievances to court, because they were unlikely to win their cases. Even when they went to court, their complaints were limited; conciertos might charge that an hacendado saddled them with unfair debts, but they rarely complained of physical abuses, and they could no longer liquidate their debts and leave one estate for another.[77] In a political atmosphere where state officials on all levels were largely unsympathetic to Indians' plight, conciertos had little choice but to tolerate all aspects of hacienda paternalism, even those forms with which they would take issue in a more favorable political climate.

The liberal era of 1895–1925 opened new opportunities for concierto resistance. Despite the significant limitations to liberal reforms, liberal discourse on Indian matters, especially regarding concertaje, once again provided indigenous estate workers with tools to negotiate better treatment on haciendas. These abilities were further bolstered by liberal reformers' claims that they would incorporate Indian men into the nation. In one case, a concierto complained that a mayordomo was acting as if he had the same rights to make decisions about conciertos as the actual owner of the estate did.[78] Conciertos also tried to gain freedom from their obligations to hacendados by playing on the sympathies and claims of the liberal state, much like their nineteenth-century predecessors did. When Benedicto Caranqui and other conciertos of the hacienda Cesel in the civil parish of Cebadas petitioned the court to free them from their contract with hacendado Leopoldo Noriega, they made several references to Noriega beating his workers.[79] Though the grievances were familiar, they were placed in a new context, reinforcing liberal reformers' insistence that highland estate owners were abusive, backward patriarchs who were responsible for Indians' misery and who threatened to keep the nation mired in feudalism.

Conciertos took collective as well as individual action against hacendados during the liberal period. An excellent example can be found in a 1920 criminal case against indigenous workers from the hacienda Gatazo Hospital. Since this case offers vital information on several levels, it is worthwhile to describe it at length, and then analyze its significance.[80] Luis Benigno and Jorge and Alberto Gallegos, renters of Gatazo Hospital, initiated a criminal complaint against ten indigenous laborers on the estate (nine men and one woman), claiming that the Indians had attacked and tried to kill Moisés Hernandez (the mayordomo) and Margarito Tene (the mayoral). The plaintiffs claimed that after the initial assault, the insurgent Indians—armed with clubs, machetes, and revolvers—went into the town of Cajabamba intending to kill the Gallegos brothers. Several townspeople verified this version of events by testifying that they heard the Indian defendants proclaiming their murderous intentions toward the Gallegos brothers.[81] They went on to tell the court that the Indians were subdued only when men from the town joined together and fought back. In the process, a gun was fired—the plaintiffs and their witnesses claimed not to know who shot the weapon—and the Indian rebel José Ñamo was wounded (he died during the course of the investigation).

The Indian defendants told a far different story. According to them, the mayordomo and mayoral arrived at a concierto's house on the morning in question and announced that the workers had to leave the estate because they had refused to work for the Gallegos on another property (the hacienda Virginia). The defendants claimed that a group of them left the hacienda to lodge a complaint with police officials in Cajabamba, but on the way to town they were attacked and imprisoned. They demanded that the court find them innocent of "an infraction in which we were defenseless victims, not actors." Two of the defendants stated that they suffered from obstruction of justice because their imprisonment barred them from bringing a legitimate concern to police authorities.[82] As for José Ñamo's fatal gunshot wound, the Indians indicated that it was either Luis Benigno or Jorge Gallegos who had shot their peer.

Even Isidrio Cordóvez, the governor of Chimborazo, got swept into this conflict. The defense lawyer called on the governor to testify that the Indian residents of the hacienda Gatazo Hospital had sought his help and protection on several previous occasions when the renters had tried to expel them from the estate. The governor confirmed this and stated that after many such visits, he directed the Indians to go to the police commission in Colta for future assistance.[83] Toward the end of the proceedings, the governor wrote to the court again: "Due to the grievous situation in which these Indians, fathers of large families, find themselves, and on the recommendation of the President of the Republic and the Minister of Justice, I am obliged to again bring your attention to the case against the Indians of the hacienda Hospital for rising up against the señores Gallegos ... it is not possible to keep them indefinitely within the four walls of the prison; moreover, according to the declarations received to the present, no responsibility [for these events] falls on them."[84] The governor ordered .officials to set the prisoners free; the court complied.

This case came only a month after an indigenous insurrection in the civil parishes of Calpi, San Juan, and Licto—all communities in the canton of Riobamba—against registration for property tax lists (which would serve as the basis for conscripting laborers for public works projects). A. Kim Clark found that even in communities far from the epicenter of rebellion, Indians were able to take advantage of the fear that this uprising generated among elites.[85] This rebellion probably colored the testimony of Cajabamba's townspeople: they were shaken by Indian uprisings nearby and therefore described the disgruntled Indians in this case as savagely rebellious.[86] The truth probably lay somewhere between the plaintiffs' and defendants' claims: the indigenous defendants may have been angry, threatened violence, and even carried clubs—yet it is doubtful that they had revolvers or tried to kill the Gallegos brothers. In many ways, each side's *impressions* of events were more important than the events themselves. The happenings of the month before also strongly affected the government response to the incident, helping to explain why central government intervened, through the governor, on behalf of the prisoners.

Conciertos in this case (and their lawyer) were also making use of the liberal state's goal to become the mediator of interethnic relations on haciendas.[87] There were two critical precedents for the Indians' actions in this case: first, when Eloy Alfaro reformed concertaje in 1899, he stated that governors, jefes políticos, and local police were obligated to ensure that hacendados did not abuse their authority; although this case took place after concertaje had been officially abolished, the central state retained the right to intervene in local interethnic disputes.[88] Second, the hacienda Gatazo Hospital was one of the estates that the government had taken over when it confiscated lands owned by Church orders in 1904, and the Gallegos brothers were renting the estate from the government. Indian residents on the hacienda thus actively employed liberal policies when they sought the intervention of the governor or local police in disputes they had with the estate's renters.[89] Elites at the time commonly attributed Indians' actions to the influence of those most hated rural lawyers, tinterillos. While it is true that the lawyer in this dispute certainly chose the language used to persuade the court, the Indians' own actions—especially their long history of lodging complaints with the governor in Riobamba—show that the conciertos had already been actively manipulating liberal law and ideology even before this case came to court.

Though one woman, Tomasa Shullag, was arrested along with the nine men accused in the case, there is no information about or discussion of her in the court proceedings. The male defendants were all questioned and gave their version of the day's events; Tomasa Shullag was never interrogated, and during much of the case, her name did not even appear on the list of defendants. References to her appeared again briefly toward the end of the case, but when the governor of Chimborazo ordered the courts to pardon the defendants, the records mentioned only that indigenous men were set free. However important Shullag's actions may have been, state officials consistently excluded her as a relevant participant in the episode in June 1920. Since court officials did not ignore male defendants, the evidence suggests that they considered Shullag less important than her fellow defendants precisely because she was a woman. The silences in this case, however, can be quite telling when they are combined with other information about gender relations on sierra haciendas. Tomasa Shullag was probably a widow who lived on the hacienda, and it is possible that indigenous men on haciendas still considered it a widow's right to defend her own interests, even if hacienda structure generally undermined female independence. If this was the case, then hacienda workers maintained some level of autonomous identity in spite of hacendados' attempts to control all aspects of social relations on their properties.

Still, there is a marked difference between Indian women's participation in and leadership of resistance movements in autonomous peasant communities and patterns of resistance on haciendas. Unlike peasant communities, where indigenous women's rights to land and their socioeconomic roles positioned them for a say in community defense, hacienda structures worked against women's participation in struggles between indigenous workers and hacendados. Since the hacienda system promoted Indian women's dependence on men, men dominated protest against hacienda owners and renters. State policies and ideologies further bolstered Indian men's—and weakened Indian women's—capacity for protest on haciendas. These factors, along with laws that allowed Indian men the right to represent their wives in all civil disputes, gave Indian men a much stronger connection to legal protest than Indian women had. This helps to explain why the governor of Chimborazo, when ordering the release of the Indian defendants, referred to them as "fathers of large families." As fathers (and husbands), the men had the right—perhaps even the responsibility—to defend their families. In this way, hacienda structure and state policies, seemingly at odds during the liberal period, combined to foster male activism and discourage female activism.

The Spectrum of Paternalisms on Haciendas

Clearly, the move from life in Indian peasant communities to life on haciendas meant more than simply replacing an autonomous peasant economy with economic dependence on an elite landowner. Hacienda owners used unequal reciprocity, marriage, and morality as tools to strengthen the social control they were able to exercise on their estates. While these changes frequently affected Indian women more intensely than Indian men, they were used to manipulate male as well as female workers. For indigenous men who became conciertos, the impact of the estate's familial hierarchy was mixed: marriage, for example, both cemented their ties of dependent, unequal reciprocity with patrones and formalized conciertos' control of women. These two aspects of indigenous men's status on estates were continually in flux and inherently contradictory. The hacendado could always undermine a concierto's patriarchal authority and symbolically emasculate him by stripping and whipping him, or by raping his wife or daughter. Patrones held workers to stringent moral codes, but they were free to act as they pleased, disregarding Church teachings. Rather than seek to discover who wielded patriarchal authority as if such power were singular and absolute, it is more fitting to look at a spectrum of paternalisms on highland estates, where the estate owner was the foremost father figure, mayordomos and mayorales exercised considerable patriarchal powers, and conciertos were lesser paternal authorities. Even the hacendado's considerable patriarchal power did not go unchecked: he was bound to fulfill at least some of his claims to paternal benevolence, and he owed his conciertos at least a modicum of masculine power.

I would argue that Indian men's patriarchal rights over women compensated the men for at least some of the negative effects they experienced as permanent indebted workers on highland estates. Therefore, while the shift from peasant communities to hacienda residence was difficult for all the indigenous peoples who made it, it was a particularly stressful and negative experience for Indian women, for whom the contrasts between peasant life and estate life were more striking. Unlike peasant communities, where the importance of Indian women's socioeconomic roles and the need for community solidarity often set limits on Indian men's patriarchal rights, highland haciendas constricted Indian women's socioeconomic power and reinforced Indian men's patriarchal rights within their homes. The contrast between gender relations in autonomous communities versus those in haciendas was due to the central role that gender played in constructing and legitimizing social and economic power relations between Indian men and hacendados. Indigenous women, excluded from the formal hierarchy and alienated from land, were largely a means of exchange or negotiation between hacienda owners and male workers. This does not mean that Indian women were entirely powerless on large estates or that indigenous men and women were always at odds with each other; but rigid patriarchal ideologies and practices on haciendas left few opportunities for indigenous women to see to either their own or their communities' interests and concerns. It would take some time for indigenous women to reorient their strategies and find ways to become pivotal players in the defense of indigenous rights on highland estates, but some of them would do so by the middle of the twentieth century.

⤜ 7 ⤛

Gendered Foundations

Contradictions in Indian-State Relations

We know that indigenous villagers envision men and women as part of one
whole; we are complementary, not opposed, united, reciprocal, equal.
—María Vicenta Chuma Quishpilema[1]

Male companions have always been trampling on us, we were underneath
their shoes. That was what they learned from so many years past in which
the hacendados had us under their shoes. For that reason there are still
male companions today who don't give women priority.
—"Juana," 1997[2]

Vicenta Chuma and Juana describe indigenous gender relations quite
differently: while Chuma's depiction emphasizes inherent gender harmony, Juana's focuses on gender inequality. One would think that they
were discussing different societies, or at least different time periods.
In fact, they are both from the Quichua-speaking Ecuadorian highlands, and their statements came within a decade of each other. Their
divergent views of gender relations reflect their personal experiences.
Chuma is a nationally renowned activist leader, while Juana struggled
to establish herself—without her family's support—as a local political
leader. Their opposing evaluations of indigenous life likewise represent
distinct strategies within the indigenous movements. After centuries of
having whites and mestizos degrade Indians, many activists adamantly defend every aspect of their community customs. Emphasis on

community accord also results from activists' assertions that their own cultures and ways of life can serve as a standard for recreating the nation. Machismo is not exactly denied, but it is treated only generally, and even then leaders tend to blame gender inequalities on Western influences. Even Juana suggests that hacendados ultimately caused gender discord among Indians, rather than depicting these problems as original to her culture. Juana's concern with discussing the specific nature and depth of indigenous patriarchy shows, however, that there are multiple voices and views on gender within indigenous movements. These two interpretations of indigenous gender relations speak to how complex and difficult it has been for indigenous activists to address gender issues.

These divergent views of contemporary indigenous gender relations return us to the interplay between the past and the present in Ecuadorian history, and to the three premises on which this monograph is based. This book opens with the question, How and why are indigenous women simultaneously central to and marginalized within contemporary indigenous activism in Ecuador? I suggest that to understand indigenous women's paradoxical relationships to cultural identity and political activism in recent decades, it is necessary to examine the past. Specifically, the nineteenth-century process of nation-state formation laid important foundations for gender dilemmas that developed later in Indian-state relations. Second, I maintain that gender analysis offers a useful lens for examining Ecuadorian nation-state formation precisely because gender was an important means through which the inter- and intraethnic struggles associated with nation making played out. An important part of this process was the masculinization of Indian-state relations, in which indigenous men's capacity for interacting with the state increased in ways that indigenous women's did not. Finally, I argue that patriarchy is not a single and timeless category; rather, it is culturally specific and adaptable, and it functions in a state of constant historical motion.

Summarizing important themes in Ecuadorian nation-state formation from 1830 to 1925 will locate these three overlapping arguments in the broader contexts of nineteenth-century Ecuadorian history. State formation was the ultimate source of the patriarchal paradoxes in nine-teenth-century Indian-state relations, since state makers manipulated gender concepts to justify policies that exploited and excluded indig-enous peoples. Gender also gave indigenous men and women ways to confront, take advantage of, or adapt to the conflicting impacts of nation-state development; how they did so depended on the particu-lar situations in which individuals or communities found themselves. Indigenous peoples sometimes called on state-generated patriarchal precepts, while at others, they adhered to their own, alternative patri-archy. Over time, state officials had increasing success in penetrating indigenous communities with white-mestizo gender ideologies. The rising power of the state more often enabled Indian men than Indian women to manipulate contradictory interethnic politics, and concier-tos frequently did so more successfully than autonomous peasants. All of these contradictions generated opportunities to create and interpret the nation from multiple points, with numerous groups—some power-ful, some weak—participating in this multilayered process. At the same time, contradictions also set limits on each group's relative abilities to shape the nation. The interplay of these different openings and closures drove the nation-state forward, while determining the basic parameters of social struggles yet to come.

To follow through with the impact of these gendered foundations of modern Indian-state relations, I examine issues in the rise and devel-opment of indigenous movements from the 1940s through the early years of the twenty-first century, with attention to the ways in which nineteenth-century transformations helped to shape more recent indigenous history. First, mid-century changes offer evidence of both the positive and negative legacies of nineteenth-century nation-state formation. Dolores Cacuango was an important indigenous leader in the 1930s and 1940s, helping to found the Federación Ecuatoriana de Indígenas (Ecuadorian Indigenous Federation, or FEI), Ecuador's first national indigenous organization. Cacuango also worked to establish bilingual schools for indigenous children. Another major event was the 1964 agrarian reform law, which redistributed land in the Ecuadorian highlands. This law failed to meet the needs of the majority of poor Indians in the highlands, and indigenous women gained least of all. Finally, I discuss the new politics of ethnicity beginning in the mid 1980s, in which indigenous women have worked to mark out a place for themselves as activists, while struggling to address gender inequalities within their own communities as well as in the nation-state. Close examination of selected secondary, and a few Internet, sources on these periods reveals numerous ways in which nineteenth-century developments in Indian-state relations have shaped indigenous women's achievements and struggles throughout the twentieth century and into the new millennium. All three periods of history are full of multifaceted contradictions regarding Indians, gender, and the Ecuadorian nation. Rather than trying to resolve incongruities, however, my aim is to delve more deeply into the ambiguities themselves as a way to make sense of historical and contemporary Indian-state relations.

Patriarchal Contradictions and the Ecuadorian Nation, 1830–1925

Though the Indian problem loomed large over nation-state development from Independence forward, each proposed solution failed to resolve the dilemma of Indians' place within the imagined community of the nation. Instead, inequalities, racism, and exclusion remained central features of Ecuadorian society and politics. It was not simply that nothing changed in Indian-state relations, but that for every change or accomplishment, one encounters an equal and opposite limitation or failure. From 1830 to 1857, Ecuadorian state officials wrestled with the problem of Indian tribute. Though they worried over abolishing a system that kept both the government and the hacienda system afloat, lawmakers firmly believed in the necessity of terminating this holdover from the colonial period. When the abolition of tribute intensified rather than rectified racial inequalities, state officials had to find ways to justify Indians' ongoing secondary status. García Moreno ultimately denied the Indian problem, leaving Indian matters in the hands of local authorities, but this simply postponed the need to address Indians' status within the nation. Liberals picked up the theme again in 1895, constantly discussing and debating Indians' plight within the nation. Their vision, however, was to incorporate Indians as workers rather than citizens, and their limited reforms once again failed to get at the heart of indigenous problems within the Ecuadorian nation.

Permeating these three phases of nation-state formation was the specter of liberal individualism. Despite their many differences from each other, most leaders from Independence forward envisioned a nation-state based on the principles of individualism, equal rights, and participatory government. For all of them, indigenous peoples posed a considerable challenge to achieving their goal, a problem that resulted from three (interacting) sources. First, there was the legacy of colonial sociopolitical structures that had divided Indians and Spaniards into separate republics. In addition to clearly benefiting white-mestizo elites in ways they were reluctant to give up, the system of two republics provided indigenous peoples with protections, tax exemptions, and land rights that they wished to maintain. Second, elites' association of modernity and progress with European culture, politics, and society reinforced their conviction that indigenous people were unfit for incorporation into the nation. Indians represented backwardness, and their inclusion threatened to weaken the emergent nation, at least until they could be properly civilized out of their Indianness with education. Finally, there were problems with European-derived liberal theories, which had always excluded certain groups from citizenship rights based on their presumed inability to reason. However, political elites had proclaimed the goal of equality before the law, and indigenous peoples presented too large a portion of the population to ignore in the process of nation making. Because abolition intensified rather than relieved interethnic tensions, subsequent national leaders had to become increasingly creative as they rhetorically included, but in practice excluded, indigenous peoples from the nation.

Contradictory Indian-state relations were therefore a product of nation-state development that was itself paradoxical. Ecuadorian statesmen, court officials, and scholars turned to gender ideas to conceal the internal conflicts of nation-state formation and to rationalize policies of exclusion. Using gender to disguise racial inequalities was not new, and each ruling regime built on its predecessors' interethnic patriarchal constructs, whether they reinforced them overtly or proclaimed to reject them. Underlying every regime, from Flores's presidency in 1830 through Córdova's in 1925, one finds descriptions of Indian men who failed to achieve the masculine, rational maturity deemed necessary for their full inclusion in the political nation. The Indian problem was no less crucial in the early twentieth century than in 1830, and gendered solutions were just as elusive. However, by this time the nation-state was also taking more definitive shape, and the central state asserted itself in local politics and private spheres more deeply and successfully than it had in earlier eras. Furthermore, previous changes—especially the reduction of indigenous communal lands under García Moreno—made it easier for liberal reformers to hide the fundamental racism of their own policies. In many ways, liberals combined various elements of Garcian and Urvinista rhetoric and policies, placing them within a new modern and regional agenda.

Further complicating Indian-state relations were conflicts between state-sanctioned and indigenous gender ideologies. State officials and hacienda owners viewed gender norms as absolute and male powers as extensive, whereas indigenous patriarchy was more flexible and set limits on men's authority. Therefore, while both state and indigenous gender ideologies assumed women's subservience to and dependence on men, the contours of patriarchy were ethnically distinct. It was in the divergent aspects of these patriarchies that many important inter- and intraethnic developments took place. The alternative patriarchy practiced among indigenous peasants provided Indian men and women with a means to resist, or at least respond to, the underlying racism that went along with economic and political developments. Differing indigenous and state gender norms help to explain, for example, why indigenous women were critical to community defense even though they were largely overlooked in official state discourse. Indian peasant communities recognized women's capacity for independent action based on their economic, social, and cultural contributions to their families and villages. Such acknowledgement not only gave indigenous women negotiating power with their male peers but also enabled them to defend their communities. Indigenous men and women often showed a clear preference for their own gender ideas and practices, ignoring state-generated gender policies such as concubinage or divorce laws. In doing so, Indian peasants did more than continue to follow age-old gender customs; they also set limits on the reach of the state into the countryside.

The clash of indigenous and elite patriarchies also contributed to rising contradictions in indigenous gender relations. By 1900, Indian women were in a paradoxical position: they remained important to family and community survival, yet state policies and hacienda structure had rendered them vulnerable to elite gender ideologies. Both state policies and hacienda structures aimed at making indigenous women fit into elite gender norms, and this gave indigenous men leverage against their female peers. Indian women experienced their greatest limitations and losses on large estates, where they lacked any formal recognition of their labor value or access to land. This made their reliance on Indian men much greater, and it limited (but did not preclude) their participation in resistance. The links between indigenous and state-sanctioned patriarchies were more convoluted in autonomous peasant communities, where elite gender norms did not completely replace long-standing indigenous gender ideologies or practices. Instead, the two gender standards coexisted, leaving indigenous men and women to navigate between them in their relationships both with each other and with the state.

Contradictions in nation-state formation left indigenous men and women with uncertain status in the nation, albeit in different ways. Indian men, caught from Independence forward between manliness and minority status, often took advantage of their paradoxical position in the nation to advance their own or their communities' interests. Indian women's status was often ambiguous, but they were more clearly on the margins of nation making than were their male counterparts. At times this made them key defenders of their communities, but overall it left them in relatively weak positions to negotiate with political and economic elites.

Though there were tensions over Indian men's childlike condition versus their patriarchal rights, each ruling regime more adamantly identified and supported Indian manliness. Even Garcian officials acknowledged that all men had the right to rule over their families, though they asserted that Indian men abused their patriarchal power. By the early 1900s, liberal reformers recognized Indian men as rightful patriarchs with a place in the nation. A variety of political, social, and economic factors determined the extent to which Indian men could use the rising emphasis on their manliness to their own benefit. Certainly liberal rhetoric and policies of the 1850s and early 1900s encouraged indigenous men to seek state intervention; yet state officials were far more likely to support conciertos' rather than peasants' petitions. The negative views of Indians during Garcianismo made it harder for indigenous men to call on state assistance, but at times officials intervened on behalf of Indians when they thought estate owners had pushed their power too far. As images of Indian manliness became more prominent, interethnic paternalism was transformed, but it did not fade from view.

Indigenous peasant men's status was more deeply contradictory than conciertos'. In some ways, indigenous peasant men had the greatest flexibility to maneuver between indigenous and state gender ideologies, giving them an advantage over conciertos as well as over indigenous women. Peasant men also had the most secure patriarchal claims, because they did not formally answer to higher father figures as conciertos did. Yet when indigenous peasants defended their manhood, they met mixed reactions from state officials. Individual men asserting masculine authority over indigenous women were likely to succeed, mainly because they typically called on state-sanctioned gender ideologies to uphold their claims. They were, however, far less successful when they stood up to white-mestizo authorities to defend their manly dignity. Indian peasant men were more likely to win a case against an abusive state official by emphasizing their childlike vulnerability than their manly rights. They were least likely, even in the liberal period, to triumph in conflicts against hacendados, because members of the central state considered indigenous subsistence agriculture and communalism barriers to modernity and economic growth. Furthermore, indigenous peasants held fast to non-European customs that state officials identified as antiprogressive. Therefore, as much as hacienda owners and central statesmen disagreed on many issues, they agreed that indigenous peasants failed to advance the nation's economic and cultural interests and therefore had to be kept in check. In short, Indian men were obstacles to achieving European-style modernity and liberal individualism.

Conciertos were likewise caught between childlike dependence and masculine maturity; however, their relations with the state were often less openly strained than peasants' were. As Independence movements waxed and waned, when liberals came to power in the 1850s, and when they returned to power in the 1890s, government officials pondered how to resolve a system like concertaje with a nation founded on the concept of equality before the law. Conciertos could take advantage of these political moments to increase their demands against hacendados, asserting their manly dignity as well as addressing their economic needs. In fact, conciertos appear to have had greater success doing this than indigenous peasants did. This happened for two reasons: first, conciertos' predicament more clearly contradicted the tenets of liberal individualism than did indigenous peasants' situations. Moreover, concertaje provided central government officials with a useful tool in intra-elite power struggles; in contrast, upholding peasant rights did little to advance liberal statesmen's interests. With conciertos, statesmen focused on how to make them into better, and more dignified, manly workers—not undermine the large estate system itself. In spite of these limitations, conciertos found meaningful opportunities to improve their conditions by taking advantage of contests between elite patriarchs.

Largely absent from the discourse on the Indian problem, Indian women were nonetheless critical to developments in Indian-state relations. State-generated gender norms changed little over time, emphasizing women's inherent passivity and need for patriarchal protection. Even liberal reforms for women failed to challenge long-standing ideas about proper gender roles. These continuities make it easy to fall into the trap of seeing indigenous women's place in nation-state formation as either marginal or unchanging, but in fact it was neither, because Indian women were both the literal and figurative bodies on which social, economic, and political struggles between men occurred. Many of these contests were between elite men themselves, particularly in liberal regimes when tensions between the state and highland hacendados ran high. In these periods, the image of Indian women suffering because their husbands could not provide for them was crucial to state officials' attacks on the hacienda class. During Garcianismo, Indian women were supposedly accomplices to a deviant indigenous patriarchy that, in turn, helped to justify Indians' ongoing marginalization. Alliances, rather than struggles, between political and economic elites led to this particular image of indigenous women. Indian men, too, could use the symbol of Indian womanhood to their advantage. In the court system, indigenous men could point to their obligation to protect and provide for wives (and children) to strengthen complaints against elites, or to support their land rights. Though these strategies promised to improve women's as well as men's conditions, at other times indigenous men used women's peripheral position to undermine them. Women were also symbolically important to interethnic relations on large estates, despite their absence from hacienda records, because their presence established indigenous men's place within hacienda hierarchy. Estate owners and administrators who abused indigenous women did so as a means of keeping workers in their place and reminding indigenous husbands of their lowly status. There were therefore numerous ways in which Indian women's marginal and seemingly unchanging status was crucial to the conflicts and negotiations that went hand in hand with nation-state formation.

Patriarchy Reconsidered

Patriarchy—like nation, culture, or state—is a term that defies simplistic definitions or classification because it is both culturally specific and in constant historical motion. Patriarchy presents a process that is inextricably linked to and complicated by politics and culture, just as politics and culture are bound to and problematized by gender. Rather than obfuscate history, these untidy but tenacious connections between politics, ethnicity and race, and gender help to clarify the various influences that continue to shape the politics of ethnicity. In particular, the multiple and conflicting patriarchies at the heart of Ecuadorian nation-state formation help to resolve several questions. Though elite discourses on the Indian problem seemed to change little, the evolution of state patriarchy highlights important, if subtle, transformations in Indian-state relations. Attention to culturally distinct patriarchies not only explains different ways in which Indians and elites understood the struggle to make the nation, but also clarifies how and why one finds differing indigenous engagements with the formative nation-state. Women and men, conciertos and peasants, all found themselves in slightly different positions within the web of gender, culture, and nation. Lastly, these patriarchies reveal new ways in which top-down and bottom-up views of state formation interacted with each other to produce the modern nation in Ecuador. The rising importance of state-sanctioned gender concepts in this process explains indigenous women's declining roles in these encounters.

These findings for Ecuador relate to broader patterns in the growing field of historical studies of gender, race, and nation. Dominant groups tried to enforce European concepts of gender and nation on subalterns in cities as well as on indigenous peoples in the countryside. They did so in Peru, Bolivia, and Mexico as well as in Ecuador. They manipulated gender constructs to justify and legalize the marginalization of the poor and non-whites as well as women.[3] Yet members of nonwhite and poor societies who incorporated European-based ideas and rules did not simply reject their own customs; rather, they blended European models with their own convictions and traditions. As a result, both elite and subaltern concepts were transformed. Whether engaging in alternative patriarchy or fashioning alternative nationalisms, less-powerful groups reshaped and multiplied the meanings of gender and honor, nation and liberty.[4] Both elite and subaltern manipulations of gender tended to constrict women. For political elites, it was critical that women be excluded from politics and tied to strict honor codes, because this made the partial or potential inclusion of poor, nonwhite men in the nation more tangible.[5] The importance of patriarchal norms to political elites, combined with patriarchal ideas and practices among subalterns, meant that any democratizing aspects of citizenship and nation making rested on the exclusion and subordination of women.[6]

Parallel findings for cities as well as the countryside, or for Mesoamerica as well as the Andes, suggest the need to rethink long-used concepts and terms. Combining an examination of gender, Indians, and the nation requires that each of these categories be problematized and related to each other. The nation did not have a single or unchanging definition; rather, it carried multiple meanings that changed over time and according to one's socioeconomic and cultural position.[7] Political elites did not alone determine what the nation meant, and notions of inclusion and exclusion were relative rather than absolute. Gender concepts, and patriarchy in particular, functioned in a similar way. Though all patriarchies are founded on notions of male authority and female subservience, the meaning of male and female roles has fluctuated over time and differed among cultures.[8] Further, gender rights and obligations operated on a continuum, with men and women seeking to improve their conditions whenever and however they could.[9] Because gender, ethnicity, and nation were intertwined in history, they functioned in relation to each other in ways that made individuals' (and groups') experiences of historical change multidimensional. Opportunities in one arena often shut off possibilities in another, and vice versa. For example, interethnic paternalism that excluded indigenous men and women from the nation fostered a stronger sense of their shared local connections, including their commitment to indigenous gender norms. Conversely, when state officials successfully reached out to indigenous men as fellow patriarchs, indigenous gender ideologies were often compromised. Recognizing the connections between gender and ethnicity therefore deepens our understanding of the complex give-and-take that went into nation-state development. Specifically, while state officials used gender to *mask* their roles in perpetuating exploitation, gender helps the historian to *unmask* the uneven and contradictory development of the nation-state and its impact on indigenous peoples. The interplay between gender, Indians, and nation from 1830 to 1925 also set parameters for struggles yet to come. It is to these legacies that the next sections turn.

Indigenous Women at Mid-century

The masculinization of Indian-state relations in the liberal period was relative rather than absolute, and Indian women would over time find new ways to contribute to indigenous struggles. They would also face unprecedented challenges. To elaborate on some of these changes, it is useful to examine the life and accomplishments of Dolores Cacuango and the gender-specific effects of the 1964 agrarian reform law. Cacuango's life shows Indian women's adaptability as well as their rising importance as maintainers of authentic indigenous identity, whereas the 1964 law demonstrates that even as the Ecuadorian government altered landholding patterns in the highlands, it clung to preestablished gender ideas that widened the gender gap in power relations among indigenous men and women.

Dolores Cacuango was born on an hacienda in the canton of Cayambe (Pichincha) in 1881. She received no education and spent much of her childhood helping her parents with their work on the hacienda. As a youth, she worked as a domestic servant in Quito to help her parents pay off debts; there she learned Spanish and became convinced that education was crucial for indigenous peoples. After marrying another indigenous hacienda worker and having children of her own, she sent her only surviving son, Luís Catacuamba, to school; however, she had to pay her son's mestizo teacher to educate him rather than treat him like a servant. These experiences left her determined to establish bilingual programs for indigenous children, in which they would benefit from learning Spanish while also maintaining the Quichua language and Indian customs that were central to their identity.[10]

Cacuango's dream became a reality when she formed a friendship and partnership with Luisa Gómez de la Torre, who helped finance a school.[11] This school, where mostly indigenous (rather than mestizo) teachers taught the children of indigenous laborers, quickly became controversial. Hacienda owners fought the project, and some of their worst fears were fulfilled when children who attended Cacuango's school began accompanying their parents to review hacienda records, pointing out areas where the owners were either underpaying or over-charging workers. The state never intervened on behalf of the school, which was extralegal insofar as it was not state run, and it survived only because of the sheer will of its founders, teachers, and students.[12]

As impressive as her bilingual education project was, it was not Cacuango's only great achievement; she was also one of the leading indigenous political activists of her time.[13] Cacuango emerged as a leader in struggles against the hacienda system in Cayambe, and she worked to do away with the payment of diezmos. Drawn to leftist poli-tics, she was long associated with the Communist Party and some of its key leaders.[14] She was also cofounder, with fellow hacienda worker Jesús Gualavisí, of the FEI. Essentially, the FEI served as the peasant sector of the Ecuadorian Workers' Federation, which in turn had strong links to leftist political parties.[15] The FEI's stated goals strongly reflected Cacuango's longstanding commitments: to improve pay and working conditions on haciendas, end forced labor for women, and advance indigenous cultural dignity.[16]

Many themes in Cacuango's life story can be connected to devel-opments in nineteenth-century Indian-state relations. First, there is the prevalence of motherhood in her political involvements. Consider Cacuango's own description of her early attempts to move forward with her bilingual education project: "I don't remember the number of times, but each time I went to Quito, my job was also to go to the Ministry of Education, to the Administrative Office for the Province of Pichincha, to the Journalists' Union. . . . I always brought a petition, signed by the inhabitants where I lived, so that the petition would be more effective. They never gave me an answer, but I continued to insist so that one day they would understand that the Indian child also has the right to an education."[17] Cacuango—and many of those who later wrote about her—focused on her commitment to Indian children's education, which in turn was closely connected to her own motherhood experiences. She was clearly publicly active, as her political positions and frequent trips to Quito show. Yet she never blatantly discarded the idea that her primary role in life was as a mother; instead she reinforced this preconception. Scholars in the 1970s likewise implied that her experiences as a wife and mother led to her politicization and emergence as an indigenous leader.[18]

Cacuango's extension of her motherhood experiences into the public sphere took the notion that women belonged to the domestic sphere and turned it into a source of political strength. Rising emphasis on Indian motherhood was one of the central ways in which indigenous women were coming to represent authentic indigenous identity in mid-twentieth-century Ecuador. This was reinforced on haciendas by a socioeconomic system that rendered women invisible, while women in autonomous peasant communities became associated with indigenous culture because of rising male migration. Indian men were more frequently migrating either temporarily or permanently to the coast or to highland cities in search of work. In the process, many of them discarded the outward symbols of Indianness, speaking Spanish instead of Quichua and no longer wearing indigenous dress. Indian women, by default, became the symbols of authentic Indian identity because they more often stayed at home, maintained indigenous dress and customs, and were monolingual in Quichua.[19] Although indigenous motherhood became tactically important only in the mid-twentieth century, the ideological precedents for it came much earlier. It could well be that the identification of all Indian women with the home—attempted under Garcianismo, established on haciendas, and strengthened in the liberal period—affected Indian women's forms of protest in the mid-twentieth century.

It is hard to know how many indigenous women were able, like Dolores Cacuango, to use their domesticity as a springboard for political activism, but some evidence suggests that most women probably found this difficult. It appears, for example, that despite Cacuango's advances, far more indigenous men than women were involved in leftist politics.[20] Further, while Indian girls as well as boys went to Cacuango's bilingual school, the class list from the first year shows twice as many male as female students.[21] Evidence from contemporary studies on indigenous women suggests that a strong bias against girls' education runs deep and has a long history. As Juana stated, her own limited education resulted largely from the fact that "they said in earlier times that women don't need to know how to read and write . . . my father heard this and didn't let me finish primary school."[22]

Cacuango's exceptional achievements derived from her own character, but they also built on a history in which indigenous women made critical contributions to resistance. Though state officials assumed Indian women were inherently passive, the historical record reveals that they actively defended their individual and community interests. Like indigenous men, indigenous women made the most of elite ideologies whenever possible, often emphasizing their female vulnerability when they interacted with state officials. When Indian-state tensions ran high, as they did from 1869 to 1895, Indian women were critical to community defense. If a local official unfairly jailed indigenous men, or an hacendado forced them to work without formal contract, it was often female relatives who initiated grievances to release them. At other times Indian women stood alongside their husbands, or widows alongside married and widowed men, to defend their rights. When this happened, however, state officials often factored women out of cases, ignoring indigenous women and dealing directly with men. The phenomenon of indigenous women fading out of court records resulted from state-sanctioned gender ideologies and the laws that they generated, which assumed male action and female passivity. The hacienda system similarly marginalized indigenous women, making them difficult to find in historical records. In the nineteenth century, white-mestizo tendencies to ignore indigenous women meant that their ability to negotiate with state or landowning elites was quite limited. Beginning in the 1920s, however, the rise of leftist parties opened new avenues of political action for Indians, including women.[23] Further, because women were tied through custom rather than contract on haciendas, they did have greater mobility than indigenous men on these estates. That mobility enabled some women to become pivotal members of emerging labor organizations.[24]

Whereas Dolores Cacuango's life and work show indigenous women's changing political strategies, the 1964 agrarian reform law reveals how state officials' gender biases worked against indigenous women. Although liberals abolished imprisonment for debts in 1918, debt peonage on highland haciendas remained intact for several more decades. By the early 1960s, however, the system was coming under assault, and 1960 and 1961 saw rising agitation among hacienda workers, who demanded not only improved conditions, but also land redistribution and education. Some hacendados were themselves advocates of agrarian reform, though their reasons for supporting reform have been a subject of scholarly debate.[25] When a military government enacted the agrarian reform law in 1964, it gave any resident hacienda laborer who had lived on and farmed the same subsistence plot for at least ten years ownership of this parcel of land. The law also created the Ecuadorian Institute of Agrarian Reform and Colonization to mediate relations between estate owners and peasants and compensate hacienda owners for the expropriated lands.[26] The law marked only minimal improvements for indigenous peoples: because they received old subsistence plots, former hacienda workers gained control of only the poorest land from large estates.

Anthropologist Lynne Phillips has shown that the law was least beneficial to indigenous women. The government distributed plots of land only to men based on the assumption that they were the natural heads of their households, and that they would be the family members responsible for farming the land. State officials identified women with domestic duties rather than productive activities and excluded them from land redistribution. Yet peasant women (the majority of whom were Indians) were often the primary agriculturalists in their households, particularly since many men migrated to the coast and left women in charge of agricultural production.[27] Phillips's work shows that while the 1964 agrarian reform law benefited Indians in some ways by terminating the old hacienda system, it simultaneously disrupted power relations between indigenous men and women. The government's refusal to award land to Indian women was even more extreme than hacendados' previous practices with subsistence plots, since estate owners occasionally allowed Indian widows land rights after their husbands died. The agrarian reform law therefore intensified inequalities within indigenous communities by reinforcing Indian men's rights over both land and women. This was typical of development programs of the mid-twentieth century, which often resulted in gender imbalances due to project designers' own gender preconceptions.[28]

Such gender inequalities were neither new nor the product of timeless or universal patriarchal concepts. Historic relations between hacendados and conciertos were founded on women's exclusion; agrarian reform in the 1960s formalized this custom, giving it the weight of law. Additionally, one can find the influence of gender assumptions dating back to the liberal period, in which government leaders reinforced Indian men's patriarchal rights as a means of including them in the nation. In the 1960s, this practice was expanded to bolster Indian men's involvement with capitalist development at Indian women's expense. The 1964 reform law exacerbated indigenous gender inequalities, but the basic masculine ties between Indians and the state were rooted in the gender-specific state policies around the turn of the century.

Gender, Culture, and Politics since 1980

Indigenous women face multiple, overlapping, contradictory challenges in contemporary Ecuador. On the one hand, indigenous leaders recognize and celebrate women's past and present contributions to resistance. On the other hand, when women face gender discrimination within their communities, they have difficulty addressing it. Development programs, once geared exclusively toward men, are becoming more gender sensitive—yet they often focus on gender norms and expectations that reflect Western rather than indigenous views and practices. No single organization seems to be able to address indigenous women's problems: indigenous activists are reluctant to attend to the extent of gender problems, while feminists fail to incorporate indigenous women's views and goals. In short, many indigenous women are caught between their feelings of solidarity with indigenous men based on race and class oppression and their need to address gender inequalities within their communities.

Indigenous leaders tend to emphasize women's importance to cultural identity and activism, and they formally encourage female participation and leadership in the movement.[29] As Vicenta Chuma and Josefa Lema expressed, "We women essentially maintain the culture of our forebears, recreating it in everyday life . . . and keeping alive our principles and ethics."[30] Women are therefore guardians of the indigenous culture on which CONAIE's political actions are based.[31] Likewise, women's historical leadership in indigenous movements is celebrated. Yet these positive images also relegate women to traditional and domestic spaces that are supposedly timeless. Trying to change them, let alone critique them, is therefore incredibly complicated. Scholars have noted that the link between indigenous women and authentic identity derives not only from motherhood, but from sexism as well.[32] The association between indigenous women and culture has been mixed, at once opening and closing off opportunities for indigenous women.[33] Similar to the history of gender and Indian-state relations from 1830 to 1925, women's experiences of and responses to these roles varies depending on the particular situation in which they find themselves.

One outstanding feature of Ecuadorian indigenous movements is the prominent role of women leaders at the regional and national levels. The most famous is perhaps Nina Pacari, who has served over the years as legal counsel for CONAIE, a member of the Ecuadorian National Assembly, a minister of government, and a participant in the United Nations Permanent Forum on Indigenous Issues. Carmen Yamberla, María Vicenta

Chuma, and Josefa Lema are also prominent women leaders. Many of the women who establish themselves in leadership roles come from activist families, with fathers who have modeled and encouraged their political growth. Even more interesting is the fact that, despite the emphasis on maternalism in activist discourse, most national women leaders are themselves single and childless.[34] Married women have advanced more in local than national politics, though often not without some marital conflict along the way.[35] The paucity of married mothers, or women who rise to activism independent of male family members, harks back to patterns in the nineteenth century. Both state laws and indigenous gender norms tended to restrict married indigenous women's formal participation in community defense, while extralegal events like rebellions allowed women to surface as leaders. Now, weighted by both community and national history, indigenous women face the challenge of carving out unprecedented spaces in formal political arenas.[36]

These contexts make it difficult for indigenous women to confront indigenous patriarchy. Since the 1990s, however, increasing numbers of indigenous women have been speaking out about their male peers' attitudes, and about inequalities within their societies.[37] The tensions over addressing gender issues results from the combination of indigenous and state gender norms, and more specifically the interactions between the two systems over time. Indigenous masculinity is a sensitive issue, which is perhaps why many indigenous peoples point to Western culture as the source of indigenous patriarchy. The complexity of addressing indigenous gender inequalities is multilayered and grounded in the historical process of nation-state formation. Indigenous men are protective of their masculinity because racial hierarchies have long feminized them.[38] Such emasculation was (and is) not only personally humiliating, but also politically significant. This history makes the problem of indigenous domestic violence, at once the most urgent and controversial topic in this debate, highly charged in both indigenous and national cultures. As Prieto and colleagues have pointed out, "In the national imagination there exists the idea that indigenous women are naturally and systematically objects of violence which they resist only passively . . . [and] within the indigenous world gender violence plays upon the complex theme of communal and collective relations, articulated by the notion of complementarity."[39] These scholars point to two distinct yet interacting concepts that are well rooted in Ecuadorian national history. Not only does the idea of rampant indigenous domestic violence have a long history in white-mestizo culture, but it is an image that is inexorably bound to the history of the nation as well. Likewise, indigenous requirements for men's and women's complementary duties and rights have allowed men to punish their wives for a very long time, even if that right was subject to community rules and regulations.

Although more indigenous women are addressing gender inequalities, they do not often turn to feminists or feminist discourse to do so. In part, this is because feminists have tended to overlook indigenous women, though this has begun to change in recent years.[40] Yet indigenous women often openly state that they do not seek feminist solutions to their problems. As Ana María Guacho claimed, "we do not work for feminism, but rather for the integration of man and woman, for gender equity."[41] Indigenous women tend to see feminist goals as combative and are wary of white-mestizo feminists who may not understand the importance of indigenous culture. Despite the many shared concerns of white-mestizo feminists and indigenous women, their distinct cultures and histories have led them mostly to organize separately from each other. The foundations for this division lie in political and cultural histories tied to nation-state formation. Not only were indigenous and white-mestizo patriarchies at odds, but state policies treated the woman question and the Indian problem as separate categories, overlooking indigenous women in both cases. This separation led indigenous peoples and feminists to develop very different strategies when demanding change. It remains to be seen if indigenous women and white-mestizo feminists in Ecuador will be able to overcome this deep and historically rooted divide.

Both indigenous activists and feminists in Ecuador not only seek incorporation within the state but also advocate its transformation.[42] The problems these groups face, in bridging the gaps between women of different cultures and indigenous peoples of different genders, are embedded in the history of Ecuadorian nation making. By 1925, nation-state formation had divided women from Indians, and it had widened the gender gap between indigenous women and men. The fact that these separations continue speaks to the importance of gender in the process of nation-state formation, and the impact of the past on the present. In particular, the combination of long-established cultural and gender divisions helps to keep the state primarily in the hands of elite white men. Though Indian women have transformed their roles and found new ways to contribute to indigenous political movements, the masculine precedents of Indian-state relations established by 1925 help to explain the continuing obstacles that these women face in their quest to defend, dignify, and democratize indigenous political culture. In addition to confronting the state, they will have to contend with their past to build a better future.

Notes

Abbreviations Used in the Notes

Archivo Nacional de la Historia, Quito

ANH/Q:Cr	Criminales
ANH/Q:Gb	Gobierno
ANH/Q:I	Indígenas
ANH/Q:Tr	Tributos

Archivo Nacional de la Historia, Riobamba

ANH/R:Civ	Civiles
ANH/R:Cr	Criminales
ANH/R:Gb	Gobiernos
ANH/R:Hac	Haciendas

Preface

1. Mujeres Indígenas de la CONAIE, *Memorias*, 103, 95. All translations from Spanish are my own unless otherwise noted.

2. Information on CONAIE and modern Indian issues in Ecuador is abundant; for a few examples of interesting work, see CONAIE, *Las nacionalidades indígenas*; Almeida et al., *Sismo étnico*; Cornejo Menacho, *Indios*; Wray et al., *Derecho, pueblos indígenas*.

3. While indigenous peoples make up much of the membership and leadership of Pachakutik, the party is an umbrella organization that is open to men and women of all walks of life, not just indigenous peoples.

4. See Selverston, "The Politics of Culture." On the coup of January 2000, see Hernández et al., *21 de enero*; Lucas, *La rebelión*; O'Connor, "Indians and National Salvation."

5. For an example, see Indigenous Alliance of the Americas, "Declaration of Quito."

6. Mujeres Indígenas de la CONAIE, *Memorias*, 2–4; CONAIE, *Las nacionalidades indígenas*, 272.

7. Chatterjee, *The Nation*.

8. Hyman, *Gender and Assimilation*.

9. See, for example, CONAIE, "Political Declaration."

10. The mid-twentieth century also was a critical period in shaping indigenous activism and gender relations. See Becker, "Class and Ethnicity"; Pallares, *From Peasant Struggles*.

11. Scott, "Gender," 42, 45. For other foundational discussions of gender, see Gordon, "What's New"; Tilly, "Gender"; McGee Deutsch, "Gender and Sociopolitical Change."

12. Lerner, *The Creation of Patriarchy*, 239.

13. Premo, *Children*, 10.

14. The concept of studying terms "in historical motion" is from Joseph and Nugent, "Popular Culture," 13.

15. For other discussions of multiple and changing patriarchies and gender codes, see Chatterjee, *The Nation*, 9; McClintock, "No Longer in a Future Heaven," 109; Christiansen, *Disobedience*, 1–4; Dore, *Myths of Modernity*, 60.

16. Christiansen, *Disobedience*, 40–49; Barragán Romano, "'Spirit' of Bolivian Laws," 67–68.

17. Chambers, *From Subjects to Citizens*, especially 8 and 254.

18. Walker, *Smoldering Ashes*, 69.

19. Dore, *Myths of Modernity*, 61.

20. Walker, *Smoldering Ashes*, 81–83; Christiansen, *Disobedience*, especially chapter 5.

21. For three excellent discussions of the usefulness of criminal cases for peasant histories, see Taylor, *Drinking*; Stern, *The Secret History*; Kanter, "Hijos del Pueblo."

22. Christiansen, *Disobedience*, 12, 17.

Chapter 1. National Dilemmas

1. Ministro del Interior, *Exposición* 1856, 17–18.

2. Cueva, "Nuestra organización social," 50, 58.

3. I use the term "statesmen" because political officials during the period under study were all men; a gender-neutral term would be misleading.

4. For classic studies, see Anderson, *Imagined Communities*; Hobsbawm, *Nations and Nationalism*; Corrigan and Sayer, *The Great Arch*. For questions of these views, see Chatterjee, *The Nation*, 6, in which he states that Indian nationalism was both material (political, borrowed from the West) and spiritual (cultural, developed in contrast to the West).

5. Abrams, "Notes on the Difficulty," 72, 75–77, 82.

6. Guerrero, "Administration of Dominated Populations."

7. Anderson, *Imagined Communities*; Hobsbawm, *Nations and Nationalism*; Corrigan and Sayer, *The Great Arch*.

8. Thurner, *From Two Republics*, 2.

9. Ibid., 5–6; Guardino, *Peasants*, 11.

10. My understanding of the importance of liberal individualism resulted from the November 2002 meeting of the Washington Area Symposium on the History of Latin America, held that year at the University of Maryland. Symposium members' generous comments and insights on my work pushed me to think about gender, race, and nation in new ways.

11. Mehta, "Liberal Strategies of Exclusion," 427.

12. Ibid., 430–31, 436 (quotation on 436).

13. Mallon, *Peasant and Nation*; Guardino, *Peasants* and "Barbarism or Republican Law?"

14. Mallon, *Peasant and Nation*; Guardino, *Peasants* and "Barbarism or Republican Law?" Also see Grandin, *The Blood of Guatemala*; Thurner, *From Two Republics*; Walker, *Smoldering Ashes*.

15. For particularly nice discussions of Peru, see Walker, *Smoldering Ashes*, and Méndez, *The Plebeian Republic*.

16. Thurner, "'Republicanos.'"

17. Mallon, *Peasant and Nation*; Guardino, *Peasants*, and "Barbarism or Republican Law?"

18. Walker, *Smoldering Ashes*, 209–19.

19. Some scholars who advanced the field through seemingly gender-neutral work are now beginning to add gender to their analytical toolbox. See, for example, Guardino, "Community Service, Liberal Law."

20. For examples of important studies that have taken commoners' views into account, see Méndez, *The Plebeian Republic*; Sattar, "An Unresolved Inheritance." Walker's *Smoldering Ashes* also includes various indigenous perspectives.

21. For some top-down studies, see Van Aken, "Lingering Death"; Muratorio,

"Nación, identidad, y etnicidad"; Guerrero, "Construction" and "Administration of Dominated Populations." For studies that consider indigenous responses, see Guerrero, "Curagas y tenientes politicos"; Ibarra, *Nos encontramos amenazados*; M. Moscoso, "La tierra" and "Comunidad"; Clark, "Indians."

22. Sattar, "An Unresolved Inheritance"; Williams, "Negotiating the State" and "Indian Servitude."

23. Clark, *The Redemptive Work*, 215.

24. For excellent studies on the formation of Indian culture in colonial Ecuador, see Salomon, *Native Lords of Quito*; Powers, *Andean Journeys*; Newson, *Life and Death*.

25. See Moreno Yánez, *Sublevaciones indígenas*, 392–94; Guerrero, "Curagas y tenientes politicos."

26. A good, concise, and classic discussion of these ideas can be found in Taylor, *Drinking*, 17–19, 43–44, 105–6.

27. Typically, estates in the north-central highlands of the late colonial and early republican eras combined haciendas where sheep were raised and obrajes where textiles were produced.

28. Both the coastal cacao boom and the obraje decline were related to the Bourbon reforms, particularly trade policies that undermined highland textile businesses while opening new markets for cacao. Eighteenth-century economic crises in the highlands were also due to natural disasters, mainly earthquakes. For discussions of the differential coastal and highland economies in the late colonial period, see Hurtado, *Political Power in Ecuador*, 7, 28–32; Phelan, *The Kingdom of Quito*; Chiriboga, *Jornaleros y gran propietarios*; Contreras, "Guayaquil y su región," 196.

29. See Saint-Geours, "La sierra centro y norte," 147; Chiriboga, *Jornaleros y gran propietarios*, 93.

30. The southern highlands had a different economic pattern. See Palomeque, *Cuenca*.

31. For an example of the ways the new categories of mestizos and forasteros led to disputes between religious orders and secular priests, see Powers, "Battle for Bodies and Souls."

32. Hurtado, *Political Power in Ecuador*, 28–32; Chiriboga, *Jornaleros y gran propietarios*, 13; Contreras, "Guayaquil y su región," 196.

33. Van Aken, "Lingering Death," 444, 447, 449.

34. "Supresión del tributo indígena (1857)," in Ayala Mora, *Nueva historia*, 15:161–62.

35. Silva, "Estado, iglesia, e ideología," 17–20. For information on García

Moreno's youth, see Demélas and Saint-Geours, *Jerusalén y babilonia*, chapter 9; also see Efren Reyes, *Breve historia*, 134.

36. Demélas and Saint-Geours, *Jerusalén y babilonia*, 152.

37. Efren Reyes, *Breve historia*, 145; Ayala Mora and Cordero, "El período Garciano," 226–30. By the late nineteenth century, the Church owned a great deal of property, especially in the north-central highland provinces of Pichincha and Chimborazo.

38. Williams, "Making of Ecuador's Pueblo Católico," 210, 221.

39. Demélas and Saint-Geours, *Jerusalén y babilonia*, 163–64.

40. This stipulation was made in the 1869 constitution, known as the *carta negra* (black letter) by its opponents.

41. Williams, "Making of Ecuador's Pueblo Católico," 207–8.

42. Ibid., 221.

43. Borrero won more votes for his presidency than any other Ecuadorian presidential candidate in the nineteenth century, but the expectations that various elite groups placed on him were so high and conflicting that he was unable to maintain political power for long.

44. Ventimilla's rule raises an interesting aspect of liberalism in this period: coastal liberals—including Eloy Alfaro and many other members of the 1895 liberal revolution— were responsible for getting Ventimilla into the presidency and taking him out of it.

45. Ortiz Crespo, "Panorama histórico."

46. Coastal liberals declared a new national government in Guayaquil in June 1895. After a few months of battles between liberal and conservative forces, the liberal regime was more securely established and had control of the capital city, Quito. Intermittent battles did still break out, however, until about 1900.

47. See the 1904 "Ley de Cultos" in Ayala Mora, *Nueva historia*, 15:223.

48. For an example of conciertos described as good workers, see ANH/Q:Cr, May 4, 1901.

49. Espinosa, "Hacienda, concertaje y comunidad," 139.

50. During the liberal era, highland landowners proved they could handle modern crises with great skill. See Clark, "El 'bienestar nacional,'" 62–64, 66–68.

51. Jaramillo Alvarado, *El indio ecuatoriano*, 3.

52. Saint-Geours, "La sierra centro y norte," 168.

53. Guerrero, *La semántica*, 82–83.

54. Clark, *The Redemptive Work*.

55. Corrigan and Sayer, *The Great Arch*, 12, 36–37; McClintock, "No Longer in a Future Heaven," 89.

56. Dore, "One Step Forward."

57. Earle, "Rape and the Anxious Republic," 140; Dore, *Myths of Modernity*, 63–64.

58. Chambers, *From Subjects to Citizens*, especially p. 5 and chapters 5 and 6.

59. Barragán Romano, "'Spirit' of Bolivian Laws"; Guerrero, "Administration of Dominated Populations."

60. Chambers, *From Subjects to Citizens*.

61. Caulfield, Chambers, and Putnam, "Introduction"; Dore, "One Step Forward."

62. For a discussion of the limitations of male power in colonial Ecuador, see Gauderman, *Women's Lives*. Though I disagree with Gauderman's assertion that colonial society was "not patriarchal," she offers crucial evidence of substantial limits and complexities to patriarchal authority at the time.

63. Examples are numerous: see Caulfield, Chambers, and Putnam, *Honor, Status, and Law*; Dore and Molineaux, *Hidden Histories of Gender*; Fowler-Salamini and Vaughan, *Women of the Mexican Countryside*; Besse, *Restructuring Patriarchy*.

64. Grandin, *The Blood of Guatemala*, particularly 36, 185–97.

65. Mallon, *Peasant and Nation*, especially xix, 74–85.

66. There are clear parallels, in this sense, between Mallon's work on Latin America and Chatterjee's work on India. Chatterjee's work, however, lacked gender analysis for the peasantry. He even refers to the peasant as "he" on a few occasions. See *The Nation*, chapter 8.

Chapter 2. Making Ecuadorians?

1. Noboa, *Recopilación*, 2:336.

2. This law is available in numerous texts. See, for example, Freile-Granizo, "Leyes indigenistas," 234–35.

3. For a few of the most important examples, see Van Aken, "Lingering Death"; Platt, *Estado boliviano*; Thurner, *From Two Republics*.

4. Andrea and Overfield, *The Human Record*, 21.

5. Premo, *Children*, 27, 31–40.

6. Milton and Vinson, "Counting Heads," paragraph 6.

7. Walker, *Smoldering Ashes*, 203–4.

8. Taylor, *Drinking*, 17–27; also see Premo, *Children*, 40.

9. The Incas also collected tribute from adult men as representatives of their households, but they focused exclusively on married men; the Spanish collected the tax from adult Indian men regardless of their marital status. See Silverblatt, *Moon, Sun, and Witches*, 126–31.

10. "Ley de Octubre de 1821," cited in Sattar, "An Unresolved Inheritance," 118.

11. Earle, "Rape and the Anxious Republic," 132–35.

12. Bolívar's quotations are cited in Cherpak, "Participation of Women," 222, 230. Also see Earle, "Rape and the Anxious Republic," 132–35.

13. "Establecimiento de la contribución personal de indígenas (1828)," in Ayala Mora, *Nueva historia*, 15:112.

14. Rodríguez O., *The Independence of Spanish America*, 220, 234; Ayala Mora, *El Bolivarianismo*, 37, 39.

15. "Constitución del Estado del Ecuador (1830)," in Ayala Mora, *Nueva historia*, 15:136.

16. Ministro del Interior, *Exposición* 1856, 17, emphasis in the original.

17. *Primer registro auténtico nacional*, November 8, 1831. The transcript of Flores's speech, made on January 15, 1841, appeared in the national newspaper *Gaceta del Ecuador*, no. 372, on January 24, 1841.

18. Guerrero, "Administration of Dominated Populations," 277–84. Also see Van Aken, "Lingering Death," 445.

19. Sattar, "An Unresolved Inheritance," 152–55.

20. Ayala Mora, "La fundación de la república," 149–55; Guerrero, "Administration of Dominated Populations"; Williams, "Indian Servitude."

21. Bolívar, "Establecimiento de la Contribución Personal de Indígenas," arts. 16, 18, and 23, in Ayala Mora, *Nueva historia*, 15:115–17.

22. Van Aken, "Lingering Death," 457.

23. Freile-Granizo, "Leyes indigenistas," 41–43.

24. *Primer registro auténtico nacional*, no. 9, 1935. Also see no. 46, 1837.

25. In addition to statements already cited, see the 1847 statement by Carlos Tamayo, secretary of the House of Representatives, in Costales and Costales, "Recopilación," 623–25.

26. Freile-Granizo, "Leyes indigenistas," 39–41.

27. Ibid., 65, regarding an 1853 law to expand primary schooling in Imbabura province. While in theory this law was meant to help Indians, it was to be funded with a salt tax that would be especially burdensome on the rural poor, the majority of whom were indigenous.

28. *Primer registro auténtico nacional*, no. 27, 1836.

29. *El seis de Marzo*, no. 132, December 5, 1854, art. 8. For colonial foundations to these shifting requirements of castas, see Milton and Vinson, "Counting Heads."

30. *Primer registro auténtico nacional*, no. 9, 1835.

31. Van Aken, "Lingering Death," 437.

32. Ibid.

33. ANH/Q:Tr, May 30, 1849, folio 101.

34. Freile-Granizo, "Leyes indigenistas," 41–43.

35. Noboa, *Recopilación*, 2:196.

36. *El deis de Marzo*, no. 132, December 5, 1854.

37. Ministro del Interior, *Exposición* 1856, 17–18.

38. *El seis de Marzo*, no. 132, December 5, 1854, art. 47.

39. *El nacional*, no. 52, December 22, 1846; the circular in which the communication appeared was dated October 22, 1846.

40. Costales and Costales, "Recopilación," 620.

41. A good synopsis of these roles is in the National Convention's 1851 "Ley de contribución de indígenas," in which the role of protectors was defined, reprinted in Freile-Granizo, "Leyes indigenistas," 62.

42. Noboa, *Recopilación*, 2:195–97; for the 1854 law, see *El seis de Marzo*, no. 132, December 5, 1854.

43. Sattar, "An Unresolved Inheritance," 155–56, based on Costales and Costales, "Recopilación," 640.

44. Guerrero, "Curagas y tenientes politicos," 334–35.

45. Costales and Costales, "Recopilación," 644–45.

46. Emphasis mine; ANH/Q:I, May 13, 1820; September 5, 1818. Indigenous peasants of Guasuntos won the first case, in which they charged that they were being illegally subjected to fines and forced payments for celebrations that were not sanctioned by law; in the second case, conciertos from Ibarra made a similar plea but lost because the judges decided that the hacendado had a right to hold them to other payments because of the conciertos' childlike status.

47. Freile-Granizo, "Leyes indigenistas," 41–43.

48. For an excellent discussion of hacendados' position relative to the central state in this period, see Williams, "Negotiating the State," 33.

49. The relationship between resident workers and owners or renters of haciendas was complex and ripe with manipulations of gender ideas and practices; see chapter 6 for in-depth discussions of these dynamics.

50. Minister of the Interior Manuel Gomes de la Torre sent a circular to all provincial governors in 1849 to have them put a stop to such practices. See *El nacional*, no. 223, March 13, 1849.

51. *Gaceta del Ecuador*, no. 349, August 16, 1840.

52. My analysis of multiple patriarchs was influenced by Stern, The *Secret History*, especially chapter 4.

53. *El seis de Marzo*, no. 132, December 5, 1854.

54. Williams, "Negotiating the State," especially chapter 2.

55. *El seis de Marzo*, no. 187, January 27, 1856. Thanks to Derek Williams for initially bringing this document to my attention.

56. ANH/Q:I, February 7, 1811; April 29, 1811; August 7, 1811; May 24, 1816; February 7, 1817. On hacendados' views in the 1850s and 1860s, see Williams, "Negotiating the State," 108–11.

57. ANH/Q:Cr, September 10, 1856. I say here that the court "appear to have" dismissed the case because the final decision was not available. However, the prosecutor himself recommended dismissal of charges, suggesting de la Guerra was freed. It also appears that de la Guerra was at the center of local political power struggles in Alausí, where he was jefe politico in the 1850s, because other local officials brought criminal charges against him several times.

58. In one instance the Indians' attorney indicated that the dispute was with don Ventura Mancheno, rather than with Carlos Zambrano, who was at one point referred to as Mancheno's successor. Information on this dispute comes from five separate documents in the Riobamba archive: ANH/R:Civ, August 19, 1845; October 10, 1845; October 25, 1845; November 18, 1845; "Seguidos por el sor Carlos Zambrano," n.d.

59. ANH/R:Civ, October 10, 1845.

60. Zambrano's most ardent arguments appear in ANH/R:Civ, October 25, 1845, and in "Seguidos por el sor Carlos Zambrano," n.d.

61. See Williams, "Negotiating the State"; and Palomeque, *Cuenca*.

62. *Primer registro auténtico nacional*, no. 21, 1836.

63. Noboa, *Recopilación*, 2:167.

64. Seeking protection from a local hacendado, however, did not necessarily mean giving up one's own parcel of land in his community of origin, particularly in regions with labor shortages, as Palomeque notes in *Cuenca*, 144.

65. The relationship between hacienda owners or renters with indigenous workers involved sophisticated gendered rules of interaction. For further information, see chapter 6.

66. ANH/Q:Tr, November 27, 1847. This hacienda was in Baños, near Cuenca.

67. Van Aken, "Lingering Death," 437.

68. ANH/Q:I, May 17, 1834. By the republican period, this response had already been well established. For example, conciertos from the Independence period called upon Supreme Court judges to protect them "as Judge *and Father* of us miserable, defenseless Indians," or proclaimed "I implore that with your caring heart you look upon me *as a Father*." Emphasis mine. See ANH/Q:I, March 12, 1818, and November 14, 1814, respectively.

69. ANH/R:Civ, October 28, 1845.

70. A summary of the petition and the congressional response appeared in *Primer registro auténtico nacional*, no. 40, 1837.

71. Costales and Costales, "Recopilación," 682.

72. Ibid.

73. Van Aken, "Lingering Death," 435–37.

74. ANH/R:Cr, January 29, 1831.

75. ANH/Q:Cr, April 3, 1856. In the end, Supreme Court judges threw the case out on a series of technicalities regarding the officials involved in the proceedings at the local and regional levels.

76. ANH/Q:I, March 18, 1823.

77. ANH/Q:Cr, March 24, 1857, folio 53; for similar pleas in the next case on this same matter, see ANH/Q:Cr, April 24, 1857.

78. Even Indian men living and working on highland haciendas asserted their masculinity and patriarchal rights at certain times; see chapter 6 for detailed discussion.

79. See ANH/Q:I, November 5, 1846; January 20, 1847; October 14, 1847; January 18, 1848; November 7, 1848; January 31, 1849; March 14, 1849; June 6, 1849. Of these, only the last petition was denied.

80. Guerrero has been concerned with this issue in recent years. See his "Administration of Dominated Populations," 299–304, and "Construction," 588–89.

81. Minister of the Interior, *Exposición* 1858, 6–9.

82. ANH/Q, vol. 1, 1858, as cited in Fuentealba, "La sociedad indígena," 56. There were also a number of uprisings in the southern highland province of Loja.

83. Minister of the Interior, *Exposición* 1858, 7; on page 6, he also referred to indigenous uprisings that resulted from new and even increased burdens Indians experienced after the abolition of tribute.

84. ANH/Q:Cr, January 29, 1858.

85. ANH/Q:Cr, April 21, 1858. It is not clear who won this dispute between Paredes and the Indian peasants of Pelileo.

86. ANH/Q:Cr, February 18, 1858. Though this court record shows that Pulla was absolved of the charges, in another case in the same folder, dated August 20, 1858, the state prosecutor requested that the first case be voided and Pulla punished; the results of that case were unclear. For another uprising in which a similar defense was used, see ANH/Q:Cr, June 18, 1858, in which Acencio Mantilla and associates were charged with initiating an uprising in Guano (Chimborazo). In this case, however, the defendants were not clearly labeled indigenous as

they were in other cases mentioned here, and they may have been mestizos, since Guano was a predominantly mestizo town by the nineteenth century. This case therefore offers a reminder that the language of interethnic and interclass political paternalism was not the exclusive domain of Ecuador's indigenous peoples.

87. Williams, "Negotiating the State," especially chapter 3.

88. *El nacional*, no. 44, June 11, 1861. This requirement is in article 26 of the law.

89. These patterns are evident from review of nineteenth-century civil and criminal court cases from the superior court in Riobamba. See chapter 3 for further discussion.

90. ANH/Q:I, February 15, 1873; see also ANH/R:Gb, January 14, 1874. Though Pinto claimed that Indians were regularly exempt from court fees, my review of court cases from Chimborazo province suggests that the practice was inconsistent.

91. *El nacional*, no. 426, May 11, 1870.

92. Guerrero, "Curagas y tenientes políticos," 327–28, 334–35, 350. Guerrero also notes, on 350, that even after the abolition of tribute, caciques helped to gather Indians for the trabajo subsidiario.

93. Palomeque, "Estado y comunidad," 398. This information also comes from my own review of civil and criminal cases in the ANH/R for the 1860s and 1870s.

Chapter 3. Garcianismo

1. "La voz del deber." Thanks to Derek Williams for bringing this document to my attention.

2. ANH/Q:Cr, December 19, 1874, folios 3–4.

3. Guerrero, "Construction," 558.

4. Saint-Geours, "La sierra centro," 155–56; M. Moscoso, "La tierra," 367–69, 375; Fuentealba, "La sociedad indígena," 56–73.

5. See Costales and Costales, "Recopilación," 700–3.

6. For examples of court disputes over abuses of these requirements, see ANH/Q:Cr, August 30, 1867; January 5, 1869; December 22, 1869; October 29, 1871. There was one exception to the age and gender parameters for the contribución subsidiaria: if a person—regardless of age or gender—had property valued at two hundred pesos or more, or rental property of at least five hundred pesos in value, they had to pay the contribución subsidiaria (subsidiary contribution).

7. República del Ecuador, *Diario*, 1861, as cited in Ayala Mora and Cordero, "El período Garciano," 217.

8. Gustavo de Almenara, 1876, as cited in G. Moscoso, "Las imágenes," 95.

9. República del Ecuador, *Código civil* (1860), art. 1734. See also arts. 124, 128,

130, 134, and 136 for further details on the limitations on wives' actions in the public sphere.

10. Such use of patriarchy was typical to state formation. See Corrigan and Sayer, *The Great Arch*, particularly pages 22, 36–37, 132–34, and 169. These passages highlight how both class-based state paternalism and the exclusion of women were central to state formation.

11. See M. Moscoso, "Discurso religioso," 24–25.

12. Ibid., 35–38, especially 38.

13. República del Ecuador, *Código civil* (1860), arts. 162–69.

14. *El nacional*, May 22, 1869. This decree also stipulated the punishment for incest, sedition and rebellion, and "abominable offenses"—the last of which was most likely male homosexuality.

15. For examples of such decisions, see ANH/Q:Cr, October 21, 1871 (acquitted); November 3, 1871 (guilty); January 13, 1872 (acquitted); March 2, 1872 (acquitted); May 7, 1872 (acquitted); August 9, 1872 (acquitted); January 22, 1873 (acquitted); March 29, 1873 (guilty); November 29, 1873 (acquitted); October 20, 1873 (guilty); February 18, 1874 (acquitted); September 23, 1874 (guilty); September 30, 1874 (guilty).

16. For rusticidad arguments, see ANH/Q:Cr, November 17, 1871; October 30, 1872; March 1873. For "good reputation" arguments, see the same document series: August 9, 1872; May 10, 1873; April 22, 1875.

17. ANH/Q:Cr, December 17, 1873, and May 10, 1873, respectively.

18. *El nacional*, March 15, 1870.

19. It is likely, though not yet closely studied, that concubinage charges may have sometimes been brought against innocent men and women by their social enemies or competitors as a way of harming their reputations. Even in this case, the state itself gained power by mediating such interpersonal disputes.

20. *El nacional*, February 27, 1875. Goetschel identified Bertram as the author of the piece in her article "El discurso," in a footnote on 87. However, no author was listed in the national newspaper itself. Segments of this opinion piece appear in 1875 editions of *El nacional* between February 17 and March 10.

21. Ibid., February 27, 1875.

22. Ibid., February 17, 1875. Reference to this ability of alcohol to turn a man into a virtual beast appeared in an earlier opinion piece (most likely originally from France, though translated from a United States English version) in *El nacional*, October 6, 1871. For more general examples of the impact of drinking on morality, see *El nacional*, February 20 and 24, 1875.

23. García Moreno, *Escritos*, 217–19.

24. *El nacional*, February 24, 1875. Other references to drunken men's financial

irresponsibility, by wasting money on drink or failing to work to bring in money for the family, appear on February 13 and February 24.

25. Ibid., February 20, 1875.

26. Ibid., February 24, 1875. Other tragic consequences of drunkenness cited in this series of articles included suicide (to which a reference appears on March 3), and beating one's own father (a different kind of disdain for patriarchal authority. Reference on February 20).

27. Such claims were not unique to Ecuador: Nicaraguan president Fruto Chamorro made a similar claim about his own nation in 1853. See Dore, *Myths of Modernity*, 64.

28. León Mera, *Catecismo*, 33.

29. Ibid.

30. Ibid., 34.

31. For one of the more important discussions of how these notions fit into the broader ideas of progress in nineteenth-century Latin America, see Burns, *The Poverty of Progress*.

32. Orton, *The Andes and the Amazon*, 111–12.

33. Fermín Cevallos, *Resumen*, 86.

34. ANH/Q:Cr, May 3, 1871. Also see ANH/Q:Cr, September 5, 1872, in which the defense attorney questioned Indians' ability to understand the law and asserted the fatherly role of employers. Both of these were concubinage cases.

35. *El nacional*, September 21, 1870.

36. García Moreno, *Escritos*, 283. García Moreno's reference to the interior provinces here reflects an important distinction made between Ecuadorian Indians in the nineteenth century, in which highland Indians were seen as "socialized" and tropical Indians as completely "savage." A good example is Fermín Cevallos, *Resumen*, 160–67, in which he discusses the gendered brutality of "savage" Indians like the Shuar (to whom he gave the derogatory label Jívaros), who practice polygamy and bury wives with their husbands. He claimed on 167 that "the state of war is the natural state for savages … for them, woman is a conquest, the spoils of glory." Such claims do not hold up to ethnographic scrutiny, and there is evidence that the Shuar considered women independent individuals with rights of their own. For further discussion of this, see Lane, *Quito 1599*, 146–47.

37. Whether or not literate Indians would have been able to exercise this legal right to vote is another matter, considering that literate Indians had trouble voting in the twentieth century. Thanks to Marc Becker for pointing this out.

38. Ministro del Interior, *Exposición 1867*, 14–16.

39. For an analysis of this statue, see Muratorio, "Nación, identidad, y etnicidad," 169–73; a photo of the statue appears on 171.

40. ANH/Q:Cr, December 19, 1874, folios 3–4; emphasis added.

41. Ibid.

42. Ibid.; emphasis added.

43. Examples of leniency in cases of indigenous domestic violence appear in ANH/R:Cr, November 11, 1880, and in ANH/R:Cr, February 6, 1875. For cases of sexual assault, see ANH/R:Cr, January 21, 1875; ANH/Q:Cr, June 21, 1873; and ANH/R:Cr, June 19, 1872. Also see G. Moscoso, "La violencia," 196–200.

44. G. Moscoso, "La violencia," 190, 192–93, 195–96.

45. Examples in ANH/R:Cr, February 25, 1870; January 9, 1865; January 30, 1908; February 25, 1870; October 27, 1870; February 28, 1873; March 19, 1870, folios 44–47.

46. Hassaurek, *Four Years*, 132.

47. ANH/R:Cr, April 23, 1864, folio 69; emphasis added.

48. Fermín Cevallos, *Resumen*, 86 and 131, respectively.

49. This idea was not new to the republican period, though the ways men in power manipulated the notion were. See Taylor, *Drinking*, chapter 2.

50. ANH/R:Cr, August 16, 1870; October 31, 1870.

51. García Moreno, *Escritos*, 292.

52. Ministro del Interior, *Exposición 1873*, 4.

53. For further discussions and questions regarding this uprising and how it has been analyzed, see chapter 5.

54. *El nacional*, nos. 407, February 17, 1875, and 408, February 20, 1875.

55. Ibid., no. 408, February 20, 1875; emphasis added. The reference to "lack of education" could well refer to poor upbringing, which the elite readership of the national newspaper would identify as a trait of Indians and other poor, marginalized groups.

56. ANH/R:Cr, July 24, 1872. The defense lawyer was Vicente Espinosa, whose clients Mauricio Heredia and Francisco Perez were charged with the arbitrary arrest of indigenous peoples in Licto. The defense claimed the Indians had failed to pay required diezmos; Espinosa also emphasized that the Indian witnesses did not understand what they were testifying to, and that they were simply being manipulated. The outcome of the case is unknown.

57. ANH/R:Civ, April 15, 1872, and July 31, 1872.

58. For tierras baldías, see ANH/R:Civ, July 7, 1870; September 5, 1870 (quoted); September 30, 1870.

59. Examples are numerous for Chimborazo: see ANH/R:Civ, October 22, 1866; December 5, 1866; June 25, 1866; June 28, 1867; November 27, 1867; July 6, 1869; December 18, 1870; February 6, 1871; June 10, 1874; August 22, 1874; July 6, 1875.

60. For discussions of hacienda expansion, see Chiriboga, *Jornaleros y gran propietarios*; and Saint-Geours, "La sierra centro," 143–88.

61. In addition to the Asencio López case from ANH/Q:Cr, December 19, 1874, see ANH/R:Cr, October 12, 1865.

62. ANH/R:Civ, July 25, 1870; the plea did not work because the complaint was found "sin lugar" (without cause).

63. ANH/R:Cr, February 23, 1871.

64. This claim reflects an Ecuadorian proverb from the nineteenth century: "For the rich who robs the garden there is no law, no judge, no prison; but if a poor man steals a crumb the thief goes to jail." This quotation appears in Burns, *The Poverty of Progress*, 95.

65. ANH/R:Civ, June 19, 1866.

66. ANH/R:Civ, January 16, 1873; for similar assertions, see ANH/R:Cr, December 29, 1890.

67. ANH/R:Cr, September 11, 1871, folio 18.

68. Ibid., folio 17.

69. ANH/R:Cr, June 3, 1871. Sepada was found guilty, and possibly Biqui was as well, but Cárdenas was found innocent.

70. ANH/R:Civ, June 16, 1866. The outcome of the case is unknown.

71. Ibid., folio 2.

72. ANH/R:Civ, January 16, 1866.

73. ANH/R:Cr, November 17, 1874. Officials emphasized their patriarchal honor in other ways and for other reasons, as when Antonio Cárdenas, facing charges for not fulfilling his duty to pursue charges against Roberto Burbano for beating indígena Santos Guevara, successfully pled with the court to dismiss him so that he might seek to make his living as a merchant to provide for his wife and children. See ANH/R:Cr, June 2, 1871 (folio not numbered). One can find such references throughout the rest of the nineteenth century, as when, in 1890, diezmero Antonio Mosquera brought several indigenous men in Licto to court for injuring his good reputation when they accused him of taking advantage of them as infelices and equated diezmo collection with extortion. Witnesses supported Mosquera's claims, and the indigenous defendants were found guilty, restoring the collector's honor. See ANH/R:Cr, December 29, 1890.

74. M. Moscoso, "Mujer indígena," 231, 240.

75. See, for example, ANH/R:Civ, December 15, 1866, no. 5. Also see Lyons, "In Search of 'Respect,'" 188.

76. The feminization of indigenous communities would also play a key role in Indian women emerging as the "authentic" bearers of indigenous cultural identity in the mid- to late twentieth century.

77. ANH/Q:I, March 12, 1873, folio 1.

78. ANH/R:Cr, October 31, 1870; folio 5 has doctors' references to the men's wounds. Also see ANH/R:Cr, March 3, 1915.

79. ANH/R:Civ, October 14, 1869 (the original dispute, in which the women's names appear, began in 1867). See chapter 5 for further discussion of why it would be important to have both men and women represent the community.

80. In addition to the Daquilema rebellion, to be discussed at length, other examples come from the 1858 uprising in Calpi. References were also made to a minor skirmish between Francisco Mayacela and the women and men of Yaruquíes in the case Paula León brought to court against Mayacela; ANH/R: Cr: October 31, 1870. Several accounts of the rebellion dynamics of nineteenth-century Ecuador can be found. See Ibarra, *"Nos encontramos amenazados,"* 46–49, 57; Fuentealba, "La sociedad indígena," 69; Ayala Mora and Cordero, "El período Garciano," 64. Though Indians usually used the court system to address incursions onto their communal landholdings, they did take group action and at times even rioted against hacendados. For examples of such actions, see ANH/R:Cr, October 12, 1865, and January 16, 1873.

81. Costales Samaniego, "Fernando Daquilema," 151. Maldonado y Basabe noted that churches were spared in the burnings; *Monografía*, 63.

82. Comunicación del Gobernador de Chimborazo, December 23, 1871, cited in Ibarra, *"Nos encontramos amenazados,"* 34–35. Also see ANH/R:Gb, December 19, 1871.

83. Tobar Donoso, *El Indio*, 160–62; Costales Samaniego, "Fernando Daquilema," 181–87.

84. Ibarra, *"Nos encontramos amenazados,"* 40–41.

85. *El nacional*, January 13, 1872; also see January 17, 1872, which describes a local official from Chimborazo's letter to the minister of finance to point out that work was not being done on public roads because workers had not been paid in months.

86. For a good discussion of the shift in Indian-state relations behind the rebellion, see Sattar, "An Unresolved Inheritance," chapter 7. This chapter includes an interesting speculation that perhaps Fernando Daquilema's coronation as a leader in the uprising reflected intracommunity conflict during the era, with commoners mocking caciques' authority by granting this title to a young man who held no position of authority himself.

Chapter 4. Liberalism

1. Noboa, *Recopilación*, 4:334.

2. Jaramillo Alvarado, *El indio ecuatoriano*, 178–79.

3. M. Moscoso, "Imagen de la mujer," 67.

4. The debates, and the law itself, can be found in Congreso ordinario de 1902, cámara de senadores, September 15, República del Ecuador, *Anales de senadores*.

5. Ibid., September 6.

6. Ibid., September 15.

7. Ibid. M. Moscoso noted the similarity between divorce laws and Catholic practices in "Discurso religioso," 38.

8. Congreso ordinario de 1902, cámara de senadores, September 6 (H. Riofrío), República del Ecuador, *Anales de senadores*. In the first part of the quotation here, Riofrío claimed to be quoting another (unnamed) congressman.

9. Ibid., September 15 (H. Banderas).

10. Ibid. (H. Riofrío).

11. Ibid., September 16.

12. For the 1910 law and debates over divorce by mutual consent, see Congreso ordinario de 1910, cámara de diputados, September 22, República del Ecuador, *Anales de diputados*.

13. Ibid.

14. See chapter 5 for the differing responses to the 1910 law for divorce by mutual consent between Indians and non-Indians. Again, arguments presented here are from Congreso ordinario de 1910, cámara de diputados, September 22, República del Ecuador, *Anales de diputados*.

15. Ibid.

16. The bishops' manifestos can be found in González Suárez, *La polémica sobre el estado laico*. The quotation is from page 265; also see 251–53.

17. "Protestas de las Matronas de Cuenca," November 2, 1902, and "Protestas de las Matronas de Quito," September 21, 1902, cited in M. Moscoso, "Imagen de la mujer," 70.

18. For Alfaro's decree regarding postal and telegraph work, see ANH/Q:Gb, 1893–1905, decree of December 19, 1895. For an example of statements about the need for female teachers, see Alfaro, *Ley orgánica*. For the law pertaining to women's financial rights within marriage, see Congreso ordinario de 1911, cámara de diputados, República del Ecuador, *Anales de diputados*.

19. ANH/Q:Gb, 1893–1905, December 19, 1895, folio 42.

20. Noboa, *Recopilación*, 4:335.

21. Congreso ordinario de 1911, cámara del senadores, September 9, República del Ecuador, *Anales de senadores.*

22. Ibid., September 11.

23. Ibid., September 15.

24. Ibid.

25. This consideration was debated at length in Congreso ordinario de 1911, cámara del senadores, September 15, República del Ecuador, *Anales de senadores.*

26. ANH/Q:Cr, May 12, 1911.

27. The extent to which middle-class and elite women adhered to or rejected the changing family and gender laws during Ecuadorian state formation still requires further research. For some important preliminary studies, see M. Moscoso, *Y el amor.*

28. Congreso ordinario de 1910, cámara de diputados, September 7, República del Ecuador, *Anales de diputados.*

29. Ibid., September 9.

30. See Clark, "Género," 226.

31. See, for example, Noboa, *Recopilación*, 4:335, for Alfaro's eloquent speech arguing that women's education and experiences in the workplace before marriage would make them better wives and mothers, rather than threaten their honor or morality.

32. Delgado Capeáns, *Deberes de la madre Cristiana.*

33. Ugarte de Landívar, "Nuestro ideal," *La mujer*, 2.

34. Ibid., 31–32.

35. A good example of this is in Veintemilla, "La mujer," *La mujer*, 8–9.

36. M. Moscoso, "Imagen de la mujer," 78.

37. Noboa, *Recopilación*, 4:292–93. Also see Viteri Lafronte and Nuñez, "La escuela rural," 274, 279.

38. Alfaro, *Ley orgánica de instrucción pública*, chapter 1, arts. 3, 77, and 78.

39. Patricia de la Torre Arauz noted that a school began functioning on the hacienda El Dean only in 1927, in spite of a 1910 law that required all estates with over twenty workers to provide educational facilities. See *Patrones y conciertos*, 20. Also see chapter 7 regarding Dolores Cacuango.

40. Cueva, "Nuestra organización social," 58.

41. Congreso ordinario de 1918, cámara del senadores, República del Ecuador, *Anales de senadores*, 7, 38, 389, 514.

42. See Guerrero, *La semántica*, 82–83.

43. Congreso ordinario de 1918, cámara del senadores, República del Ecuador, *Anales de senadores*, particularly senators Arzube (925) and Cueva García (927) in

support of the law, and senators Iturralde (927, 929) and Lasso (946) in opposition to the law.

44. Freile-Granizo, "Leyes indigenistas," 104.

45. Asamblea Nacional, *Constitución de . . . 1897*, as it appears in Trabuco, *Constituciones*, arts. 30 and 138, respectively.

46. For other laws and decrees that related to Indian backwardness and childlike passivity, see Freile-Granizo, "Leyes indigenistas," 113 and 134; Alfaro, *Decreto ejecutivo*. For Supreme Court cases in which Indians' rusticity and vulnerability were emphasized, see ANH/Q:Cr, March 13, 1916; November 25, 1896 (this case referred to a concierto, in particular, being coerced into making a false confession); August 20, 1918.

47. Cueva, *El concertaje de indios*, 14–15 (regarding religion), 21–26 (for all other characteristics).

48. Delgado Capeáns, *El problema indígena*, 5.

49. Ibid., 19–20, for his discussion of alcoholism; other myths are addressed on pages 20–24. His discussion of education begins on page 4 and is intertwined throughout the essay.

50. ANH/Q:Cr, July 15, 1918, folios 29–29v.

51. Ibid., folio 30.

52. ANH/Q:Cr, December 21, 1918; for another reference to indigenous violence brought to the Supreme Court, see ANH/Q:Cr, June 26, 1916.

53. Cueva, "Nuestra organización social," 35; emphasis added.

54. Alfaro, *Decreto ejecutivo*, art. 6.

55. Until the middle of the twentieth century, courts regularly upheld landowners' right to receive unpaid labor from Indian women and children on their estates. Personal correspondence with Marc Becker, May 2006.

56. Quevedo, "El salario del concierto," 71.

57. See, for example, Leonidas Plaza's message to Congress in 1905 in Noboa, *Recopilación*, 291–92. Also see Cueva, *El concertaje de indios*, especially pages 5, 8, 11, and 16; to rectify the situation, Cueva—unlike other reformers—claimed, on page 45, that Indian women should be paid for their work on haciendas.

58. Quevedo, "El salario del concierto," 72–73.

59. For example, Fermín Cevallos observed in 1889 that the increasing debts a concierto incurred were often related to his wife's and children's needs. See *Resumen*, 144–45.

60. Viteri Lafronte and Nuñez, "La escuela rural," 281. In ANH/Q:Cr, January 25, 1908, Supreme Court officials, like Viteri Lafronte and Nuñez, recognized that "peasant women work as much as the men." Indigenous women's work was also

recognized in practice; see ANH/Q:Cr, January 25, 1908, in which one of the lawyers noted that "rural women work just as much as men … in all classes of labor." One can find occasional references to Indian women's labors in the nineteenth century, though these were much rarer than in the liberal period. See Fermín Cevallos, *Resumen*, 144–45.

61. Viteri Lafronte and Nuñez, "La escuela rural," 282.

62. Cueva, "Nuestra organización social," 48, and Delgado Capeáns, *El problema indígena*, 37–38.

63. ANH/R:Cr, October 3, 1908; also see June 23, 1920, n. 141.

64. ANH/R:Cr, August 22, 1890; Vinueza was found guilty. In another case, ANH/R:Cr, October 31, 1892, attorneys used a similar argument, but it was not successful.

65. ANH/R:Cr, April 9, 1892. The plaintiffs' charges are first found on folio 1, while Rivadeneira's defense first appears on folio 7.

66. ANH/R:Cr, December 29, 1890. Indigenous plaintiffs first addressed their grievances to the governor of Chimborazo. Mosquera, like the priest in Licán, blamed a tinterillo for provoking the Indians of Licto.

67. ANH/R:Cr, October 3, 1892. The court found insufficient evidence for a guilty verdict and dropped the charges.

68. See Clark, "Indians," 51; and Ibarra, "La identidad," 337.

69. ANH/R:Cr, October 3, 1908. For other references from the superior court in Riobamba, see December 3, 1901; June 23, 1920. For examples from the Supreme Court, see ANH/Q:Cr, March 13, 1916; November 25, 1896 (in which the defense claimed that the concierto was coerced into making a confession without being provided an interpreter); December 11, 1915.

70. ANH/R:Cr, October 3, 1908. Quishpi's claims failed to have an impact, however, and he was found guilty of the lesser charge of slander.

71. ANH/Q:Cr, August 2, 1921.

72. ANH/R:Cr, April 4, 1921.

73. See, for instance, ANH/R:Civ, January 14, 1901, and June 17, 1913. The second case was against a female hacienda owner in Guaranda (Bolívar province; the hacienda was named Casaichi). Another case, dated April 18, 1907, was similar to the two above, although only men were involved in the dispute.

74. In the above-mentioned case from 1901, six of the thirty-six participants were widows; in the 1913 case, one participant was a widow. Discussion of female leadership and widows' rights—for these cases and in other instances throughout the period under study—appear in chapter 5.

75. See Clark, "Indians," 58, and chapter 6 of this monograph.

76. ANH/R:Cr, June 23, 1920, folios 47, 58–58v. See chapter 6 for a full discussion

of this case, which took place on one of the estates formerly owned by the Catholic Church and taken over by the central government in 1904.

77. Examples here are ANH/Q:Cr, April 9, 1921; January 21, 1897.

78. ANH/Q:Cr, April 9, 1921.

79. ANH/Q:Cr, November 25, 1896. Not all tensions in these cases were between state officials of different levels of government; some were between elites within a local or regional area. An example of this comes up in ANH/Q:Cr, April 28, 1909, in which indigenous men in the Alausí region of Chimborazo complained that local elite don Emeterio Palacios had used his connections at court to rob them of land, and that the court had held the indigenous litigants responsible for 340 sucres in court costs as well. Several local officials and other non-Indians labeled "señor" or "doctor" testified on the Indians' behalf, verifying their charges of corruption in local judicial practices. Palacios claimed that many of these witnesses were unreliable because they were his enemies.

80. Clark, "Indians," 55–56.

81. ANH/Q:Cr, January 1, 1897.

82. Examples of cases in which elite views of Indian violence can be found are ANH/R:Cr, April 3, 1902; April 4, 1921; June 23, 1920; ANH/Q:Cr, April 28, 1916.

83. ANH/R:Cr, January 27, 1896, folio 1.

84. See ANH/R:Cr, April 9, 1892; January 27, 1896; April 4, 1921.

85. M. Moscoso, "Imagen de la mujer," 80.

86. Corrigan and Sayer discuss this in *The Great Arch*, particularly pages 80 and 132–34. Much of their discussion of the issue is based on Barker, "Regulation of Marriage."

Chapter 5. Alternative Patriarchy

1. ANH/R:Cr, February 25, 1870.

2. Ibid., folios 3–4v.

3. Ibid., folio 5–5v.

4. Ibid., folios 6–9. To the end of the case, Ñaula denied any relationship with Tenemasa, and Tenemasa denied living with Ñaula.

5. Ibid. Tenemasa's confession appears on folios 9v-10, and Ñaula's statements on folios 26–26v.

6. Ibid. Ñaula's attorney's assertions, and witnesses' denials of them, appear on folios 38–40, and Tenemasa's lawyer's claims are on folio 42v.

7. Guerrero also found that in the northern sierra, during the first half of the nineteenth century, caciques sometimes married whites as a means of strengthening their own authority. See "Curagas y tenientes politicos," 333.

8. For similar dynamics in rural interethnic politics in Nicaragua, see Dore, *Myths of Modernity*, chapter 3.

9. *El nacional*, no. 26, March 8, 1871, as cited in Costales and Costales Samaniego, "El concertaje de indios," 84. Evidence of such patterns has also been found for the 1980s in Weismantel, *Food, Gender, and Poverty*, 170.

10. While I do not have data on specific courtship or marriage costs in Ecuador between 1850 and 1925, there were certainly costs for both, since hacendados often lent money for these rituals to young Indian men as a means of establishing bonds of permanent debt servitude.

11. This may be the reason wills by single women with children are sometimes found. Examples of this are ANH/R:Civ, December 11, 1909; ANH/R:Civ, December 17, 1919.

12. The centrality of gender complementarity as an organizing principle for Andean peasant communities—both past and present—is now generally recognized, thanks to groundbreaking works by many scholars. One pioneering historical examination of gender and community is Silverblatt's *Moon, Sun, and Witches*; see also Zulawski, "Social Differentiation." Examinations for the nineteenth century have been few thus far, but Martha Moscoso does explore complementarity to some extent within her essay "Mujer indígena." For contemporary gender relations in Ecuador, see Harrison, *Signs, Songs, and Memory*, particularly chapter 5; Hamilton, *The Two-Headed Household*. For the Potosí region, see Harris, "Complementarity and Conflict" and "Condor and Bull." For the Peruvian highlands, see Allen, *The Hold Life Has*.

13. Most information on Indian men's and women's labors comes from criminal cases in the national historical archive in Riobamba, from the 1860s through 1925. Civil cases also include many references to women's contributions to agricultural production. M. Moscoso found similar patterns for the southern sierra; see "Mujer indígena," 235–36.

14. These patterns are typical within Indian peasant communities. See Stern, *The Secret History*, especially chapter 4; Kanter, "Hijos del Pueblo," chapter 4; Weismantel, *Food, Gender, and Poverty*, chapter 6.

15. Indigenous gender complementarity had both patriarchal and egalitarian tendencies, and it is difficult to determine how these played out. Contemporary studies suggest that women's positions relative to their husbands varied among communities, even within the central highlands of Ecuador. While Weismantel found that it was wives' obligation to serve their husbands and overall concluded that husbands generally had more (but not absolute) power in marriages, Hamilton has argued that indigenous peasants in the community of Chanchaló had egalitarian marriages, and divisions of duties were not so clearly drawn. Some

perceptions of differences could derive from the distinct research agendas of the two anthropologists: Weismantel was studying food and its importance to gender and poverty, while Hamilton was focused on gender and rural development. My assessment of complementary but largely unequal gender relations is based on the majority of the literature, both past and present, and suggestions from the documentary records I encountered.

16. For a discussion of these relations in contemporary Chimborazo, see Botero, *Chimborazo de los indios*, 138, 143, 144.

17. República del Ecuador, *Código civil* (1860), arts. 967, 970, 973, and 974, 138–39.

18. Allen, *The Hold Life Has*, 78.

19. Ibid., 85. Also Weismantel, *Food, Gender, and Poverty*, 183–84.

20. Allen, *The Hold Life Has*, on page 33 notes that "Through routine activities, habitually carried out, a cultural identity takes shape: the sense of the self as *Runa*."

21. Some examples of these responses can be found in ANH/R:Cr, March 19, 1870; January 9, 1865; November 11, 1880; January 30, 1908.

22. ANH/R:Cr, February 6, 1875. Other cases in which witnesses supported husbands by testifying that the injuries to their wives were less severe than charges suggested are ANH/R:Cr, November 11, 1880, and January 9, 1865. The latter was a homicide case against an indigenous man who was a concierto rather than a peasant.

23. ANH/R:Cr, March 19, 1870.

24. ANH/R:Cr, February 25, 1870.

25. ANH/R:Cr, March 19, 1870.

26. See ANH/R:Cr, October 27, 1871. The defendant, Juan de Dios Daquilema, was found guilty and was sentenced to death. This was one of the cases in which the protagonists lived and worked on an hacienda, yet indigenous peasant familial connections remained strong influences in interpersonal relationships.

27. ANH/R:Cr, June 1, 1874. Also see Christiansen, *Disobedience*, 74–75, where she asserts that for men, adultery was a symbolic threat, whereas for women, it was also a threat to subsistence.

28. This parallels Stern's findings on contested patriarchy in Mexico, *The Secret History*, 75–82.

29. Weismantel, *Food, Gender, and Poverty*, 181.

30. Examples here can be found in such cases as ANH/R:Cr, March 19, 1870, folios 44–47; February 28, 1873; April 10, 1901.

31. State officials' images of Indian male brutality derived not only from their

racial prejudices, but also from encountering intra-indigenous discord only when the violence was extreme, most commonly when outbursts resulted in severe injury or death.

32. In addition to court cases cited, see Lyons, "In Search of 'Respect,'" 170.

33. When Angamarca did not strike Francisco and Plácido Rea forcefully enough to suit Ribadeneira, the priest whipped Angamarca to demonstrate how a proper beating was administered. This case is from ANH/R:Cr, April 9, 1892. The plaintiffs lost this case.

34. ANH/R:Cr, April 7, 1907. Dore found similar accusations in Diriomo, Nicaragua. See *Myths of Modernity*, 61.

35. There are no records of Indians involved in the concubinage disputes that reached the Supreme Court in Quito, and only three exist in the archive of the superior court in Riobamba (two between Indians). Unfortunately these records are incomplete and do not reveal any specific information on indigenous gender dynamics.

36. Thanks here to personal communication, April 2006, with Nick Racheotes, who helped me to elaborate on the multiple public and private spheres in which indigenous peasants maneuvered.

37. Cajas and Carrillo mentioned Josefa Mariño's deceased father, Manuel Mariño, as their *padre político*. While this term could mean either father-in-law or stepfather, I suspect that in this case it meant father-in-law, and the two men had staked a claim to some of the land and goods on behalf of their wives. They would not, however, be able to lay claim to all the land, since Josefa Mariño had rights to some of it. All discussion of these disputes comes from ANH/R:Cr, August 30, 1865.

38. This situation may have been especially tense because the county of Guano, unlike most of the areas discussed in this chapter, was an overwhelmingly mestizo (rather than indigenous) area in Chimborazo province.

39. Some examples of these cases can be found in ANH/R:Cr, November 8, 1865; February 26, 1887; December 12, 1890; March 5, 1892; February 2, 1896; March 6, 1909; July 3, 1915.

40. This is one issue on which Indian women and white-mestizo women had much in common. Both state and indigenous patriarchies held women far more responsible than men for moral purity. The pattern held true not only for Ecuador, but also for urban and semiurban Peru. See Chambers, *From Subjects to Citizens*, and Christiansen, *Disobedience*, chapter 5.

41. Christiansen, *Disobedience*, 101–2, notes that a woman's sexual reputation affected her husband's honor.

42. See, for example, ANH/R:Cr, March 6, 1909; July 3, 1915. Though it was usually husbands who were accused of being pimps, brothers were also vulnerable to this charge. See ANH/R:Cr, March 19, 1870, folios 44–47.

43. The only exception to this rule that I found was in ANH/R:Cr, July 3, 1915. This case, from the civil parish of Yaruquíes, included specific countercharges by defendant Simón Tenelema, in which he asserted that plaintiff Jerónimo Hipo's wife, María Aguagallo, was living "in illicit union with her grandfather" (folio 3). While this charge may indicate some form of intermarriage between close family members, it might simply mean that there was a significant age difference between Aguagallo and Hipo that the community frowned on. Still, the main slander charge in the case, and most of the countercharges, fit into the general pattern noted.

44. See Christiansen, *Disobedience*; Chambers, *From Subjects to Citizens*.

45. Some examples here are ANH/R:Civ, October 15, 1888; December 4, 1909; November 17, 1919.

46. See ANH/R:Civ, January 14, 1901, and March 13, 1901 (both land disputes against the same estate-owning religious order). See also Rosero Garcés, "Comunidad, hacienda, y estado," 165 and 183.

47. República del Ecuador, *Código civil* (1860); see for example arts. 1306 and 1307 regarding the partition of goods.

48. Ibid., book 3, title 2, governing inheritance.

49. ANH/R:Civ, May 27, 1882, folio 5. Other examples of this phenomenon are ANH/R:Civ, May 16, 1900; July 25, 1905; April 15, 1913.

50. A few times Indian women even indicated, by referring to a woman by the title doña, that pieces of land were originally inherited through a *cacica*. For an example of this, see ANH/R:Civ, July 25, 1890, folios 17–18.

51. I suspect that some particular crisis or family argument led Cavadiana to request court intervention, because five years had elapsed between the time of his wife's death and the beginning of the court case.

52. ANH/R:Civ, January 23, 1890, folio 2. Tomás Cavadiana and Vicenta Carguaitongo also had a son named Gaspar, who died, leaving behind a daughter named Carmen. Juan was named to represent Carmen's interests, because he had married Gaspar's widow.

53. Ibid.; examples appear on folios 13 and 17.

54. Ibid., folio 5.

55. Ibid. Folios 6v and 9 include references to Castro sowing land; the inventory of all eleven parcels of land ranges from folios 6 to 11v. There was one property, shared by Tomás and Juan Cavadiana, that was about five times the size of the other parcels, as shown on folio 8.

56. Ibid., folio 19v.

57. Ibid.; examples can be found on folios 21v, 22v, 31v.

58. Ibid. For communications in which Tomás and Juan Cavadiana mentioned Castro, see folios 21 and 22; for the shift in their references, see folios 30 and 32v.

59. Ibid., folio 48v, emphasis mine; another piece of land was awarded, with similar wording, on folio 49.

60. República del Ecuador, *Código civil* (1860), title 5, regarding second marriages. Later civil codes reiterated marriage laws; see República del Ecuador, *Código civil* (1889).

61. ANH/R:Civ, January 23, 1890. Folio 6v includes mention that Castro was tilling land adjacent to family member María Cavadiana, and discussion of another parcel of Castro's land that bordered land owned by Juan Cavadiana appears on folio 9.

62. A few examples in which this might have been the case are ANH/R:Civ, March 23, 1876; September 6, 1905; October 20, 1906; December 5, 1908. Though widows did not always win these cases, they at least had a means to fight for land via indigenous gender norms.

63. Weismantel, *Food, Gender, and Poverty*, 190; Babb, "Producers and Reproducers." Also see ANH/R:Cr, August 28, 1914.

64. See ANH/R:Cr, June 23, 1920, folios 65–66v.

65. Martha Moscoso notes similar patterns in urban chicherías during the nineteenth century in "Mujer indígena," 241.

66. Ibid.

67. There are similar findings for eighteenth-century Mexico: see Stern, *The Secret History*, 51; Taylor, *Drinking*, chapter 2.

68. For examples, see ANH/R:Cr, March 12, 1874; August 3, 1915.

69. ANH/R:Cr, June 21, 1872.

70. This practice seems to have been common to Indian women in many areas of Latin America, and perhaps even women of all social classes. For an example from late colonial Mexico, see Kanter, "Hijos del Pueblo," 14.

71. See, for example, ANH/R:Cr, April 9, 1918; August 14, 1871.

72. ANH/R:Civ, June 14, 1876, folio 6.

73. M. Moscoso, "Mujer indígena," 230.

74. Costales Samaniego, "Fernando Daquilema." Examples of this can be found throughout Costales's work, but see in particular pages 152 and 158.

75. Ibid., 168–69.

76. María Misachi was under the age of twenty-one; Juana Misachi was over twenty-one. Both considered themselves orphaned—their mother had died years before, and their father had passed away four months before the incident in question. All information on this dispute comes from ANH/R:Cr, June 16, 1872.

77. These traitors were probably all Indian men, and not women, but the Misachi sisters never made this explicit in the court proceedings.

78. Ibid., folio 1–1v.

79. Or possibly a combination of sheep and llamas, since Aucansela referred to *ganado lanar* (wool-producing livestock).

80. ANH/R:Cr, August 26, 1876.

81. ANH/R:Civ, October 15, 1888, folio 1.

82. Ibid., folios 40–42.

83. ANH/R:Civ, June 10, 1901. The case offers evidence back into the 1880s also.

84. ANH/R:Civ, May 8, 1878, folio 40. As with the case involving Rosa Castro, no mention was made in this case about the specific nature of the problem that led Vinlasaca to initiate legal proceedings. Nor was it clear whether the grievance between the two parties began before or after Soledad Laso's death.

85. Ibid.; see folio 38 for Cuenca's assertions, and folios 39–40v for confirmation of her claims from witnesses Fernando Caranqui, Cornelio Sinchi, and Tomás Aucansela.

86. Ibid., folios 47–47v; emphasis mine. Unfortunately, documentation to which he refers on folios 13 and 15 are not part of the surviving court record.

87. Ibid., folios 49–50.

88. Ibid., folio not numbered.

89. ANH/R:Civ, June 21, 1883, folio 1. Not all plaintiffs named carried the surname Cabay, but the men who did not were married to members of the Cabay family.

90. Ibid., folio 3 for the quotation, and folio 5 for del Pino's demand that Quisnancela supply Rosa Guillcasunta's will for the court.

91. Ibid. For the exchanges over whether the will was submitted, see folios 6–8; for the civil judge of Calpi's reference to the will when he granted formal title of the land to Quisnancela, see folio 22v.

92. Ibid.; folio 27v for the court decision, and folios 39–40 for del Pino's final plea before the court.

93. Ibid., folios 45–59.

94. For an excellent discussion of this, see Guerrero, "Construction," 558, 568–70.

Chapter 6. Family Matters

1. ANH/Q:I, May 13, 1820; emphasis added.

2. Cueva, "Nuestra organización social," 35; emphasis added.

3. Hurtado, *Political Power in Ecuador*, 53–54. Hurtado paints too stark a picture in which Indians appear essentially powerless. An example of a hacendado vouching for one of his conciertos can be found in ANH/R:Cr, February 26, 1874.

4. Sometimes mayordomos' wives fulfilled a similar intermediary role between patronas and conciertos' wives who did domestic labor, although this function was

not officially recognized and remunerated the way that a mayordomo's own position was. See Lyons, "In Search of 'Respect,'" 12.

5. de la Torre Arauz, *Patrones y conciertos*, 29, 34–36; Lyons, "In Search of 'Respect,'" 118–19, notes that in spite of the general pattern described here, some mayordomos were thought of as good rather than evil.

6. Becker, "Peasant Identity, Worker Identity," 12.

7. ANH/R:Hac, 1873, "Descargo delos frutos de las haciendas de Pul, Totorillas, y Sulchán, que ha ingresadelo apoder e depositorio del Señor Juan Dávalos."

8. Lyons, "In Search of 'Respect,'" 117.

9. Other laborers were crucial in an estate's productive capacity, as most haciendas periodically hired Indians from surrounding communities. However, because I am interested mainly in the "permanent family" of the hacienda, my focus is on the Indian resident workers.

10. Saint-Geours, "La sierra centro," 157.

11. This two-way benefit of loans is well established in Ecuadorian scholarship. For the benefits to hacendados, see de la Torre Arauz, *Patrones y conciertos*, 64. For benefits to conciertos, see Espinosa, "Hacienda, concertaje, y comunidad," 136.

12. Gleaning for crops after the formal harvest was another type of redistribution at harvest time. See Lyons, "In Search of 'Respect,'" 105.

13. Costales and Costales Samaniego, "El concertaje de indios," 59; Lyons, "In Search of 'Respect,'" 11; ANH/R:Civ, March 13, 1892. In the civil case cited here, the new and former owners went to court against each other partly because of a disagreement over the new owner's specific rights to indigenous laborers.

14. Workers were sometimes able to negotiate with estate owners to allow them to leave and work seasonally on coastal estates. Such migration patterns were, however, a source of conflict between estate owners in the sierra and on the coast. See Lentz, "De regidores," 192.

15. See Becker, "Peasant Identity, Worker Identity," for an excellent discussion of the complex class consciousness that emerged out of this system.

16. Lyons, "'To Act Like a Man,'" 56–57.

17. See Guerrero, *La semántica*, 145–47. Lyons found in Chimborazo, however, that parents often borrowed the money for the wedding feast; see "In Search of 'Respect,'" 85.

18. For examples of this, see ANH/R:Hac, 1871 and 1876 (both from the hacienda Guacona in the civil parish of Sicalpa, canton Colta); Guerrero, *La semántica*, 145; de la Torre Arauz, *Patrones y conciertos*, 64.

19. Exactly when a married concierto could get a huasipungo varied. In some instances the land would be given to a male worker upon marriage, but in others, he would have to wait. In the latter case, the young concierto's father might even give him

a piece of his own huasipungo. See de la Torre Arauz, *Patrones y conciertos*, 58; Lyons, "In Search of 'Respect,'" 84–85. The most obvious reason for this variation would be the amount of land available for distribution to workers. It is unclear if there were also differing regional customs.

20. Guerrero, *La semántica*, 273–79.

21. See ANH/R:Hac, 1893, "Cuaderno de los granos."

22. Household activities were in fact intertwined with hacienda production, or production in peasant societies. In addition to issues of household and subsistence discussed in chapter 5, see Carmen Diana Deere's superb discussion of these connections in *Household and Class Relations*.

23. Costales and Costales Samaniego, "El concertaje de indios," 49; de la Torre Arauz, *Patrones y conciertos*, 37.

24. Pasturing animals, however, was sometimes done by a concierto's older children, rather than by his wife.

25. Lyons, "In Search of 'Respect,'" 105.

26. The position of lechero was another duty that rotated among conciertos and included responsibilities to gather cows for milking, oversee women who milked cows, and measure the amount of milk produced for sale.

27. A young unmarried woman might also take over her aging relatives' duties on the hacienda, performing the work required of the official concierto. See Lyons, "In Search of 'Respect,'" 112–13.

28. Lentz, "De regidores," 192.

29. Guevara, *Puerta de El Dorado*, 336.

30. Other scholars have noted this as well. See M. Moscoso, "Mujer indígena," 233; de la Torre Arauz, *Patrones y conciertos*, chapter 4; Deere, *Household and Class Relations*, 105.

31. Deere, *Household and Class Relations*, 110.

32. Deere notes this also; *Household and Class Relations*, 110.

33. As with the discussion of chicheras in Indian peasant communities, information about chicherías on haciendas often comes from criminal cases in which a chichera's house is mentioned in testimony.

34. ANH/R:Hac, 1871 (hacienda Guacona), in which Rosa Yubailla was accountable for a debt of twenty-two pesos that her husband, José Duche, had left behind when he died; also ANH/R:Civ, July 27, 1907.

35. ANH/R:Hac, 1871 and 1876 (both for the hacienda Guacona).

36. ANH/R:Cr, October 14, 1870.

37. ANH/R:Cr, March 14, 1871.

38. Deere came to the same conclusion in *Household and Class Relations*, 110, 120.

39. This was likely true for debt peonage throughout much of Latin America, though the combination of gender and racial domination manifested in different specific practices in different regions. For comparisons and contrasts with Ecuador, see Dore, *Myths of Modernity*, chapter 7.

40. See Espinosa, "Hacienda, concertaje, y comunidad," 171–75.

41. On haciendas of the northern sierra, the main religious celebration was the feast of San Juan. See Guerrero, *La semántica*, 11–41.

42. Lentz, "De regidores," 199. The translation used here was done by Lyons, "In Search of 'Respect,'" 105.

43. Ibid., 197.

44. For a discussion of this issue in early modern France, which greatly influenced my own interpretation of Ecuadorian dynamics, see Davis, *Society and Culture*, especially 131–42.

45. *Doctrinas* were mandatory morning prayer meetings that the entire estate workforce attended, and *doctrineros*, who were often mayorales, made sure that workers attended these meetings. Lyons discusses the overlap between religious and secular authorities on haciendas on 180–82; also see Lentz, "De regidores," 193–94.

46. Lyons, "In Search of 'Respect,'" 180–83.

47. Though the estate was not named, it was in the civil parish of Quimiag, Chimborazo.

48. ANH/R:Cr, June 10, 1874. The charges were eventually dropped because Guamán had thought Remache was dead when she remarried.

49. Unfortunately, because most issues of morality and sexuality were handled within haciendas themselves, no court records offer evidence of these patterns. For evidence based on interviews with former hacienda workers, see Lyons, "In Search of 'Respect,'" 138–43, 195–96.

50. For discussions of sexual assault and abuse and ethnic domination in Nicaragua, see Dore, *Myths of Modernity*, 61–62, 158.

51. ANH/Q:I, February 28, 1820.

52. ANH/Q:I, January 15, 1821. Other examples of conciertos making references to owners falling short of paternal kindness are in ANH/Q:I, January 20, 1803; March 12, 1818; December 13, 1821; June 30, 1849.

53. ANH/Q:I, 1816.

54. ANH/Q:I, February 24, 1833. ANH/Q:I, January 20, 1821, makes a similar reference, to laws passed by the Cortes in Spain against the mistreatment of Indians.

55. ANH/Q:I, November 14, 1814, folio 2.

56. ANH/Q:I, June 11, 1803.

57. Williams, "Negotiating the State," 109–11.

58. ANH/Q:I, January 20, 1803.

59. ANH/Q:I, February 7, 1817. The hacendado in this case did use the term "nation," though it was certainly a word whose deeper meaning was under construction at the time.

60. ANH/Q:I, November 14, 1814.

61. Ibid., folios 4v, 18–21, 14v–15.

62. Ibid., folios 26–26v.

63. Examples can be found in ANH/Q:I, November 14, 1814; February 7, 1817; January 20, 1821. For ways mistreatment threatened to undermine family bonds or separate them, see ANH/Q:I, July 4, 1813; February 7, 1817.

64. ANH/Q:I, February 14, 1803.

65. ANH/Q:I, February 7, 1817.

66. ANH/Q:I, November 14, 1814. Also see ANH/Q:I, December 13, 1821; 1816.

67. ANH/Q:I, June 11, 1803.

68. ANH/Q:I, April 29, 1811; emphasis mine.

69. ANH/Q:I, November 14, 1811; emphasis mine.

70. Also see ANH/Q:I, August 15, 1816, in which a concierto refers to his loss of his home and woman as part of his suffering.

71. Williams, "Negotiating the State," 76–79.

72. The petition appears in full as an appendix to Becker, "Peasant Identity, Worker Identity."

73. Lyons, "'To Act Like a Man,'" especially 45–47. Lyons has a more extensive discussion of concierto-hacendado conflicts in "In Search of 'Respect,'" 107–17 and 169–70, but in this work he does not do the close gender analysis that he offers in "'To Act Like a Man.'"

74. ANH/Q:I, April 29, 1832.

75. ANH/Q:I, May 17, 1834. This is the second case that appears in this folder. No outcome is available.

76. ANH/Q:I, April 9, 1867.

77. See, for example, ANH/R:Civ, June 26, 1867, a complaint by conciertos Tomás and Juan Remache, who worked on the hacienda Gatazo in the canton of Colta and sought to have an unfair claim of debt rectified.

78. ANH/R:Civ, July 5, 1897; though this hacienda was not named in the record, it was in the parroquia of Quimiag, and its owner was Rafael Gonzalez. It is therefore likely that this was the same hacienda where Gregoria Guamán was forced to marry by hacienda owner Miguel María Gonzalez.

79. ANH/R:Civ, December 31, 1904; see also ANH/R:Civ, June 30, 1906. The latter case is similar to the first case cited here but offers far less information.

80. All discussion of this dispute is from ANH/R:Cr, June 23, 1920.

81. Ibid., folios 10 and 28. The number of Indian insurgents was never pinpointed; most witnesses claimed there were about twenty, though others claimed there were far more or that the rebels in town were waiting to be reinforced by Indians who were "lurking around in the páramo" of the hacienda.

82. Ibid., folio 43, 15v; most of the defendants' testimonies are on folios 12–15.

83. Ibid., folios 47 and 58–58v.

84. Ibid., folio 73.

85. Clark, "Indians," 62–63.

86. Their descriptions also indicate that even if the state's official image of Indians was no longer barbarically brutal, many white individuals still felt that way.

87. For another discussion of this, see Guerrero, *La semántica*, 60, 82–83.

88. Alfaro, *Decreto ejecutivo*, especially art. 13.

89. Clark, "Racial Ideologies," 373–93. Clark goes over the history of these haciendas and also notes that Indian residents of these haciendas often had conflicts with renters in the 1930s and 1940s.

Chapter 7. Gendered Foundations

1. Chuma Quishpilema, "Las mujeres."

2. Quoted in Cervone, "Engendering Leadership," 188.

3. Christiansen, *Disobedience*; Barragán Romano, "'Spirit' of Bolivian Laws"; Guerrero, "Administration of Dominated Populations."

4. Christiansen, *Disobedience*; Chambers, *From Subjects to Citizens*; Mallon, *Peasant and Nation*; Guardino, *Peasants*; Grandin, *The Blood of Guatemala*.

5. Chambers, "Private Crimes, Public Order"; Earle, "Rape and the Anxious Republic."

6. For different aspects of this, see Guardino, "Community Service, Liberal Law"; Chambers, *From Subjects to Citizens*; Mallon, "Patriarchy."

7. Thurner, *From Two Republics*; Guardino, *Peasants*; Mallon, *Peasant and Nation*; Walker, *Smoldering Ashes*; Méndez, *The Plebeian Republic*; Grandin, *The Blood of Guatemala*.

8. Dore, *Myths of Modernity*, 159, made a similar assumption about patriarchy varying according to social class.

9. See Christiansen, *Disobedience*, 177. Her discussion of honor functioning on a continuum greatly influenced my conclusions on patriarchy here.

10. Biographical information on Cacuango is from Rodas, *Crónica de un sueño*.

11. For further information on Gómez de la Torre as well as other indigenous and elite women activists at mid-century, see Becker, "Race, Gender, and Protest."

12. Ibid., pp. 39–45.

13. Another was Tránsito Amaguaña. Again, see Becker, "Race, Gender, and Protest."

14. Becker, "Class and Ethnicity," 234.

15. Albornóz, *Dolores Cacuango*, 17–18.

16. Becker, "Class and Ethnicity," 236–37.

17. Rodas, *Crónica de un sueño*, 21.

18. See, for example, Albornóz, *Dolores Cacuango*, 7–8, 25–26.

19. Lentz, "De regidores," 192; Weismantel, *Food, Gender, and Poverty*, 182–83; Crain, "The Gendering of Ethnicity."

20. Albornóz, *Dolores Cacuango*, 23.

21. Rodas, *Crónica de un sueño*, 30.

22. Cervone, "Engendering Leadership," 187. Also see Radcliffe, Laurie, and Andolina, "The Transnationalization of Gender"; Prieto et al., "Respeto, discriminación y violencia," 160.

23. See Becker, "Class and Ethnicity," and "Race, Gender, and Protest."

24. Crespi, "Mujeres campesinas."

25. Some scholars see hacendados as a driving force behind the agrarian reform law, while others maintain that the estate owners were merely embracing reform out of fear of indigenous protests. For a good synopsis of events and scholarly debates, see Becker, "Class and Ethnicity," 301–4.

26. Barsky, "Los terratenientes serranos," 180–81, 187–201. See also Phillips, "Women, Development," 112.

27. Phillips, "Women, Development," 105, 111–12, 114–15.

28. See, for example, Babb, "Women and Men."

29. This is not unique to Ecuador. See de la Cadena, "'Las mujeres.'"

30. Chuma and Lema, "Construimos la vida."

31. Prieto et al., "Respeto, discriminación y violencia," 157.

32. Radcliffe, Laurie, and Andolina, "The Transnationalization of Gender."

33. Prieto et al., "Respeto, discriminación y violencia," 155.

34. Ibid., 160, 163; Cervone, "Engendering Leadership," 185.

35. For two examples, see Cervone, "Engendering Leadership."

36. CONAIE activists, with foreign financial assistance, have established a school to encourage indigenous women's leadership in the movement. See Palacios and Chuma, "La construcción de una utopia," regarding the aptly named Dolores Cacuango School for the Formation of Indigenous Women Leaders.

37. In addition to Cervone, "Engendering Leadership," see Radcliffe, Laurie, and Andolina, "The Transnationalization of Gender."

38. Radcliffe, Laurie, and Andolina, "The Transnationalization of Gender."

39. Prieto et al., "Respeto, discriminación y violencia," 167–68.

40. Radcliffe, Laurie, and Andolina, "The Transnationalization of Gender."

41. Cited in Prieto et al., "Respeto, discriminación y violencia," 164. See also Chuma Quishpilema, "Las mujeres"; Radcliffe, Laurie, and Andolina, "The Transnationalization of Gender."

42. For an excellent discussion of the indigenous movement, see Pallares, *From Peasant Struggles*. For women's movements, see Lind, *Gendered Paradoxes*.

Bibliography

Archival Sources

Archivo Nacional de la Historia, Quito (ANH/Q)

Criminales (ANH/Q:Cr), 1820–1920
Gobierno (ANH/Q:Gb), selected years
Indígenas (ANH/Q:I), 1800–1925
Tributos (ANH/Q:Tr), 1800–1857

Archivo Nacional de la Historia, Riobamba (ANH/R)

Civiles (ANH/R:Civ), 1860–1925, plus selected years 1830–1859
Criminales (ANH/R:Cr), 1860–1925, plus selected years 1830–1859
Gobiernos (ANH/R:Gb), selected years
Haciendas (ANH/R:Hac), selected years

National Newspapers

Gaceta del Ecuador, 1840, 1841
El nacional, 1846, 1849, 1861, 1869–1875
Primer registro auténtico nacional, 1831, 1835, 1836, 1837
Registro oficial, 1895–1918
El seis de Marzo, 1854, 1856

Published and Internet Primary Sources

Academia de Abogados. "El concertaje." *Revista forense* (Quito) 7, no. 57 (1918): 249–84.

Actas del congreso constitucional. Vol. 1. Quito: Imprenta del Gobierno, 1893.

Actas de la convención nacional del Ecuador, año de 1835. Quito: Imprenta del Gobierno, 1890.

Alfaro, Eloy. *Decreto ejecutivo sobre concertaje de indios.* Quito: Imprenta Nacional, 1899.

———. *Ley orgánica de instrucción pública.* Quito: Imprenta Nacional, 1907.

Arízaga, Rafael M. "Algo sobre concertaje." *Revista forense* (Quito) 7, no. 57 (1918): 223–34.

Borja, L. F. *El indio ecuatoriano y la agricultura en la sierra.* Quito: Tip. y Encuad. de la "Prensa Católica," 1923.

Borrero, M. M. "De la responsabilidad de la mujer para el pago de las deudas contraidas durante el matrimonio." *Revista forense* (Quito) 6, no. 48 (1917): 3–9.

Chuma, Vicenta, and Josefina Lema. "Construimos la vida, llamando a la paz." *Boletín ICCI "Rimay"* 2, no. 14 (2000). Http://icci.nativeweb.org/boletin/mayo2000/chuma.html (accessed June 2006).

Chuma Quishpilema, María Vicenta. "Las mujeres en la construcción del estado plurinacional." Presented in the Segunda cumbre continental de los pueblos y nacionales indígenas de Abya Yala, July 21–25, 2004. Http://icci.nativeweb.org/cumbre2004/chuma.html (accessed June 2006).

CONAIE. *Las nacionalidades indígenas del Ecuador: Nuestro proceso organizativo.* Quito: TUNCUI/Abya-Yala, 1989.

———. "Political Declaration of Ecuador's Indigenous Peoples." From the Fourth Congress of CONAIE, December 15–18, 1993. Http://conaie.nativeweb.org/conaie4.html (accessed June 2006).

Costales, Alfredo, and Piedad Costales, eds. "Recopilación de las leyes indígenas de 1830 a 1918." Special issue, *Llacta* (Quito) 3, no. 19 (1964).

Cueva, Agustín. *El concertaje de indios.* Quito: Instituto de Investigaciones Económicas, 1912.

———. "Nuestra organización social y la servidumbre." *Revista de la sociedad jurídico-literaria* (Quito) 14, nos. 25–27 (1915): 29–58.

Delgado Capeáns, R. P. *Deberes de la madre Cristiana.* Quito: Tip. y Encuad. de la "Prensa Católica," 1923.

———. "La escuela laica." *El derecho* (Quito), August 25, 1922.

———. *El problema indígena: Organización y educación del indio.* Quito: Tip. Editorial Chimborazo de V. A. Cabrera M., 1925.

Destruge, G. "Un problema social." *Revista de la sociedad jurídico-literaria* (Quito) 21, nos. 62–64 (1918): 131–39.

Fermín Cevallos, Pedro. *Resumen de la historia del Ecuador.* Vol. 6. Guayaquil: Imprenta de la Nación, 1889.

Freile-Granizo, Juan, ed. "Leyes indigenistas: Compilación." Special issue, *Sarance* (Instituto Otavaleño de Antropología), no. 19 (August 1994).

García Moreno, Gabriel. *Escritos y discursos de Gabriel García Moreno.* Vol. 2, ed. D. Manuel María Polit. Quito: Imprenta del Clero, 1888.

González Suárez, Federico. *La polémica sobre el estado laico.* Ed. Enrique Ayala Mora. Quito: Banco Central del Ecuador/Corporación Editora Nacional, 1980.

Hassaurek, Friedrich. *Four Years among the Ecuadorians.* Cincinnati, Ohio: Robert Clarke and Co., 1892 [1867].

Indigenous Alliance of the Americas on 500 Years of Resistance. "Declaration of Quito." July 1990. Http://www.nativeweb.org/papers/statements/quincentennial/quito.php (accessed June 2006).

Jaramillo Alvarado, Pio. *El indio ecuatoriano: Contribución al estudio de la sociología nacional.* Quito: Biblioteca Ecuatoriana, 1922.

León Mera, Juan. *Catecismo de geografía del Ecuador.* 2d ed. Guayaquil: Imprenta de Nación, 1884 [1874].

Ministro del Hacienda. *Exposición del ministro de hacienda y relaciones interiores.* Quito: Imprenta Nacional, 1867, 1873.

Ministro del Interior. *Exposición del Interior, relaciones exteriores e instrucción pública.* Quito: Imprenta del Estado, 1854, 1856, 1857, 1858.

Mujeres Indígenas de la CONAIE. *Memorias de las jornadas del foro de la mujer indígena en el Ecuador.* Quito: CONAIE/UNFPA, 1994.

Niles, Blair. *Casual Wanderings in Ecuador.* New York: Century Co., 1923.

Noboa, Alejandro. *Recopilación de mensajes dirigidos por los presidentes de la república, jefes supremos y gobiernos provisorios a las convenciones nacionales desde el año 1819 hasta nuestros días.* Vols. 2–5. Guayaquil: Imp. De El Tiempo, 1907.

Orton, James. *The Andes and the Amazon.* New York: Harper and Brothers, 1870.

Palacios, Paulina, and Vicenta Chuma. "La construcción de una utopia." *Boletín ICCI "Rimay"* 3, no. 28 (2001). http://icci.nativeweb.org/boletin/28/palacios.html (accessed June 2006).

Palacios, Polvio C. "El concertaje y el liberalismo." *La patria ecuatoriana* (Guayaquil), November 5, 1915.

Pérez Borja, Francisco. "Estudio de la ley de emancipación de la mujer casada." *Revista de la sociedad jurídico-literaria* (Quito), no. 3 (1913): 123–32; no. 4 (1913): 235–42.

Quevedo, B. "El concertaje y las leyes naturales de la sociedad." *Revista de la sociedad jurídico-literaria* (Quito) 16, no. 36 (1916): 283–87.

———. "El salario del concierto." *Revista de la sociedad jurídico literaria* (Quito) 16, no. 33 (1916): 67–76.

República del Ecuador. *Anales de diputados*. Quito: 1902, 1910, 1911, 1916, 1917, 1918.

——. *Anales de senadores*. Quito: 1902, 1910, 1911, 1917, 1918.

——. *Código civil de la República del Ecuador*. Quito: Imprenta de los Huérfanos de Valencia, 1860.

——. *Código civil de la República del Ecuador*. New York: Imprenta de "Las Novedades," 1889.

Saenz, Moisés. *Sobre el indio ecuatoriano y su incorporación al medio nacional*. México: Publicaciones de la Secretaria de Educación Pública, 1933.

Tobar y Borgoño, Carlos M. "Prejuicios y errores con respecto al indio." *Revista de la sociedad jurídico-literaria*. (Quito) 16, no. 36 (1916): 288–92.

Torres, Adolfo A. "La prisión por deudas." *Revista forense* (Quito) 7, no. 57 (1918): 235–48.

Trabuco, Federico, ed. *Constituciones de la República del Ecuador*. Quito: Editorial Universitaria, 1975.

Ugarte de Landívar, Zoila. "Nuestro ideal." *La mujer* (Quito) 1, no. 1 (1905): 1–4.

Veintimilla, Josefina. "La mujer." *La mujer* (Quito) 1, no. 1 (1905): 7–9.

Viteri Lafronte, Homero, and Pedro L. Nuñez. "La escuela rural y los indios." *Revista de la sociedad jurídico-literaria* (Quito) 16, no. 36 (1916): 269–82.

La voz del deber de unas mujeres católicas. Quito: Hojas Volantes, Biblioteca Ecuatoriana Aurelio Polit, 1878.

Secondary Sources

Abrams, Philip. "Notes on the Difficulty of Studying the State (1977)." *Journal of Historical Sociology* 1, no. 1 (March 1988): 58–89.

Albornóz, Oswaldo. *Dolores Cacuango y las luchas indígenas de Cayambe*. Guayaquil: Edit. Claridad S.A., 1975.

Allen, Catherine J. *The Hold Life Has: Coca and Cultural Identity in an Andean Community*. Washington, D.C.: Smithsonian Institution Press, 1988.

Almeida, José, Hernán Carrasco, Luz María de la Torre, Andrés Guerrero, Jorge León, Antonio Males, Nina Pacari, Galo Ramón, Alberto Taxo, Jorge Trujillo, and León Zamosc. *Sismo étnico en el Ecuador: Varias perspectives*. Quito: CEDIME/Abya-Yala, 1993.

Anderson, Benedict. *Imagined Communities: Reflections on the Origins and Spread of Nationalism*. Rev. ed. New York: Verso, 1992.

Andrea, Alfred, and James Overfield, eds. *The Human Record: Sources of Global History*. Vol. 2, *Since 1500*. 4th ed. Boston: Houghton Mifflin, 2001.

Arcos, Carlos G. "El espíritu del progreso: Los hacendados en el Ecuador del 900." *Cultura* (Quito) 7, no. 19 (1984): 107–34.

Arcos Cabrera, Carlos, and Carlos Marchán. "Apuntes para una discusión sobre los cambios en la estructura agraria serrana." *Revista ciencias sociales* (Quito) 2, no. 5 (1978): 13–51.

Ayala Mora, Enrique. *El Bolivarianismo en el Ecuador*. Quito: Corporación Editora Nacional, 1991.

————. "La fundación de la república: Panorama histórico (1830–1859)." In Enrique Ayala Mora, ed., *Nueva historia del Ecuador*, vol. 7. Quito: Corporación Editora Nacional, 1983, 143–95.

————. "El municipio en el siglo XIX." *Procesos* (Quito) 1, no. 2 (1991): 69–86.

————. "De la revolución alfarista al régimen oligárquico liberal." In Enrique Ayala Mora, ed., *Nueva historia del Ecuador*, vol. 9. Quito: Corporación Editora Nacional, 1983, 117–66.

Ayala Mora, Enrique, ed. *Nueva historia del Ecuador*. Vol. 15. Quito: Corporación Editora Nacional, 1983.

Ayala Mora, Enrique, and Rafael Cordero. "El período Garciano: Panorama histórico." In Enrique Ayala Mora, ed., *Nueva historia del Ecuador*, vol. 7. Quito: Corporación Editora Nacional, 1983, 197–235.

Babb, Florence E. "Producers and Reproducers: Andean Market Women in the Economy." In June Nash and Helen Safa, eds., *Women and Change in Latin America*. New York: Bergin and Garvey, 1986, 53–64.

————. "Women and Men in Vicos, Peru: A Case of Unequal Development." In William W. Stein, ed., *Peruvian Contexts of Change*. New Brunswick, N.J.: Transaction Books, 1985, 163–210.

Barker, Diana Leonard. "The Regulation of Marriage: Repressive Benevolence." In Gary Littlejohn, Barry Smart, John Wakefield, and Nira Yuval-Davis, eds., *Power and the State*. New York: St. Martin's Press, 1978, 239–66.

Barragán Romano, Rossana. *Indios, mujeres y ciudadanos: Legislación y ejercicio de la ciudadanía en Bolivia (siglo XIX)*. La Paz, Bolivia: Fundación Diálogo, 1999.

————. "The 'Spirit' of Bolivian Laws: Citizenship, Patriarchy, and Infamy." In Sueann Caulfield, Sarah C. Chambers, and Lara Putnam, eds., *Honor, Status, and Law in Modern Latin America*. Durham, N.C.: Duke University Press, 2005, 66–86.

Barsky, Osvaldo. "Los terratenientes serranos y el debate político previo al dictado de la ley de reforma agraria de 1964 en el Ecuador." In FLACSO and CEPLAES, eds., *Ecuador: Cambios en el agro serrano*. Quito: Imp. Ediciones Asociados, 1980, 133–205.

Becker, Marc. "Class and Ethnicity in the Canton of Cayambe: The Roots of Ecuador's Modern Indian Movement." PhD diss., University of Kansas, 1997.

————. "Peasant Identity, Worker Identity: Multiple Modes of Rural Consciousness in Highland Ecuador." *Estudios interdisciplinarios de América Latina y el Caribe* 15, no. 1 (2004): 115–39.

————. "Race, Gender, and Protest in Ecuador." In Vince Peloso, ed., *Work, Protest, and Identity in Twentieth-Century Latin America*. Wilmington, Del.: SR Books, 2003, 125–42.

Besse, Susan K. *Restructuring Patriarchy: The Modernization of Gender Inequality in Brazil, 1914–1940*. Chapel Hill: University of North Carolina Press, 1996.

Botero, Luis Fernando. *Chimborazo de los indios*. Quito: Abya-Yala, 1990.

Bromley, Rosemary D. F. "The Functions and Development of 'Colonial' Towns: Urban Change in the Central Highlands of Ecuador, 1698–1940." *Transactions* (London), new series, 4, no. 1 (1979): 30–43.

Bromley, Rosemary D. F., and R. J. Bromley. "The Debate on Sunday Markets in Nineteenth-Century Ecuador." *Journal of Latin American Studies* 7, no. 1 (1975): 85–108.

Burns, E. Bradford. *The Poverty of Progress: Latin America in the Nineteenth Century*. Berkeley: University of California Press, 1980.

Casagrande, Joseph P. "Strategies for Survival: The Indians of Highland Ecuador." In Norman E. Whitten, ed., *Cultural Transformations and Ethnicity in Modern Ecuador*. Chicago: University of Illinois Press, 1987, 260–77.

Castillo Jácome, Julio. *La Provincia de Chimborazo en 1942*. Riobamba: Talleres Gráficos de la Editorial "Progreso," 1942.

Caulfield, Sueann, Sarah C. Chambers, and Lara Putnam, eds. *Honor, Status, and Law in Modern Latin America*. Durham, N.C.: Duke University Press, 2005.

————. "Introduction: Transformations in Honor, Status, and Law over the Long Nineteenth Century." In Sueann Caulfield, Sarah C. Chambers, and Lara Putnam, eds., *Honor, Status, and Law in Modern Latin America*. Durham, N.C.: Duke University Press, 2005, 1–24.

Cervone, Emma. "Engendering Leadership: Indigenous Women Leaders in the Ecuadorian Andes." In Rosario Montoya, Lessie Jo Frazier, and Janise Hurtig, eds., *Gender's Place: Feminist Anthropologies of Latin America*. New York: Palgrave MacMillan, 2002, 179–96.

Chambers, Sarah C. *From Subjects to Citizens: Honor, Gender, and Politics in Arequipa, Peru, 1780–1854*. University Park: Pennsylvania State University Press, 1999.

————. "Private Crimes, Public Order: Honor, Gender, and the Law in Early Republican Peru." In Sueann Caulfield, Sarah C. Chambers, and Lara Putnam, eds., *Honor, Status, and Law in Modern Latin America*. Durham, N.C.: Duke University Press, 2005, 27–49.

Chatterjee, Partha. *The Nation and Its Fragments: Colonial and Postcolonial Histories*. Princeton, N.J.: Princeton University Press, 1993.

Cherpak, Evelyn. "The Participation of Women in the Independence Movement in Gran Colombia, 1780–1830." In Asunción Lavrin, ed., *Latin American Women: Historical Perspectives*. Westport, Conn.: Greenwood Press, 1978, 219–34.

Chiriboga, Manuel. "Auge y crisis de una economía agroexportadora: El período cacaotero." In Enrique Ayala Mora, ed., *Nueva historia del Ecuador*, vol. 9. Quito: Corporación Editora Nacional, 1983, 55–115.

————. *Jornaleros y gran propietarios en 135 años de exportación Cacaotera (1790–1925)*. Quito: Concejo Provincial de Pichincha, 1980.

Christiansen, Tanja. *Disobedience, Slander, Seduction, and Assault: Women and Men in Cajamarca, Peru, 1862–1900*. Austin: University of Texas Press, 2004.

Clark, A. Kim. "El 'bienestar nacional': Experiencias del mercado interno en el Ecuador, 1910–1930." *Procesos* (Quito) no. 7 (1995): 59–87.

————. "Género, raza y nación: La protección a la infancia en el Ecuador, 1910–1945." In Martha Moscoso, ed., *Palabras del silencio: Las mujeres latinoamericanas y su historia*. Quito: Abya-Yala/DGIF/UNICEF, 1995, 219–56.

————. "Indians, the State and Law: Public Works and the Struggle to Control Labor in Liberal Ecuador." *Journal of Historical Sociology* 7, no. 1 (March 1994): 49–72.

————. "Racial Ideologies and the Quest for National Development: Debating the Agrarian Problem in Ecuador." *Journal of Latin American Studies* 30, no. 2 (1998): 373–93.

————. *The Redemptive Work: Railway and Nation in Ecuador, 1895–1930*. Wilmington, Del.: SR Books, 1998.

Contreras, Carlos. "Guayaquil y su región en el primer boom cacaotero (1750–1820)." In Juan Maiguashca, ed., *Historia y región en el Ecuador, 1830–1930*. Quito: FLACSO/CERLAC, 1994, 189–250.

Conway, Jill K., Susan C. Bourque, and Joan W. Scott. "Introduction: The Concept of Gender." *Daedalus* 116, no. 4 (1987): xxi–xxix.

Cornejo Menacho, Diego, ed. *Indios: Una reflexión sobre el levantamiento indígena de 1990*. Quito: ILDIS/Abya-Yala, 1992.

Corrigan, Phillip, and Derek Sayer. *The Great Arch: English State Formation as Cultural Revolution*. Oxford: Basil Blackwell, 1985.

Costales, Piedad P. de, and Alfredo Costales Samaniego. "El concertaje de indios y la manumisión de esclavos." Special issue, *Llacta* (Quito) 17, no. 17 (1964).

Costales Samaniego, Alfredo. "Fernando Daquilema: Último guaminga." Special issue, *Llacta* (Quito) 16, no. 11 (1963).

Crain, Mary. "The Gendering of Ethnicity in the Ecuadorian Andes: Native Women's Self-Fashioning in the Urban Marketplace." In Marit Melhuus and Kristi Ann Stolen, eds., *Machos, Mistresses, Madonnas: Contesting the Power of Latin American Gender Imagery*. New York: Verso, 1996, 134–58.

————. "The Social Construction of National Identity in Highland Ecuador." *Anthropological Quarterly* 63 (January 1990): 43–59.

Crespi, Muriel. "Mujeres campesinas como líderes sindicales: La falta de propiedad como calificación para puestos políticos." *Estudios Andinos* 5, no. 1 (1976): 151–70.

Davis, Natalie Zemon. *Society and Culture in Early Modern France*. Stanford, Calif.: Stanford University Press, 1965.

Deere, Carmen Diana. *Household and Class Relations: Peasants and Landlords in Northern Peru*. Berkeley: University of California Press, 1990.

de la Cadena, Marisol. "'Las mujeres son más indias': Etnicidad y género en una comunidad del Cusco." *Revista Andina* 9, no. 17 (1991): 7–29.

de la Torre Arauz, Patricia. *Patrones y conciertos: Una hacienda serrana*. Quito: Abya-Yala/Corporación Editora Nacional, 1989.

Demélas, Marie-Danielle, and Yves Saint-Geours. *Jerusalén y babilonia: Religión y política en el Ecuador, 1780–1880*. Quito: Corporación Editora Nacional/IFEA, 1988.

Dore, Elizabeth. *Myths of Modernity: Peonage and Patriarchy in Nicaragua*. Durham, N.C.: Duke University Press, 2006.

————. "One Step Forward, Two Steps Back: Gender and the State in the Long Nineteenth Century." In Elizabeth Dore and Maxine Molineaux, eds., *Hidden Histories of Gender and the State in Latin America*. Durham, N.C.: Duke University Press, 2000, 3–32.

Dore, Elizabeth, and Maxine Molineaux, eds. *Hidden Histories of Gender and the State in Latin America*. Durham, N.C.: Duke University Press, 2000.

Earle, Rebecca. "Rape and the Anxious Republic: Revolutionary Colombia, 1810–1830." In Elizabeth Dore and Maxine Molineaux, eds., *Hidden Histories of Gender and the State in Latin America*. Durham, N.C.: Duke University Press, 2000, 127–46.

Efren Reyes, Oscar. *Breve historia general del Ecuador*. Vols. 2–3. Quito: Imprenta del Colegio Técnico "Don Bosco," n.d.

Espinosa, Roque. "Hacienda, concertaje, y comunidad en el Ecuador." *Cultura* (Quito) 7, no. 19 (1984): 135–209.

Espinoza, Leonardo, and Lucas Achig. "Economía y sociedad en el siglo XIX: Sierra sur." In Enrique Ayala Mora, ed., *Nueva historia del Ecuador*, vol. 7. Quito: Corporación Editora Nacional, 1983, 69–101.

Fitzell, Jill. "Teorizando la diferencia en los Andes del Ecuador: Viajeros Europeos, la ciencia del exoticismo y las imagines de los indios." In Blanca Muratorio, ed., *Imágenes e imagineros: Representaciones de los indígenas ecuatorianos, siglos XIX y XX.* Quito: FLACSO, 1994, 25–73.

Fowler-Salamini, Heather, and Mary Kay Vaughan, eds. *Women of the Mexican Countryside, 1850–1990.* Tucson: University of Arizona Press, 1994.

Fuentealba, Gerardo. "La sociedad indígena en las primeras décadas de la República: Continuidades coloniales y cambios republicanos." In Enrique Ayala Mora, ed., *Nueva historia del Ecuador,* vol. 8. Quito: Corporación Editora Nacional, 1983, 45–77.

Gauderman, Kimberly. *Women's Lives in Colonial Quito: Gender, Law, and Economy in Spanish America.* Austin: University of Texas Press, 2003.

Goetschel, Ana María. "El discurso sobre la delincuencia y la constitución del estado liberal." *Procesos* (Quito) 8, no. 2 (1995): 83–98.

———. "Educación e imagines de mujer." In Martha Moscoso, ed., *Y el amor no era todo . . . mujeres, imagines, y conflictos.* Quito: Abya-Yala/DGIS/Holanda, 1996, 59–83.

Gordon, Linda. "What's New in Women's History?" In Teresa de Lauretis, ed., *Feminist Studies, Critical Studies.* Bloomington: Indiana University Press, 1986, 20–30.

Grandin, Greg. *The Blood of Guatemala: A History of Race and Nation.* Durham, N.C.: Duke University Press, 2000.

Guardino, Peter. "Barbarism or Republican Law?: Guerrero's Peasants and National Politics, 1820–1846." *Hispanic American Historical Review* 75, no. 2 (1995): 185–213.

———. "Community Service, Liberal Law, and Local Custom in Indigenous Villages: Oaxaca, 1750–1850." In Sueann Caulfield, Sarah C. Chambers, and Lara Putnam, eds., *Honor, Status, and Law in Modern Latin America.* Durham, N.C.: Duke University Press, 2005, 50–65.

———. *Peasants, Politics, and the Formation of Mexico's National State: Guerrero, 1800–1857.* Stanford, Calif.: Stanford University Press, 1996.

Guerrero, Andrés. "The Administration of Dominated Populations under a Regime of Customary Citizenship." In Mark Thurner and Andrés Guerrero, eds., *After Spanish Rule: Postcolonial Predicaments in the Americas.* Durham, N.C.: Duke University Press, 2003, 272–309.

———. "The Construction of a Ventriloquist's Image: Liberal Discourse and the 'Miserable Indian Race' in Late 19th-Century Ecuador." *Journal of Latin American Studies* 29, no. 3 (October 1997): 555–90.

———. "Curagas y tenientes políticos: La ley de la costumbre y la ley del estado

(Otavalo, 1830–1875)." *Revista Andina* 7, no. 2 (September 1989): 321–65.

———. *La semántica de la dominación: El concertaje de indios*. Quito: Libri Mundi, 1991.

Guevara, Dario C. *Puerta de El Dorado: Monografía del Cantón Pelileo*. Quito: Editora Moderna, 1945.

Hamilton, Sarah. *The Two-Headed Household: Gender and Rural Development in the Ecuadorean Andes*. Pittsburgh, Pa.: University of Pittsburgh Press, 1998.

Harris, Olivia. "Complementarity and Conflict: An Andean View of Women and Men." In J. S. La Fontaine, ed., *Sex and Age as Principles of Social Differentiation*. London: Academic Press, 1978, 21–40.

———. "Condor and Bull: The Ambiguities of Masculinity in Northern Potosí." In Penelope Harvey and Peter Gow, eds., *Sex and Violence: Issues in Representation and Experience*. New York: Routledge, 1994, 40–65.

Harrison, Regina. *Signs, Songs, and Memory in the Andes: Translating Quechua Language and Culture*. Austin: University of Texas Press, 1989.

Hernández, José, Marco Aráuz, Byron Rodríguez V., Leonel Bejarano. *El 21 de enero: La vorágine que acabó con Mahuad*. Quito: El Comercio, 2000.

Hobsbawm, E. J. *Nations and Nationalism since 1780: Programme, Myth, and Reality*. New York: Cambridge University Press, 1990.

Hunefeldt, Christine. *Liberalism in the Bedroom: Quarreling Spouses in Nineteenth-Century Lima*. University Park: Pennsylvania State University Press, 2000.

Hurtado, Osvaldo. *Political Power in Ecuador*. Trans. Nick D. Millis, Jr. Albuquerque: University of New Mexico Press, 1980.

Hyman, Paula. *Gender and Assimilation in Modern Jewish History: Roles and Representations of Women*. Seattle: University of Washington Press, 1995.

Ibarra, Hernán. "La identidad devaluada de los 'modern Indians.'" In Diego Cornejo Menchado, ed., *Indios: Una reflexión sobre el levantamiento indígena de 1990*. Quito: ILDIS/Abya-Yala, 1992, 319–49.

———. *Indios y cholos: Orígenes de la clase trabajadora ecuatoriana*. Quito: Editorial el Conejo, 1992.

———. *"Nos encontramos amenazados por todita la indiada": El levantamiento de Daquilema (Chimborazo, 1871)*. Quito: CEDIS, 1993.

Joseph, Gilbert M., and Daniel Nugent. "Popular Culture and State Formation in Revolutionary Mexico." In Gilbert M. Joseph and Daniel Nugent, eds., *Everyday Forms of State Formation: Revolution and the Negotiation of Rule in Modern Mexico*. Durham, N.C.: Duke University Press, 1994, 3–23.

Kanter, Deborah Ellen. "Hijos del Pueblo: Family, Community, and Gender in Rural Mexico, the Toluca Region, 1730–1830." PhD diss., University of Virginia, 1993.

Kelly, Joan. "The Social Relations of the Sexes: Methodological Implications Of Women's History." In *Women, History, and Theory: The Essays of Joan Kelly*. Chicago: University of Chicago Press, 1984, 1–17.

Lane, Kris. *Quito 1599: City and Colony in Transition*. Albuquerque: University of New Mexico Press, 2002.

Lentz, Carola. *Buscando la vida: Trabajadores temporales en una plantación de azúcar*. Quito: Abya-Yala, 1991.

———. "De regidores y alcaldes a cabildos: Cambios en la estructura sociopolítica de una comunidad indígena de Cajabamba/Chimborazo." *Ecuador Debate* (Quito) 12 (1986): 189–212.

Lerner, Gerda. *The Creation of Patriarchy*. New York: Oxford University Press, 1986.

———. "Reconceptualizing Differences among Women." *Journal of Women's History* (Winter 1990): 106–22.

Lind, Amy. *Gendered Paradoxes: Women's Movements, State Restructuring, and Global Development in Ecuador*. University Park: Pennsylvania State University Press, 2005.

Lucas, Kintto. *La rebelión de los indios*. Quito: Abya-Yala, 2000.

Lyons, Barry Jay. "In Search of 'Respect': Culture, Authority, and Coercion on an Ecuadorian Hacienda." PhD diss., University of Michigan, 1994.

———. "'To Act Like a Man': Masculinity, Resistance, and Authority in the Ecuadorian Andes." In Rosario Montoya, Lessie Jo Frazier, and Janise Hurtig, eds., *Gender's Place: Feminist Anthropologies of Latin America*. New York: Palgrave MacMillan, 2002, 45–63.

Maiguashca, Juan. "El proceso de integración nacional en el Ecuador: El rol del poder central, 1830–1895." In Juan Maiguashca, ed., *Historia y región en el Ecuador*. Quito: FLACSO/CERLAC, 1994, 355–420.

Maldonado y Basabe, Rodolfo. *Monografía de la provincial de Chimborazo*. Riobamba: Imprenta Nacional, 1930.

Mallon, Florencia. "Patriarchy and the Transition to Capitalism: Central Peru, 1830–1950." *Feminist Studies* 13, no. 12 (Summer 1987): 379–407.

———. *Peasant and Nation: The Making of Postcolonial Mexico and Peru*. Berkeley: University of California Press, 1995.

Marchán Romero, Carlos. "El sistema hacendario Serrano, movilidad y cambio agrario." *Cultura* (Quito) 7, no. 19 (1984): 63–106.

Marchant, B. Perez. *Diccionario biográfico del Ecuador*. Quito: Escuela de Artes y Oficios, 1928.

McClintock, Anne. "No Longer in a Future Heaven: Gender, Race, and Nationalism." In Anne McClintock, Aamir Mufti, and Ella Shohat, eds., *Dangerous*

Liaisons: Gender, Nation, and Postcolonial Perspectives. Minneapolis: University of Minnesota Press, 1997, 89–112.

McGee Deutsch, Sandra. "Gender and Sociopolitical Change in Twentieth-Century Latin America." *Hispanic American Historical Review* 71, no. 2 (1991): 259–306.

Mehta, Uday S. "Liberal Strategies of Exclusion." *Politics and Society* 18, no. 4 (December 1990): 427–54.

Méndez, Cecilia. *The Plebeian Republic: The Huanta Rebellion and the Making of the Peruvian State, 1820–1850*. Durham, N.C.: Duke University Press, 2005.

Milton, Cynthia, and Ben Vinson III. "Counting Heads: Race and Non-Native Tribute Policy in Colonial Spanish America." *Journal of Colonialism and Colonial History* 3, no. 3 (2002). (Accessed on Project Muse, http://muse.jhu.edu/journals/journal_of_colonialism_and_colonial_history/, January 2006.)

Moreno Yánez, Segundo. *Sublevaciones indígenas en la audiencia de Quito: Desde comienzos del siglo XVIII hasta fines de la colonia*. Quito: Ediciones de la Pontífica Universidad Católica, 1976.

Morgan, Edmund. *Inventing the People: The Rise of Popular Sovereignty in England and America*. New York: W. W. Norton and Co., 1988.

Moscoso, Gladys. "Las imágenes de la literatura." In Martha Moscoso, ed., *Y el amor no era todo . . . mujeres, imagines y conflictos*. Quito: Abya-Yala/DGIS, 1996, 85–116.

———. "La violencia contra las mujeres." In Martha Moscoso, ed., *Y el amor no era todo . . . mujeres, imagines y conflictos*. Quito: Abya-Yala/DGIS, 1996, 187–209.

Moscoso, Martha. "Comunidad, autoridad indígena y poder republicano en el siglo XIX." *Revista Andina* 2 (1990): 481–500.

———. "Discurso religioso y discurso estatal: La mujer sumisa." In Martha Moscoso, ed., *Y el amor no era todo . . . mujeres, imagines y conflictos*. Quito: Abya-Yala/DGIS/Holanda, 1996, 21–57.

———. "Imagen de la mujer y la familia a inicios del siglo XIX." *Procesos* 8, no. 2 (September 1996): 67–82.

———. "Los límites de la tolerancia: Divorcio, concubinato y adulterio." In Martha Moscoso, ed., *Y el amor no era todo . . . mujeres, imagines y conflictos*. Quito: Abya-Yala/DGIS/Holanda, 1996, 119–55.

———. "Mujer indígena y sociedad republicana: Relaciones étnicas y de género en el Ecuador, siglo XIX." In A. C. Defossez, D. Fassin, and M. Viveros, eds., *Mujeres de los Andes: Condiciones de vida y salud*. Bogotá: IFEA/Universidad Externado de Colombia, 1992, 223–43.

————. "La tierra: Espacio de conflicto y relación entre el estado y la comunidad en el siglo XIX." In Heraclio Bonilla, ed., *Los Andes en la encrucijada: Indios, comunidades, y estado en el siglo XIX*. Quito: FLACSO/Libri Mundi, 1991, 367–90.

Moscoso, Martha, ed. *Y el amor no era todo . . . mujeres, imagines y conflictos*. Quito: Abya-Yala/DGIS/Holanda, 1996.

Muratorio, Blanca. "Nación, identidad, y etnicidad: Imágenes de los indios Ecuatorianos y sus imagineros a fines del siglo XIX." In Blanca Muratorio, ed., *Imágenes e imagineros: Representaciones de los indígenas ecuatorianos, siglos XIX y XX*. Quito: FLACSO, 1994, 109–96.

Newson, Linda A. *Life and Death in Early Colonial Ecuador*. Norman: University of Oklahoma Press, 1995.

O'Connor, Erin. "Indians and National Salvation: Placing Ecuador's Indigenous Coup of January 2000 in Historical Perspective." In Erick D. Langer and Elena Muñoz, eds., *Contemporary Indigenous Movements in Latin America*. Wilmington, Del.: SR Books, 2003, 65–80.

————. "Widows' Rights Questioned: Indians, the State, and Fluctuating Gender Ideas in Central Highland Ecuador, 1870–1900." *The Americas* 59, no. 1 (2002): 87–106.

Ortiz Crespo, Gonzalo. "Panorama histórico del período 1875–1895." In Enrique Ayala Mora, ed., *Nueva historia del Ecuador*, vol. 7. Quito: Corporación Editora Nacional, 1983, 197–235.

Pallares, Amalia. *From Peasant Struggles to Indian Resistance: The Ecuadorian Andes in the Late Twentieth Century*. Norman: University of Oklahoma Press, 2002.

Palomeque, Silvia. *Cuenca en el siglo XIX: La articulación de una región*. Quito: FLACSO/Abya-Yala, 1990.

————. "Estado y comunidad en la región de Cuenca en el siglo XIX. Las autoridades indígenas y su relación con el estado." In Heraclio Bonilla, ed., *Los Andes en la encrucijada: Indios, comunidades, y estado en el siglo XIX*. Quito: FLACSO/Libri Mundi, 1991, 391–417.

————. "La Sierra Sur (1825–1900)." In Juan Maiguashca, ed., *Historia y región en el Ecuador: 1830–1930*. Quito: FLACSO/CERLAC, 1994, 69–142.

Peniche Rivero, Piedad. "Gender, Bridewealth, and Marriage: Social Reproduction of Peons on Henequen Haciendas in Yucatán, 1870–1901." In Heather Fowler-Salamini and Mary Kay Vaughan, eds., *Women of the Mexican Countryside, 1850–1990*. Tucson: University of Arizona Press, 1994, 74–89.

Phelan, John Leddy. *The Kingdom of Quito in the Seventeenth Century: Bureaucratic Politics in the Spanish Empire*. Madison: University of Wisconsin Press, 1967.

Phillips, Lynne. "Women, Development, and the State in Rural Ecuador." In Carmen Diana Deere and Magdalena León, eds., *Rural Women and State Policy:*

Feminist Perspectives on Latin American Agricultural Development. Boulder, Colo.: Westview Press, 1987, 105–23.

Pineo, Ronn F. "Guayaquil y su región en el segundo boom cacaotero (1870–1925)." In Juan Maiguashca, ed., *Historia y región en el Ecuador: 1830–1930.* Quito: FLACSO/CERLAC, 1994, 251–94.

Platt, Tristan. "The Andean Experience of Bolivian Liberalism, 1825–1900: Roots of Rebellion in 19th-Century Chayanta (Potosí)." In Steve J. Stern, ed., *Resistance, Rebellion, and Consciousness in the Andean Peasant World: 18th to 20th Centuries.* Madison: University of Wisconsin Press, 1987, 280–323.

———. *Estado Boliviano y ayllu Andino.* Lima: IEP, 1983.

Powers, Karen Vieira. *Andean Journeys: Migration, Ethnogenesis, and the State in Colonial Quito.* Albuquerque: University of New Mexico Press, 1995.

———. "The Battle for Bodies and Souls in the Colonial North Andes: Intraecclesiastical Struggles and the Politics of Migration." *Hispanic American Historical Review* 75, no. 1 (1995): 31–56.

Premo, Bianca. *Children of the Father King: Youth, Authority, and Legal Minority in Colonial Lima.* Chapel Hill: University of North Carolina Press, 2005.

Prieto, Mercedes, Clorinda Cuminao, Alejandra Flores, Gina Maldonado, and Andrea Pequeño. "Respeto, discriminación y violencia: Mujeres indígenas en Ecuador, 1990–2004." Http://www.flacso.org/ec/docs/respeto.pdf (accessed June 2006).

Radcliffe, Sarah A., Nina Laurie, and Robert Andolina. "The Transnationalization of Gender and Reimagining Andean Indigenous Development." *Signs* 29, no. 2 (2004): 387–420.

Ramon Valarezo, Galo. "La visión andina sobre el estado colonial." *Ecuador Debate,* no. 12 (1986): 163–87.

Rodas, Raquel. *Crónica de un sueño: Las escuelas indígenas de Dolores Cacuango.* Quito: Ministerio de Educación y Cultura/Sociedad Alemana de Cooperación Técnica, 1989.

Rodríguez, Linda Alexander. *The Search for Public Policy: Government Finances in Ecuador, 1830–1940.* Los Angeles: University of California Press, 1985.

Rodríguez O., Jaime. *The Independence of Spanish America.* New York: Cambridge University Press, 1998.

Rosero Garcés, Fernando. "Comunidad, hacienda, y estado: Un conflicto de tierras en el período de las transformaciones liberales." *Ecuador Debate,* no. 12 (1986): 163–87.

Saint-Geours, Yves. "La sierra centro y norte." In Juan Maiguashca, ed., *Historia y región en el Ecuador: 1830–1930.* Quito: FLACSO/CERLAC, 1994, 143–88.

Salomon, Frank. *Native Lords of Quito in the Age of the Incas: The Political Economy of North Andean Chiefdoms*. Cambridge: Cambridge University Press, 1986.

Sattar, Aleezé. "An Unresolved Inheritance: Postcolonial State Formation and Indigenous Communities in Chimborazo, Ecuador, 1820–1875." PhD diss., The New School for Social Research, 2001.

Scott, Joan Wallach. "Gender: A Useful Category for Historical Analysis." In *Gender and the Politics of History*. New York: Columbia University Press, 1988, 28–50.

Selverston, Melina. "The Politics of Culture: Indigenous Peoples and the State in Ecuador." In Donna Lee Van Cott, ed., *Indigenous Peoples and Democracy in Latin America*. New York: St. Martin's Press, 1994, 131–52.

Silva, Erika. "Estado, iglesia, e ideología en el siglo XIX." In Enrique Ayala Mora, ed., *Nueva historia del Ecuador*, vol. 8. Quito: Corporación Editora Nacional, 1983, 9–44.

Silverblatt, Irene. *Moon, Sun, and Witches: Gender Ideologies and Class in Inca and Colonial Peru*. Princeton: Princeton University Press, 1987.

Smith, Carol A., ed. *Guatemalan Indians and the State, 1540–1988*. Austin: University of Texas Press, 1990.

Spindler, Frank MacDonald. *Nineteenth Century Ecuador: An Historical Introduction*. Fairfax, Va.: George Mason University Press, 1987.

Stern, Steve J. *The Secret History of Gender: Women, Men, and Power in Late Colonial Mexico*. Chapel Hill: University of North Carolina Press, 1995.

Stutzman, Ronald. "El Mestizaje: An All-Inclusive Category of Exclusion." In Norman E. Whitten, ed., *Cultural Transformations and Ethnicity in Modern Ecuador*. Chicago: University of Illinois Press, 1981, 45–94.

Taylor, William B. *Drinking, Homicide, and Rebellion in Colonial Mexican Villages*. Stanford, Calif.: Stanford University Press, 1979.

Thurner, Mark. *From Two Republics to One Divided: Contradictions in Postcolonial Nationmaking in Andean Peru*. Durham, N.C.: Duke University Press, 1997.

———. "'Republicanos' and 'la Comunidad de Peruanos': Unimagined Political Communities in Postcolonial Andean Peru." *Journal of Latin American Studies* 27, no. 2 (May 1991): 291–318.

Tilly, Louise A. "Gender, Women's History, and Social History." *Social Science History* 13, no. 4 (Winter 1989): 439–61.

Tobar Donoso, Julio. *El indio en el Ecuador independiente*. Quito: Editorial de la Pontífica Universidad Católica, 1992.

Trujillo León, Jorge. *La hacienda serrana 1900–1930*. Quito: Instituto de Estudios Ecuatorianos/Abya-Yala, 1986.

Tutino, John. "The Revolution in Mexican Independence: Insurgency and the Renegotiation of Property, Production, and Patriarchy in the Bajío, 1800–1855." *Hispanic American Historical Review* 78, no. 3 (1998): 367–418.

Urban, Greg, and Joel Sherzer, eds. *Nation-States and Indians in Latin America.* Austin: University of Texas Press, 1991.

Van Aken, Mark. "The Lingering Death of Indian Tribute in Ecuador." *Hispanic American Historical Review* 6, no. 3 (1981): 429–59.

Walker, Charles. *Smoldering Ashes: Cuzco and the Creation of Republican Peru, 1780–1840.* Durham, N.C.: Duke University Press, 1999.

Weismantel, Mary. *Food, Gender, and Poverty in the Ecuadorian Andes.* Philadelphia: University of Pennsylvania Press, 1988.

Williams, Derek. "Indian Servitude and Popular Liberalism: The Making and Unmaking of Ecuador's Anti-Landlord State, 1845–1868." *Hispanic American Historical Review* 83, no. 4 (2003): 697–733.

———. "The Making of Ecuador's Pueblo Católico, 1861–1875." In Nils Jacobsen and Cristóbal Aljovín de Losada, eds., *Political Cultures in the Andes, 1750–1950.* Durham, N.C.: Duke University Press, 2005, 207–29.

———. "Negotiating the State: National Utopias and Local Politics in Andean Ecuador, 1845–1875." PhD diss., SUNY Stony Brook, 2001.

Wray, Alberto, Rodrigo de la Cruz, Diego Iturralde, Adolfo Triana-Francisco, Ballón Aguirre, Xavier Izko, and Juan Carlos Ribadeneira. *Derecho, pueblos indígenas y reforma del estado.* Quito: Abya-Yala, 1993.

Zulawski, Ann. "Social Differentiation, Gender, and Ethnicity: Urban Indian Women in Colonial Bolivia, 1640–1725." *Latin American Research Review* 25, no. 2 (1990): 93–113.

Index

About the Author

Erin O'Connor is assistant professor of history at Bridgewater State College in Massachusetts. She received her BA in Latin American studies, summa cum laude, from Brandeis University, and her PhD in Latin American history from Boston College. Her article "Widows' Rights Questioned: Indians, the State, and Fluctuating Gender Ideas in Central Highland Ecuador, 1870–1900," was published in *The Americas* (2002). Another essay, "Indians and National Salvation: Placing Ecuador's Indigenous Coup of January 2000 in Historical Perspective," was published in Erick D. Langer, ed., *Contemporary Indigenous Movements in Latin America* (SR Books, 2003). She has essays included in upcoming publications on indigenous peoples and the state in the Andes, and an encyclopedia entry on Ecuador forthcoming in the *Encyclopedia of Modern World History* (Oxford University Press, 2008). She continues to be interested in questions of gender, ethnicity, and politics. Plans for future research include collaborative work to bring more translated archival documents to the classroom. She is also undertaking preliminary research on two projects: one examines gender, race, and domesticity in nineteenth-century Ecuadorian cities, while the other involves issues of gender, ethnicity, and resistance in Ecuador from 1780 to 1830.